WORLD CITIZEN

Journeys of a Humanitarian

JANE OLSON

*With so much love and gratitude to
my husband, Ron Olson,
and our children,
Kristin, Steven, and Amy.*

*This book is for my eight grandsons,
with the fervent hope that they will never experience
the horrors of war:*

*Will, Charlie, Tommy, Graham, James,
Matthias, Win, and Jack.*

And to the people of Ukraine.

*Sometimes our light goes out, but is blown again
into instant flame by an encounter with another human being.
Each of us owes the deepest thanks
to those who have rekindled this inner light.*

—DR. ALBERT SCHWEITZER

The soul would have no rainbow if the eyes had no tears.

—ANONYMOUS NATIVE AMERICAN ELDER, 1879

*The earth is too small and life is too short for anything to be
more important than the quest for peace.*

—RABBI LEONARD I. BEERMAN

Be who you are. Use what you have. Do what you can.

—LORRAINE LISTER TENHULZEN, MY MOTHER

CONTENTS

AFRICA

WAR AND FORGIVENESS

PROLOGUE

During decades of travel with humanitarian and human rights organizations to war zones and other devastated places around the world, I relied on an inner strength that was rooted and nurtured in rural western Iowa. In the small town where I grew up, I learned humility, for sure, and I also learned the importance of every member of a community.

When I made my first humanitarian trip to Central America during the contra wars, I was not a human rights expert, nor an international lawyer, nor a foreign policy scholar. I had no training in sociology or psychology. I didn't even have a job, other than the full-time occupation of raising three active children and supporting my husband's busy professional career. I was a woman shaken into action by what I saw as devastating conditions and treatment of people in places far from Iowa, which shattered me to the core. I wanted to witness the plight of vulnerable people and advocate on their behalf. If you want to know the consequences of human rights abuse, war zones are very good classrooms.

During my early journeys, I discovered that when we meet global "enemies" face to face, we can recognize that they are more like us than different and that we share common values, such as the love of family and a desire to live in peace. I also learned that people suffering from war, poverty, disease, and other traumas can recover faster and more fully if supported by compassionate people performing small acts, doing what they can to make a difference. In some of the worst places in the world, I experienced the best of humanity.

As I walked humbly among survivors all over the world, I captured their stories in my journals and photographs, often gripping tales of courageous people who despite devastation managed to survive by pure grit. I learned about their conditions and needs in order to advocate on their behalf. Many of those who lost so much still sacrificed to help others, a sign of human resilience, an awesome force.

History is now repeating itself in many of the regions where these chapters are set. Brutal heads of state are again sacrificing their own people in order to gain territory and personal power. Millions of people fleeing violent homelands in search of refuge once again have become objects of fear, dehumanized and labeled as criminals and terrorists. As I write this, there are many more refugees and displaced people in the world than ever before. Climate change is adding to that disturbing total, causing a phenomenon called "climigration." As war, viral diseases, and global warming all demonstrate, borders and walls offer no protection.

In this memoir, I introduce "the other," human beings suffering from extreme violence, disease, and poverty, people I came to love and still carry with me. In the midst of chaos, they taught me the difference between victim and survivor, between fear and hope. They illustrated the healing power of forgiveness, the fundamental importance of justice, and the strength that comes from choosing life. Survivors whom I met inspired my deep commitment to doing everything I can to lift up humanity. And because they trusted me with their stories, I carry an obligation to tell those stories, to put faces on victims, and to share the lessons of history that inform and illuminate current conditions, with the fervent hope of making a difference.

Simply by showing up, one caring person can hold up a mirror to people who have forgotten who they are, a mirror that can work two ways. In the reflection of "the other," I often met myself and could not distinguish between the two. At times, I experienced a tangible energy that connected me with those I meant to help, until caregiver and victim became one.

One human family.

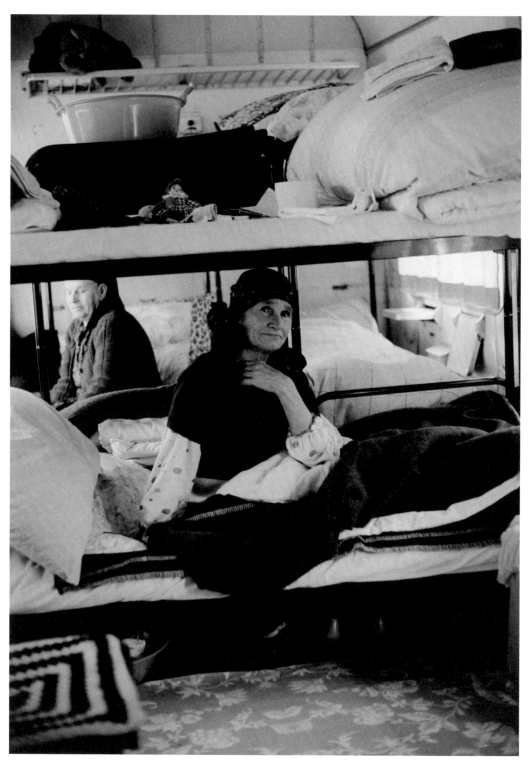

A Bosnian refugee woman carried wounds so raw and recent that she could not or would not speak.

CHAPTER ONE

KNITTING LIVES TOGETHER

It begins with an Irish fisherman sweater,
in a cold barracks filled with grief

YUGOSLAVIA, OCTOBER 1993

When we drove out of Zagreb, Croatia, on my third trip to the former Yugoslavia with the Women's Refugee Commission (WRC), I was knitting in the back seat, working on a sweater for my son, Steven, that I hoped to complete before Christmas. While living in England as a young mother, I had discovered Aran sweaters and the tactile pleasure of working with natural wool yarn because it held the scent and oils of shorn sheep. The complex cable patterns intrigued me, especially after I learned that Irish fishermen who drowned at sea could be identified by the unique designs of their sweaters.

A light snow started falling, dropping big flakes that melted instantly on the windshield of our car, a wet snow that reminded me of early winters where I grew up in Iowa. Snow always made the landscape look so clean. That thought struck me as ironic, since this war in the former Yugoslavia was called the "ethnic cleansing of Bosnia," and slaughter was anything but clean.

The snow stopped just before we reached a refugee camp, where patches of accumulated snow revealed mud puddles not yet frozen. I had not seen this camp on my previous travels through Croatia but knew it was close to a live combat zone in northwest Bosnia-Herzegovina (Bosnia). Although anxious to stretch my legs, I felt something ominous in the atmosphere and paused before exiting the car. A shiver went through my body.

I looked up to see a line of old men sitting with their backs against the wall of a concrete block building, smoking cigarettes and staring into the distance. Despite the damp cold, women and children wandered with no apparent sense of purpose beside long, windowless wooden buildings that looked like barracks, reminiscent of Nazi Germany's concentration camps. A putrid odor penetrated the car's closed windows, the stench of an outhouse coming from three small sheds nearby. My two New York–based colleagues from the WRC and our interpreter seemed to share my apprehension. Without a word, they got out and waited beside the car. We had come, just as winter approached and the war intensified, to meet with Bosnian refugee women and children who were sheltering in Croatia and to assess their physical conditions and immediate needs. This was our first stop. I carefully put down my knitting, zipped my parka, and picked up my camera. Then I tucked a spiral notebook under my arm and stuck a pencil above my left ear, habits from my newspaper reporter days.

A tired-eyed young Dutch aid worker named Hannah greeted us at the door of the first wooden building and led us into to her small office, where an improvised desk, a door laid across two sawhorses, held piles of manila folders stacked high. We briefed Hannah on the WRC's mission to assess the living conditions of refugee women and children and identify their critical needs in order to advocate on their behalf with policy makers and international relief organizations.

Hannah explained that more than three thousand people occupied this facility, which had been built to accommodate a few hundred Yugoslavian soldiers during summer military training. I took notes while she gave demographic statistics—the number of elderly people, invalids, pregnant and lactating women, school-age children, toddlers, and infants. One figure stood out because it was shocking, the number of babies who were less than four months old—fifty-two of them! We bombarded Hannah with questions. Why were there so many newborns in this camp? How old were their mothers? Did she think that they might have been victims of rape? Hannah closed her eyes and looked down. I noticed the pain in her expression and felt ashamed of our insensitivity to her feelings. We needed to slow down and take time, to listen and feel our way into the situation.

My colleagues asked to speak with some of the women, so Hannah took us across the yard, past the line of lounging men, and into the concrete block building, which housed an industrial-sized kitchen. Since kitchens have always been a comfort place, the sight of women stirring large pots of soup on a wood-burning stove helped me to relax. Several women glanced at us but continued to chop carrots, onions, and unpeeled potatoes on a worn gray linoleum countertop. I wanted to grab a knife and join them, as I had done thousands of times with my mother, sisters, grandmothers, and friends, but none of the women seemed to invite our companionship. I had never before been unwelcome in a kitchen, and this hurt my feelings, an irrational response. When our interpreter asked a few questions in Serbo-Croatian, she received grunts in reply. She pointed to my camera and gestured that I should not take any more photographs.

We left quickly and walked back to the barracks. Inside the long narrow building, shafts of light appeared through gaps in the wood-slat exterior walls. Triple-high metal bunk beds lined both sides of the room, running perpendicular to the long walls, shoulder width apart and about five feet high. Piles of bedding and other belongings covered most of the beds and the floor beneath them. Women and children watched warily as we passed.

A teenaged girl lying on a lower bed curled her body into a tight fetal position when I approached, exposing her legs, bare and red. I felt like the intruder that I was, in truth. Despite gentle prodding by our interpreter, no one wanted to talk. Wounds, both physical and emotional, seemed raw and recent. Hannah told us that international journalists had been visiting refugee camps looking for rape victims who would share their stories. By describing their experiences, she said, victims would have to relive painful traumas. I understood why they would not trust us and did not want to take advantage of their vulnerability, but I hoped somehow to reach these hurt souls.

I went out to the car and retrieved my knitting from the back seat, returned to the barracks, and walked all the way to the back wall, then sat down on the cold concrete floor and picked up my needles. Sitting against the wall, I started working on the half-completed sleeve of the Irish fisherman sweater. Soon women began to gather around me, standing back at first, then bending over to examine the complicated cable stitches. With silent awareness, I held the moment, barely breathing, as I used a four-inch, double-pointed needle to capture a few stitches, hold them to the back, knit over them, and then twist and knit them back onto the needle. I noticed that a few women left and then returned with their own knitting and sat down beside me. More followed, eventually forming a circle. I wanted to look at their faces, but I had to concentrate, squinting in the dim light, in order not to drop a stitch.

We worked quietly together, exchanging a few glances as we admired each other's work. We could have been chopping onions, digging weeds, or planting seeds. Same effect. We had created an invisible, unifying force, primal and powerful, of women doing women's work, the small tasks that sustain life.

As our circle grew, I felt the women on each side of me move closer, as if wanting our legs to touch. Gradually, some of the women began to speak, at first haltingly, and I heard our interpreter translating softly. They described their families, the towns they had fled, and horrors they had witnessed, never looking up from their knitting needles. My colleagues recorded their stories about the horrific Serbian military campaign in Bosnia, stories that made me choke with outrage and burn with compassion.

An older woman sitting directly across from me told us how soldiers had forced her to watch them shoot and kill her two teenaged grandsons. Leaving the boys' bodies on the lawn, she said, they took her away in a truck with other women of all ages. "All of us were dumped on a road many miles away and ordered to continue walking west," she said. Then she looked straight into my eyes and confessed, "All that has kept me alive is my will to return home, find my grandsons, and bury their bodies. Then I will lie down beside them and die."

I could barely see my yarn through stinging tears. I felt a strong impulse to embrace her but did not want to interrupt the emotional outpouring. When I read her words in my journal many years later, I pictured my eight beloved grandsons. Then, the depth of her grief, which I had not allowed myself to absorb at the time, completely overwhelmed me.

When I got up to leave, a slender woman, whom I guessed to be in her late fifties, approached me shyly and held out a pair of thickly knitted slippers. She pantomimed the act of unraveling yarn from a sweater, the apparent source of the yarn she had used for the gift that she now presented to me. Luckily for me, my colleague snapped a photograph of her, a red and green bandana tied under her chin, holding out the burgundy and white sock slippers, a broad smile on her face. I knew how much she would need those slippers during the cold winter months ahead. She had sacrificed a sweater, perhaps her only one, to create them. But her obvious joy in the giving made clear that I must accept her incredible gift with an equal grace. While she and other knitters followed us out to the car for tearful farewells, our interpreter expressed my appreciation. I was too choked up to speak. We drove away in stunned silence.

Holding the slippers on my lap in the back seat, I silently berated myself for failing to learn the donor's name or anything about her life. Suddenly, I looked down at the slippers and laughed, realizing that they were much too small for my size ten feet. I broke the silence and tension by calling myself "Cinderella's stepsister."

As we visited several other refugee camps in Croatia and met many other survivors of recent attacks in northwest Bosnia, I thought about giving away the slippers, because all of the women needed warm clothing, but I felt that the re-gifting of such a precious thing would violate the giver's sacrifice. I brought the slippers home to Los Angeles and took them to the next board meeting of the Women's Refugee Commission in New York. I never could have imagined the impact they would have.

I told board members about the knitting circle that had formed spontaneously in that cold barracks filled with traumatized women and children, and I suggested the obvious point that women refugees needed yarn. A board member from Boston, Babbie Cameron, volunteered to create what became the Knitting Project of the Women's Refugee Commission. She wrote articles and placed them in knitting magazines and other publications, explaining the needs and requesting that people donate wool yarn and knitting needles for women refugees in the Balkans.

In just two years, knitters from the United States and Canada donated more than twenty-one tons of yarn. The International Rescue Committee (IRC) handled distribution to refugee women on all sides of the Balkans conflict. Social workers set up knitting circles in scores of refugee camps and reported that the experience of sitting in a circle and knitting with fellow survivors provided quantifiable healing to participants. The IRC bought many of the finished garments and donated them in places of need, thus enabling knitters to support their families.

Nearly thirty years later, I met women who participated in the WRC Knitting Project in the 1990s who recently had created a similar program for refugee women from Syria who ended up at shelters in Sarajevo and various other places in the Balkans. Women of mixed nationalities, races, and religions continued to create circles of survivors, within which resilient women shared their deepest secrets with other women who fully understood the underlying pain.

When I gave the Irish fisherman sweater to Steve for Christmas in 1993, I told him about the circle of women survivors in that cold barracks. "I hope that every time you wear it," I said, "you will feel the warmth that I felt within that circle."

OPPOSITE: A teenaged refugee boy talked about escaping with his younger sisters during the heavy shelling of his village in western Bosnia; ABOVE: In northeast Croatia, a refugee camp holding thousands of Bosnian women and children looked like a World War II concentration camp.

TOP: Children could barely cope with the devastating violence and loss they had experienced so recently; BOTTOM: Countless teenaged mothers held newborn infants; OPPOSITE: The incredibly generous gift of knitted wool slippers took my breath away.

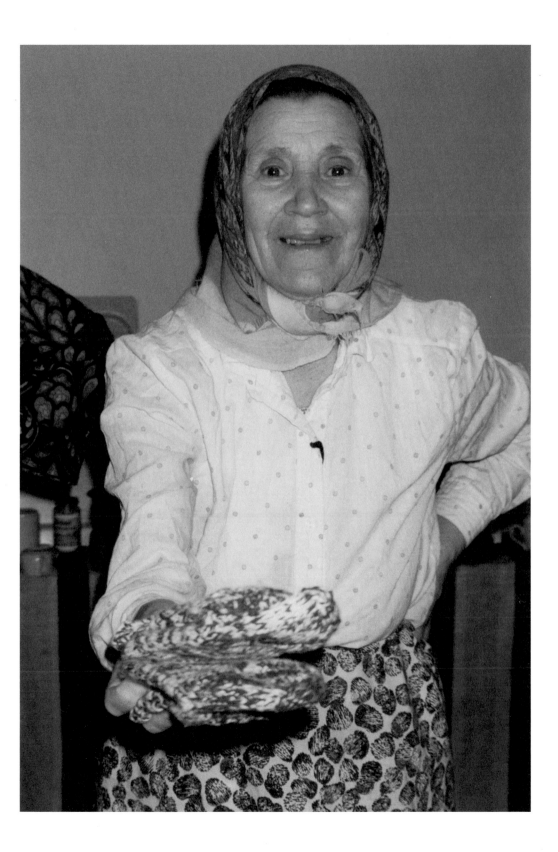

My father, Lester Dale Tenhulzen, enlisted in the U.S. Navy and served in the South Pacific during World War II as a submarine sonar operator.

CHAPTER TWO

GROWING UP IN IOWA

A small rural community provides
values and role models

Perhaps the timing of my birth in Denison, Iowa, August 1942, nine months after the bombing of Pearl Harbor, influenced the path that my life took, or at least my focus on international peace and justice issues. The heartland of America provided a solid foundation, but it was not exactly the center of action. Denison, as the seat of Crawford County, served a large region of rural western Iowa. It boasted a population of about 4,500 during the late 1950s, the Eisenhower years when I was in high school.

Denison had a Carnegie Library, a swimming pool, a roller-skating rink, a bowling alley, and a golf course. There were two doctors, two lawyers, two jewelry stores, two shoe stores, two drug stores, a J.C. Penney, and a Montgomery Ward. Best of all, we had two movie theaters on the same block, the Iowa and the Ritz, which later became the "Donna Reed Theater" in honor of the famous actress who grew up in Denison. The town's water tower still proclaims in big letters *It's a Wonderful Life*, the title of Donna's most famous film.

On Saturdays, double features at the movie theaters cost ten cents. We went early to watch black and white newsreels about world events that ran before feature films. During the Korean War, the newsreels showed reporters on battle-fields, holding microphones and describing the war taking place around them, bombs exploding in the background. I dreamed of becoming a war correspon-dent, never noticing there were no female reporters in the scenes.

The newsreels often featured our former first lady Eleanor Roosevelt, who modeled another kind of courage. Eleanor met with poor people in shanty-towns, coalmines, orphanages, and hospitals, serving as a witness and reporter of the human condition for her husband, President FDR, and becoming the conscience of our nation. I felt personal pride in her leadership role in drafting the Universal Declaration of Human Rights and creating the United Nations along with other admirable world leaders. Eleanor became my role model. I kept a list of her statements:

Do one thing every day that scares you.

You must do the things you think you cannot do.

Do what you feel in your heart to be right—for you'll be criticized anyway.

The timing of my birth indicates that my parents responded appropriately to that "day of infamy." Love serves as an antidote to fear. My parents, Lorraine and Lester Tenhulzen, had five children spread over eighteen years. I was the second of three daughters, with two brothers much younger. Dad operated a poultry business, a food-producing industry that could have given him a draft exemp-tion, but he volunteered for the Navy and became a submarine sonar operator and instructor. His father and brother ran the hatchery and feed mill while he served in the South Pacific. When the war ended, he returned home with gifts of exotic seashells and grass skirts for his wife and three young daughters, Judy, Jane, and Cynthia, who was born on my second birthday. She met our father for the first time when she was two and the war ended.

Dad would never answer our questions about World War II except to say that he did his duty. He once told us that military officers appreciated the me-chanical skills and strong work ethic of Midwestern farm boys, traits that he taught his children. I honor my father now by serving on as a trustee of the National World War II Museum in New Orleans. When museum researchers found and gave me his service records, complete with fingerprints, I learned that my father had served on the famous *Bowfin* submarine.

During the war, my mother had to make do with food rations and whatever she could grow in the garden. Like most Americans, she donated metal pans and utensils to be melted and molded into weapons of war, but she held on to her Singer treadle sewing machine. In those lean times, an ample supply of fabrics—feed sacks—could be found at Tenhulzen's Triple T Hatchery and Feed Mill, which sold finely ground chicken feed in soft cotton sacks that were woven tightly enough to prevent seepage. During the Great Depression, rural women wasted nothing; they repurposed those bags into garments. Feed sacks came in bright colors with printed designs during the 1940s, perfect for sewing dishtowels, pillowcases, and even clothing.

Before my two brothers were born, my family took many summer driving trips in our Ford station wagon to explore other regions of the country, often taking along one of our grandmothers, both of whom lived in Denison. We sisters displayed souvenirs in the bedroom we shared, including triangular pennants from many different states.

Our brother Jack joined the family when I was eight years old, a long-awaited boy. In 1952, we moved to a new ranch-style house on a hill north of Denison. I helped Dad to plant trees, and we created an instant lawn by unrolling pallets of grass sod onto our half-acre lot. As a self-proclaimed tomboy, I took pride in working with my father, and I lived for a rare compliment from him, a tough task master.

My world turned upside down when I was ten years old. My sisters and I had been doing our weekly chores, changing beds and cleaning bathrooms, while our mother tackled piles of laundry. Suddenly, Mother yelled to us that Jack, who had been playing on the lawn with older neighbor boys, was lost. I knew she was scared, because she called Dad at the hatchery and asked him to come home and then sent us out to search the neighborhood. Judy and Cynthia headed to the oak forest across the street, and I ran down our steep hill to a wooded valley. I crawled under a barbed wire fence and slid down a muddy bank to a shallow creek below, my favorite place to play. With great relief, I found my little brother along the creek, alone and frightened, his high-top white shoes buried in sticky black mud. It took all my strength to pull him out and carry him up the hill to our house, both of us covered in mud.

I felt like a hero when I opened the front door and yelled to Mother that I had found Jack, and we were going straight to the bathtub. Just then, Dad came in from the garage, and I saw anger in his face—anger that did not change to relief and gladness when he saw me holding Jack. He crossed the family room, took Jack out of my arms and set him down, then removed the belt from his khaki work uniform. Knowing what that meant, I quickly stepped between my father and little brother. The scene had shocked me, a tall angry man standing over a small frightened boy. I wanted Dad to understand that my baby brother had been abandoned by older boys, stuck in the mud and afraid. I expected him to feel the compassion that I felt, but he just looked at me sternly, his dark brown eyes ordering me to step aside. I stood my ground and held up both my arms, a determined stance that seemed to surprise my father and cause his eyes to soften just a little. In that moment, I knew I had earned my father's respect. He stepped aside and let us pass.

It took many years for me to understand that my father never got to be a child. Having grown up during the Great Depression on a poor farm in Nebraska, he had a childood imprinted by hard work and punishment. That deprivation, along with his war experience and abuse of alcohol, could explain his volatile temper, which he most often directed at Jack and our younger brother Dale, who was born when Jack was eight. I felt protective of them both.

In the autumn of that year, when I was ten, Dad said he had a surprise for me and wanted to take me for a drive in the country. Because I rarely spent any time alone with my father except for working at gardening or another chore, I greatly anticipated the experience and wanted to remember every detail to record in my new diary. It was a special treat just to sit in the front seat of the car, which allowed better viewing and less risk of motion sickness.

We drove east out of Denison on Highway 30 and turned onto a curvy dirt road. For the next few miles, I showed off my knowledge of trees, having learned in Brownie Scouts how to identify leaves. The oaks and maple trees already had dropped many of their bright red, orange, and golden leaves, but the willows remained a brilliant green. Their slender branches bent low to the ground, forming full skirts that swayed in the breeze. Wide willows and tall

sycamore trees grew along the banks of the small river we had been following since turning north from the highway. I knew the direction, because moss
grows on the north side of trees.

When we came to a narrow wooden bridge, Dad pulled off the road and
parked, then got out of the car and opened the trunk. Thinking that this must
be my surprise, I closed my eyes and waited until he opened up my car door
and showed me what he had—a gun!

"You are old enough to shoot a gun, Janie Girl," Dad said, waving a hand
pistol and laughing. He must have noticed my surprise. I had never before
seen this gun, only the shotguns he took when he hunted pheasants. This one
looked like the guns in cowboy movies. I felt a wave of fear but also excitement
as I followed Dad to the center of the little bridge. Looking upstream at the
slow-moving currents of water, I watched a flotilla of colorful leaves disappear
under the solid wooden planks on which we stood.

The bridge had two horizontal wooden railings. The top one reached my
shoulders, and I held on to it, just in case the bridge swayed, like the swinging footbridge south of Denison. Dad, who always relaxed in the countryside,
smiled as he took in the scene. He remarked that he loved the sweet fragrance
of freshly mown hay from a nearby field and the sparkle of the sunshine on the
water, a perfect fall day. Then, setting the gun on the top railing, he reached into
a pocket of his brown leather jacket, pulled out some bullets, and demonstrated
how to load the pistol and engage the safety latch.

"See that?" he asked, pointing upstream at a rusty tin can wedged between
rocks, his apparent target. Explaining every move, Dad slowly raised his right
arm, pointed the gun, closed one eye, released the safety, and squeezed the trigger. "Bang! Ping!" The can jumped up and moved closer to the bank. I clapped
my hands. That demonstration had been enough of a surprise for me, but Dad
said it was now my turn. He suggested that I kneel on the bridge and aim between the railings. The gun felt very heavy in my hand, but I carefully followed
instructions and propped my elbow on the lower rail to stop my arm from shaking. Then I aimed at the can. "Bang! Splash!" No ping. I dropped the pistol into
the river! Bowing my head and closing my eyes, I tightened my butt muscles to
receive a spanking, willing myself not to cry, but the punishment never came.

Perhaps my father realized he should have warned me that guns can buck like horses. He looked stunned as he walked down to the bank and stared into the water, now darkened by cloud cover. I offered to wade in and find the gun, but Dad seemed not to hear me. He went back to the car and told me to get in. We drove back to town in silence, until Dad stopped in front of an ice cream shop and asked what flavor I wanted. That question puzzled me. Was ice cream a peace offering? Or was I being bribed to not tell my mother? I loved butter brickle ice cream, but what I really wanted, what I really needed, was a chance to talk about what had happened on that bridge. I wanted to ask Dad if he had gotten the pistol during the war and whether he killed anyone with it. I wanted to tell him I would save my allowance and buy him a new gun. But we never again spoke of that incident—and I have forever hated guns.

During the 1950s, people in Denison rarely locked their doors, and the fragrance of fresh cookies wafting through kitchen screen doors always seemed like an invitation. I grew up thinking that neighbors wanted me to drop by. I babysat for several neighborhood families, including Leila and Walt Morrison and their three children. A native of Georgia, Leila had served during World War II as a U.S. Army nurse, one of the first group of young women trained and sent to care for Allied troops on European front lines, who landed on Omaha Beach shortly after D-Day. She talked about treating seriously wounded combat soldiers as if she were reliving those horrendous experiences and hearing bombs exploding nearby. I peppered her with questions, never tiring of the war stories Leila shared with me in her charming southern accent. As the war in Europe ended, the Army's 118th, the unit she served, retreated through Weimar, Germany, and discovered the Buchenwald concentration camp. Leila always teared up when she described how they liberated the camp and met shockingly skeletal survivors. "We just couldn't believe the horror of it!" she exclaimed. "Never will I ever forget a single image." At the end of each story, Leila would say, "Freedom comes at a high, high price," and then she would pull a handkerchief from the pocket of the ruffled apron she always wore.

Like my father, Leila's husband, Walt, grew up in Nebraska. They had met during training in Texas before being shipped to Europe, where he served in General Patton's Third Army. As director of Denison's first radio station, Walt encouraged my interest in journalism and later my enrollment at the University of Nebraska. My father approved, because he had grown up in Holland, Nebraska, and many of his Dutch relatives still lived there.

When we went to Nebraska for family reunions, we drove across the Missouri River on the old Mormon Bridge, which had facilitated pioneers traveling west to claim land under the Homestead Act. It is impossible to drive east or west out of Iowa without crossing a bridge. Iowa's entire western border with Nebraska is formed by the Missouri River, which Lewis and Clark explored. The Mississippi River traces Iowa's eastern border.

My introduction to the Mississippi River came at the age of twelve, when our parents took Judy and me to New Orleans for our first airplane trip in a bouncy Braniff Airways propeller plane that made me sick during the entire flight from Omaha. The Cajun heritage of New Orleans fascinated me, from the sidewalk vendors singing "bananas, cauliflower," and "gumbo, jambalaya," to the intricate iron railings on balconies in the old French Quarter. It seemed as if we had landed in a different country. I will forever love New Orleans, my first exotic adventure.

In Louisiana, I saw a lot of dark-skinned people for the first time. Because Denison was a homogeneous white community in the 1950s, I had not been exposed to racial diversity; but human beings always look for differences. What separated people in my home town was religion, Catholics versus Protestants. But when I was in middle school, two Jewish families moved to Denison, and we got to experience greater diversity. Both of the families had daughters in my class, Barbara and Dorothy. When Barbara and I learned that we were born on the same day, we became best friends, birthday twins.

Barbara lived beside the railroad tracks next to a junkyard operated by her father, a cemetery for old cars, farm equipment, and scrap metal of all kinds. Large machines smashed the junk and loaded the resultant rectangular bails onto flatbed train cars for recycling, a fascinating but very noisy procedure. I loved staying overnight at Barbara's house. On Friday nights, I shared pots of soup with her family, but I did not learn much about the Jewish faith. Her family never lit candles when I was there, and they never even mentioned what happened to Jews during World War II. Years later, I remembered those soup nights, the Shabbat with no rituals, when I met a Jewish leader in Sarajevo, Yugoslavia.

Food played an important role in Iowa, the breadbasket of America. Mother cooked from scratch, often incorporating produce she had canned or frozen in the fall with the help of her three daughters and our two grandmothers. During the fall season, we gathered every Saturday in the kitchen, around the yellow-tiled countertops, to process bushel baskets filled with cucumbers, green beans, tomatoes, and sweet corn, fresh vegetables that still held the sweet fragrance of Iowa's rich black soil. They had to be scrubbed and chopped, then blanched or boiled.

Every year my mother had to buy new cases of Mason jars for her preserves, because she gave away so many quarts of fruits and vegetables to people in need. Whenever friends or neighbors suffered a calamity, Iowa women never just called to ask, "Please let me know if I can do anything to help you." They simply showed up. They showed up with food, because food was always needed. In addition to preserves, Mother often prepared and delivered hot macaroni and cheese casseroles, which she called "comfort food," a tradition that I continued.

As a young child, I found a "comfort place," the Carnegie Library. During the war years, with Dad gone and no money for entertainment, Mother took us to the library several times a week. That impressive stone structure, built in 1904, stood on a corner just four blocks west of our first home. Later, my sisters and I read books in the library while Mother practiced the pipe organ in the Presbyterian Church, just across the street.

During middle school, I discovered *The Diary of Anne Frank*, a book that taught me the importance of keeping a journal. Reading Anne's story in her own words, I empathized with her experiences as a victim of prejudice and hatred. She documented personal experiences of unimaginable cruelty that destroyed her own family and millions of others. I read the book twice, the first time to learn what was happening in Holland, my ancestral heritage, and the second to soak in Anne's feelings, her yearning for life, her trust of the adult world, and the raw emotion of her terror. Keeping a diary of my own proved to be important in my world travels. Like Anne, I filled my diary and later my journals with sensory details that helped me to recall experiences. My camera preserved visual records, but I wanted to remember how I felt, what I smelled and heard, and what I learned from people I met, in their own words.

The extreme cruelty and violence perpetrated outside Anne's temporary safe haven and all across Europe began with one man, a brutal dictator, whose hate speech and bigotry led to the genocide of some six million people. After such a horrific lesson as the Holocaust, I felt certain that genocide would never happen again, but during repeated journeys to Rwanda, Cambodia, and the former Yugoslavia, I learned how wrong I had been to believe in "never again." Tragically, humanity continually fell victim to fierce tribalism, brutality, murder, torture, rape, and massive destruction. When I traveled to war zones with international human rights and relief organizations, I could never comprehend what drove such cruel and barbaric behavior.

World history, predictably, became my favorite subject in high school. Our teacher, George Dobrovolny, walked with crutches and a leg brace that he never explained, and we Iowans knew it was impolite to ask. Perhaps he had suffered polio, but I thought of him as a wounded warrior, that man who inspired in me a lifelong desire to understand the roots of world affairs and global conflicts. His animated lectures made me think that he had experienced war. He once raised his crutch and aimed it like a rifle, looking beyond the classroom walls. I had seen enough war movies to imagine what his mind had conjured.

When we got to World War II, Mr. Dobrovolny displayed devastating photographs of countless corpses and half-dead survivors in Nazi concentration camps, and also pictures of Japanese citizens devastated by atomic bombs, skin dripping off their faces. That graphic evidence of war's impact on innocent civilians burned impressions into my soul forever.

On journeys to post-conflict countries with Landmine Survivors Network, where I met countless amputee victims of landmine explosions, I thought about my high school history teacher. His inspiration, like seeds planted in the fertile topsoil of Iowa, grew substantial roots. I realize now that my sturdy resolve to confront the insanity of war and work for world peace began in Leila Morrison's kitchen and Mr. Dobrovolny's classroom.

During the summer of my fifteenth birthday, I gathered the courage to call Richard Knowles, publisher of Denison's bi-weekly *Bulletin and Review* newspaper, and ask him for a job. I had no idea what was possible, but this seemed the logical place to start if I wanted to become a war correspondent. I calmly asserted to Mr. Knowles a phrase that I had been rehearsing for many days: "No matter what you pay me, I will be worth much more." I think I surprised him with my cheekiness, and he surprised himself by hiring me. He said he would pay me out of petty cash until I turned sixteen and could legally earn a salary. I would begin by writing obituaries.

Obituaries may be the lowliest job for a reporter, but I became fascinated by accounts of the deceased. Whenever I received a very brief death report, I would call the mortuary or a family member and ask for more information. It seemed to me that every life deserved a legacy of at least three paragraphs. In response to my queries, relatives often shared long stories about the deceased, not all of them flattering. When an elderly farmer died, the only "next of kin" I could reach was his niece. When I asked about her uncle's life, there was a long pause. "Well," she finally answered, "he wasn't as mean as his brother." I made an exception and wrote just one paragraph.

I worked at the Denison newspaper throughout high school and for two summers during college, carrying a heavy Graflex camera with a strobe battery case and a spiral notebook everywhere I went. There were no wars in Crawford County, but I covered fires, burglaries, and some pretty grisly car accidents, one that resulted in a double decapitation. Through my photographs and stories, I tried to portray victims with compassion, hoping to ease the pain of those who grieved their loss.

After graduating high school in 1960, I joined my sister Judy at the University of Nebraska in Lincoln, where I majored in history and journalism. I contributed to my tuition by editing the national award–winning *Cornhusker* yearbook, a paid job that required hours of work evenings and weekends in the basement of the Student Union. My senior year, I gave leadership to the All Women Students organization, for which I served on a punitive court every Friday afternoon. Along with the dean of women students, we reviewed cases of coeds who had received ten or more demerits for rule infractions, mostly violations of the strict curfew. Some women students had to come before the court because they were pregnant, and their punishment could be suspension or expulsion. I always thought those penalties were much too severe, and I could not understand why male partners remained nameless and suffered no such consequences.

The injustice made me angry, but I lacked the confidence to speak up. When I shared my feelings on a telephone call with my long-distance boyfriend, who was going to law school in Michigan, he endeared himself by sympathizing with me about that unfairness.

For two years I had been dating Ron Olson, a handsome blue-eyed blond whom I met in Iowa. Ron grew up just south of Denison in the small town of Manilla. He was a year older and had once dated my sister Judy. Ron attended Drake University on a four-year football scholarship and then the University of Michigan Law School on a full academic scholarship. Because of the distance between our campuses, we met only on holidays and during summer months, but our love and respect for each other grew despite the distance. We got engaged on Christmas Eve, 1963, and married six months later.

Just one week after my college graduation, on the longest day of the year, Ron and I celebrated our wedding at Denison's Presbyterian Church. My parents hosted a beautiful reception in our backyard, where as a child I had helped my father lay the sod and plant the pin oak tree that now shaded the buffet table. We newlyweds then drove to the Holiday Inn in Des Moines, a luxurious splurge, before we starting the long drive to Washington, D.C., where Ron, having completed one year of law school, worked as a summer intern for a member of Congress.

I had two jobs in Ann Arbor, managing an apartment building, which reduced our rent, and working for a newspaper. *The Ypsilanti Press* had hired me as editor of its women's pages, a job I loved but had to quit after Ron accepted a summer job with a law firm in San Francisco, a delightful introduction to California.

The following school year, I served as head resident of a dormitory at Eastern Michigan University in Ypsilanti. At the age of twenty-three, I assumed responsibly for the wellbeing of three hundred women students living in Goodison Hall. When I interviewed for the job, I had not realized that most resident advisors (RAs) were older single women, many of whom had served for years. But my interview went well, and the dean of students liked my college leadership experience. She hired me even though I would likely serve only a year or two.

I felt lucky to get the RA position, because it paid as much as a teaching job and also provided free room and board, a two-room apartment near the dorm's office. Although I was barely older than the college students, they began calling me "Mom" within the first month. Every day I spent hours listening to my Goodison "daughters'" concerns about classes, family issues, boyfriends, and future jobs. After long evenings at the law library, Ron would return to Goodison Hall and encounter women students in their pajamas sitting on our sofa. They called him "Daddy," a title that helped him to prepare for the surprising news that I was pregnant.

Baby Kristin arrived shortly before law school graduation, and three hundred proud "aunties" broke all hospital visiting rules. A month before the birth, those generous aunties surprised us with a beautiful baby shower, providing all the baby equipment we needed, an incredible gift. I felt quite prepared for motherhood, having helped to raise two little brothers, but I soon learned it was more than a full-time job.

With Ron's excellent record in law school, he received a Ford Foundation fellowship that provided for a year of post-law study at Oxford University, and we set sail for England with Kristin and enough baby equipment to fill our small berth located in the bowels of the S.S. *France*. Our fondness for rural life motivated us to rent what had been described as a "hill cottage" on a farm west of Oxford. Our "gentleman farmer" landlord had converted a tarpaper tool shack into rental property but failed to insulate the wood-slat exterior walls. Fresh air flowed freely—much too freely—through all three small rooms. The cottage lost its charm during long, dark winter days, when an upright propane heater provided the only warmth. We had to leave windows ajar to replace oxygen that the heater sucked up. During the night we could hear the bleating of sheep huddled against our exterior walls.

While Ron studied at Linacre College, I took Kristin in her stroller for long walks around the city and took notes for my Fempressions from Oxford, a newspaper column that I created and mailed weekly to three newspapers that had employed me in Iowa, Nebraska, and Michigan. Our mothers clipped and collected the published articles, and I laugh now at my descriptions of baby prams, punters on the Thames, and politely proscriptive walkway signs, such as "mind the crack," "curb your dog," and "do not soil path."

During Oxford's month-long vacations, we explored most of Western Europe with our baby in a Volkswagen camper van, parking off road in nearly every country to save our limited funds. Baby Kristin served as a magnet for warm-hearted people. Instead of chasing us off their land, farm families often brought us fresh eggs and warm bread in the morning. In the mid 1960s, we traveled safely everywhere in Europe and loved exploring many countries, despite the nuisance of passport control and currency exchanges at border crossings.

From England we moved to Washington, D.C., where Ron worked in the Civil Rights Division of the Justice Department and then clerked for the Chief Justice of the U.S. Court of Appeals, D.C. Circuit. The birth of our son, Steven, in February 1968, brought us great joy and eased the stress of current events that year, as anti–Vietnam War and civil rights protests erupted in many American cities. The Poor People's Campaign in Washington began with inspirational speeches promoting economic justice for the poor, but it ended with violence and destruction.

I understood the inequalities and fully supported the goals of the march, but it began to feel like war in Washington. I stayed in our small apartment and protected our two babies, riveted to live television coverage of the riot. Ron worked through the night at city jails, interviewing people who had been arrested, explaining their legal rights and helping them enter pleas. In that time before cellphones, he did not call me for two days, but he came home full of stories from the chaotic epicenter of the march on our capital city. I felt proud of his contributions and didn't tell him how frightened I had been or how much not hearing from him had worried me. I remembered this years later, when Ron got upset if I failed to call him from war zones.

After weighing many options, Ron accepted an offer from a young law firm in Los Angeles. We packed up our Volkswagen camper in June and drove across the country with two babies, stopping in Iowa for a week to visit their grandparents in Denison and Manilla. We moved into a small rental house in the Pasadena area, where our third child, daughter Amy, was born three years later, in the summer of 1971.

As a young wife and mother, I worked as a volunteer for many local organizations, most of them involving children. I took our blond toddlers with me when I worked as a volunteer in Head Start classrooms for many years. Often, they were the only white children among poor black and brown toddlers, who thrived from the early intervention and enrichment of Head Start. One month, the head teacher asked me to work solely with a boy named Mark, a "bully boy" who constantly interrupted the class. A beautiful child, Mark had the defined muscles of an athlete at age four, and he used them to push other children away from the toys he wanted. One day I took Mark outside during reading time and put him on a swing, hoping that physical exercise would release some of his noisy, negative energy. I pushed the swing from behind his back, as I had done countless times for my own and many other children, and Mark screamed. I stopped the swing to see what was the matter, and he jumped into my arms and wrapped his legs around my waist, crying. To my surprise, I realized he had never been on a swing before. This strong child who bullied other children was just a scared little boy needing to be comforted. Working with Mark opened my heart and taught me a big lesson. From then on, I viewed bullies, even big men who were autocrats, as scared little boys seeking attention.

After looking for a church home in Pasadena, we joined All Saints (ASC), a progressive Episcopal church with a prophetic rector, the Rev. Dr. George F. Regas, who related the gospel message to contemporary life. My volunteer work then broadened to include many important programs that All Saints had initiated, programs that addressed issues such as HIV/AIDS and homelessness, and a free clinic that provided reproductive health care to low-income women. In 1979, George asked me to work at the church full time to coordinate a big conference called "Reversing the Arms Race," a two-day event that ASC co-sponsored with Rabbi Leonard Beerman and Leo Baeck Temple in West Los Angeles.

I had never planned such a major event, but I took the logical first steps, like dusting and mopping the small room assigned to me in the church office building, which looked like a converted closet. I enjoyed working away from home while the children were at school, recruiting potential speakers and filling file folders with carbon copies of letters that I wrote on a manual typewriter. Four months later, some 1,200 attendees came to learn about nuclear weapons and the great risks they posed to all life on earth. During the two-day conference, presentations by prominent physicists, economists, labor leaders, retired military officers, and clergy from diverse faiths advocated for the imperative of halting the nuclear arms race.

The Rev. William Sloane Coffin of Riverside Church, New York, described the arms race as "two men in a wooden lifeboat, each holding a drill and competing to see who could make the biggest hole in the bottom of the boat." In response to the enthusiasm that the conference generated, we created a non-profit organization called the Interfaith Center to Reverse the Arms Race, which I helped to lead for a decade, in partnership with the co-founders, my mentors George Regas and Leonard Beerman.

Besides providing substantive education and advocacy in Southern California and beyond, the Interfaith Center put a face on "the enemy" by inviting a large delegation of Soviet citizens from across the USSR to visit the United States. The Soviet group included two obvious intelligence officers (KGB spies), but most of the visitors were ordinary citizens, including an artist and a farmer. We hosted the guests in our homes and organized visits for them to other states. The Soviets seemed overwhelmed by the friendliness of their hosts, the bounty of our supermarkets, the cleanliness of our neighborhoods, and the size of our homes. At the closing session, the comments of a local Methodist minister's wife captured a common American response to their visit. "Before," she said, "I could have supported bombing Moscow, but now I know Svetlana and Yuri, and I would never hurt them."

Such wisdom grew from my association with All Saints Church, and guidance came from the benediction that ends every service: "Go forth into the world in peace, with strength and courage, to love and to serve." I heard that benediction as a commandment.

OPPOSITE, TOP: My mother sent this photograph to my father in the South Pacific of her with daughters Judy, Jane (right), and Cynthia; OPPOSITE, BOTTOM: Jane (left) with her sisters. ABOVE, LEFT: As we arrived in England on the S.S. *France* for our year at Oxford University, Ron introduced baby Kristin to a British bobby; ABOVE, RIGHT: We traveled across Europe in our Volkswagen camper van; BOTTOM: The tar-paper shed on the left served as our home on a sheep farm west of Oxford.

TOP: With my mentors, Rabbi Leonard
Beerman and the Rev. George Regas, at a
conference for the Interfaith Center to Reverse
the Arms Race; BOTTOM: Ron and I share a
passion for learning about the world through
travel and newspapers; OPPOSITE: Leading a
Human Rights Watch meeting.

THE COLD WAR

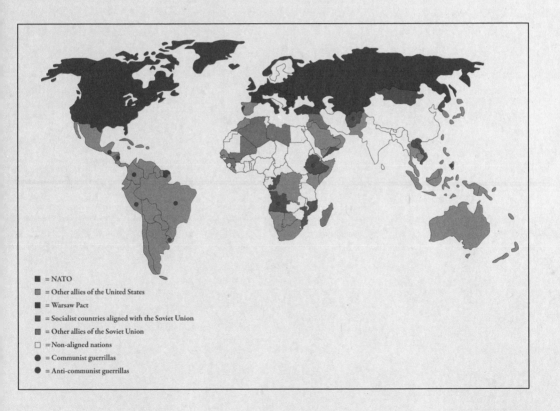

- ■ = NATO
- ■ = Other allies of the United States
- ■ = Warsaw Pact
- ■ = Socialist countries aligned with the Soviet Union
- ■ = Other allies of the Soviet Union
- □ = Non-aligned nations
- ● = Communist guerrillas
- ● = Anti-communist guerrillas

Jane Olson
Cabin 321

АВИА
PAR AVION

Olson

CA 91106

USA

An
Rep o
Dnei p

Recommande
Par avion

Куда Jane Olson

Кому

Индекс предприятия связи   и адрес отправителя
                                 Украина

ПОШТА ПОШТА
       УКРАЇНИ

v., A. A. Leontyev

IAN FOR
RISTS

March 9 - arrive Miami 5:30 pm
Ramada Inn Airport - yuck!
Kick in at 6 - Hooray & Joy.
Meeting 7-9:30 pm - yawn
No sleep - meet in lobby 5:15 am (awoke 5:10 - yum)
3 hrs in airport -
Haitian airlines - seat belt signs & instructions
printed in arabic
3 hrs in airport Havana
    Kick made friends with woman cleaning toilets
       who crocheted tops of tennis shoes

Hotel Inglaterra (England)

When I photographed a billboard displaying this revolutionary image, policemen grabbed my camera and destroyed my film. I wondered whether the sun was rising or setting for this small country caught up in super power rivalry.

CHAPTER THREE

POWER OF THE SUN

A prostitute and a comandante inspire
hope in a country devastated by war and poverty

NICARAGUA, MAY 1984

In the early 1980s, the "contra wars" propelled thousands of Central Americans to flee to the north, hoping to enter the United States and gain asylum. Although covert actions by our country had contributed to rampant poverty and violence in that region, many Americans reacted with fear and blocked them from crossing our southern border, calling them "criminals." In that turbulent environment, All Saints Church Pasadena declared itself to be a sanctuary for "illegal alien" immigrants who had reached our city. Many members provided shelter for Central American families and protected them from being sent back home, where they likely would face imprisonment, or even death. I felt so proud of our church community!

During the Cold War between the United States and the Soviet Union, small Third World nations like those in Central America served as pawns in a dangerous competition for power and influence between the two super powers. Like the nuclear arms race, the contra wars became a top foreign policy issue. Wanting to do all that I could to promote understanding and justice, I helped to organize a committee on Central America at our church, an educational program that attracted active participation and prompted a decision that ASC would send four people to Nicaragua and El Salvador in May 1984. The delegation would be charged with assessing the truth of claims by the U.S. government that these young revolutionary governments posed a grave threat of spreading communism throughout the region. An ASC priest, the Rev. Richard Gillette (Dick), would lead the delegation, because he had studied and worked in Nicaragua as a young priest. Dick invited me to join him, along with two long-time All Saints members who were a generation older than I.

Although immersed in the demands of his growing law practice, my husband, Ron, offered to handle domestic duties at home and supervise our three children, but, in truth, I felt very torn about leaving them. The last month of school was a busy time for all three of our children, especially our daughter Kristin, who would soon be graduating from high school. It felt selfish to be gone for two weeks at such an important time, but I promised I would be back before graduation and all the senior awards ceremonies.

Leaving our youngest child, Amy, concerned me for different reasons. Amy had been only eight years old when we started the Interfaith Center to Reverse the Arms Race. While I was chairing that board and working on "Nuclear Freeze Campaign" programs across Los Angeles and beyond, I often took her with me. Now in seventh grade, she confessed to me that she had watched a documentary video about the bombing of Hiroshima so many times that she hid under her wicker-framed bed in fear whenever she heard airplanes in the night sky. I felt terrible about exposing this tender child to such horrific scenes. And now, she expressed fear that I was going to a dangerous country where there had been a lot of killing. My assurances did not seem to assuage her fear. Since phone calls home would be very difficult, I asked Ron to tell Amy every night that her mother was safe.

Our son, Steven, also in high school, was more enthusiastic about my proposed adventure. Steve shared my passion for photography and had often helped me print photos in my garage darkroom. He asked me to take photos of any soldiers and tanks that I saw, a request that did not surprise me. As a child, Steve and his friend David had spent endless hours playing in our backyard

with plastic soldiers, setting up war zones with elaborate battle scenes sugges-
tive of World War II.

Even though I hated leaving our family at such a sensitive time, I felt a
strong sense of purpose on this, my first, trip to a war zone. I wanted to learn
about life in Nicaragua and El Salvador and what had made their citizens so
desperate to escape that they endured long journeys, even knowing they could
meet rejection and hatred at the U.S. border.

When we landed in Managua, Nicaragua's capital city, the setting sun cast
a deep amber glow across a low profile of buildings that had little or no interior lighting. We drove through the city in near darkness, and I had to imagine
the landscape through other sensory perceptions. The air felt hot and humid,
laden with a stink that I later learned to identify with extreme poverty. As we
neared our destination, an Episcopal seminary outside of town, the sweet scent
of orange blossoms welcomed us Californians, as did our hosts at the seminary.
After a delicious dinner of tamales and fried plantains, I retired to my small but
comfortable bedroom, exhausted.

The next morning, I slipped out the front door at dawn and headed down
a dirt road for an early morning jog in the already warm air. After running
for half an hour between fragrant citrus orchards, I noticed figures on the
road ahead, silhouetted against the rising sun. Soon I recognized the outlines
of men who were approaching me, swinging machetes in rhythm with their
steps. Fear gripped my stomach as I realized my predicament: a white woman, alone on an isolated road, wearing shorts and an LA Dodgers T-shirt. I
slowed my pace, not wanting to turn my back on danger. Suddenly, I saw a
young man raise a machete over his head, and I froze in terror. I wanted to
turn around and run back the way I had come, but my legs seemed to be
paralyzed. After a long moment, I heard a shout of *Hola!* and recognized the
word as a greeting, not a battle cry. I laughed and waved with relief as the
man threw an orange to me.

During breakfast, I shared the story of my early morning people-to-people
lesson and asked my fellow travelers not to tell Ron about the machetes, because
I had assured him that I would be careful. I must tell you that years later, when
I traveled with a Human Rights Watch delegation to Rwanda, I remembered

that machete incident. In Rwanda, machetes had served as the primary weapon in the bloody massacre in which some eight hundred thousand people were murdered in just one hundred days. That genocide took place exactly ten years after this trip to Nicaragua. I sigh as I write this, both from memories and from recognizing that such fears still drive our thoughts and actions.

After touring Managua for a day, we drove north to visit small villages along Nicaragua's border with Honduras, a journey that proved to be a photographer's dream. I kept a manual Pentax SLR camera on my lap in the front seat. Along the way I spotted an intriguing billboard and asked to stop and take a picture. When I got out of the car, a van pulled up and stopped behind us. Two men wearing tan uniforms jumped out and approached me aggressively. When I did not understand a command, one of them grabbed the strap of my camera and pulled me off balance. Although shocked and afraid, I held on tenaciously.

I could not imagine what caused such alarm. The billboard pictured a deep-orange sky with a low sun hovering over a lighter orange field. In the foreground were four raised arms with fists holding a knife, a shovel, an axe, and a rifle. It reminded me of Soviet statues and graphic images. Black lettering at the bottom spelled out *La Patria* and *La Revolución*, an open but not radical display of revolutionary spirit. Rev. Gillette came to my rescue, calmly suggesting that I give them the film from my camera. I did so reluctantly and watched the fully exposed film being pulled from the cartridge and tossed in a ditch. I almost cried, remembering all the photos I had taken the previous day, especially those of homeless people camping in Managua's central cathedral, which had been badly damaged by the major earthquake that struck Nicaragua in 1971. The church had been taped off, declared uninhabitable, but countless broken people had taken shelter within its broken walls.

After the camera experience, I realized that the political situation here was more complicated than I had realized. I got back in the car and apologized to my fellow travelers for putting them in danger, however innocent my intent. We speculated together that the building behind the billboard might have had a sensitive military or security purpose. I suddenly felt vulnerable and vowed to be more careful. This was only my second full day in a war zone. I had not seen any tanks or soldiers, but I had already caused some trouble twice.

When we reached rural settings in the north, my confidence returned. I always felt more comfortable in the countryside with people who worked the land. At each village, I delivered duffle bags filled with used children's clothing that I had collected in Pasadena. Village leaders told us that shells were sometimes fired across the border from Honduras. Pointing to a large pit in the village center, they explained that they had dug this hole in the terracotta soil in order to protect women and children from the shelling. Many of these families had moved here from Managua, we were told, after Somoza's forces poured gasoline and burned out poor neighborhoods (barrios), forcing them to flee.

"There are no jobs or schools here," a campesino (peasant) explained, when I asked why they were not planting gardens. "We have lots of sunshine and dirt here, but it's not our land, and we don't have seeds or tools," he said, adding that snipers sometimes fired at men working in fields. I wondered whether the shelling had been meant only to frighten them. If a U.S. military force had indeed been training and arming contra forces to take down Nicaragua's new Sandinista government, I figured they would not want villagers wandering near that border. I wondered to what extent the U.S. had intervened in Honduras and how that country's long-term stability would be affected.

(Thirty-five years later, in 2019, thousands of desperate families fled Honduras and walked north in huge caravans to reach our southern border. As I watched television news coverage, I remembered having wondered about such consequences back in 1984. Violence and corruption in Honduras, and also in El Salvador and Guatemala, had become so intolerable decades later that people risked a long and a torturous journey in hopes of gaining asylum. They faced rejection at the U.S. border, just as asylum seekers from Nicaragua and El Salvador experienced in the 1980s, and desperate Central Americans and Mexicans do today.)

We returned to Managua and joined a gathering at the U.S. Embassy on Thursday morning, May 24, 1984. American peace activists who came to Nicaragua traditionally held demonstrations at the embassy every Thursday. On this steaming hot day, we voiced our support for Nicaragua's efforts to secure a loan from the World Bank. Using its veto power as a major World

Bank donor, the U.S. had blocked Nicaragua's application for funds to ease its massive poverty. Most of the Americans we met outside the embassy said they had also opposed the Vietnam War, which had cost some fifty thousand American lives. The same number of Nicaraguans had died in the anti-Somoza insurrection, an incredible number, considering that Nicaragua had only three million citizens. Relative to the size of our population, the loss of fifty thousand Nicaraguans would equal several million American deaths, a loss impossible to imagine.

President Ronald Reagan frequently made enthusiastic pronouncements in support of the contras, calling them "freedom fighters and the moral equivalent of our Founding Fathers." I thought back to my Eisenhower Era school days in Iowa. Our monthly "duck and cover" emergency drills carried the voice of Ronald Reagan, then a Hollywood actor, calmly assuring us over the intercom that we would be safe under our desks if the Russians ever launched an atomic bomb. Even as a child, I had questioned Reagan's assurance that our little desks would keep us safe, and now, as an adult, I doubted his claim that little Nicaragua posed a dire threat to the United States.

After several days of driving around the country, we returned to the embassy for a formal meeting. Since we had no ambassador in residence, we assumed that the men briefing us were members of the CIA. They displayed aerial photographs taken over the Bay of Corinto in the northeast, where we had just visited. Small boats carrying one or two men could be seen in profile against a low sun.

"Those rowboats are transporting guns across the bay to El Salvador," spokesman Roger Gamble told us. When we asked for more evidence, Gamble said, "Just because there's no proof, doesn't mean that the Sandinistas are not exporting revolution." Even if this had been true, I wondered, how could it justify mining that small bay? The U.S. response seemed greatly out of proportion. I had to stop and remind myself that I, as an American, should be able to trust and believe our embassy staff, but none of these claims seemed rational.

Over dinner that night, members of our delegation discussed what we had learned. Bob Yarnall, an oil company executive and self-proclaimed conservative Republican, told us that he felt skeptical about the embassy briefing, because their claims lacked evidence. Bob suggested, "It seems that we could rebuild Nicaragua for a fraction of what it is costing us to destroy it."

I looked forward to visiting programs designed to improve the lives of poor people, some sponsored by the government and others by non-profit aid organizations, where I could meet local people and assess their living conditions and their needs. One inspiring project focused on rehabilitating prostitutes by teaching them skills that could generate income. To our surprise, we learned that women in this program would be sacrificing income by changing professions, because prostitution paid in dollars and sewing only in the local currency, which was vulnerable to rampant inflation.

Feeling a bit like an intruder in that small stuffy room, and again wishing that I could speak more fluent Spanish, I sat on a flimsy folding chair beside a young woman named Alma. I had been attracted to her because, leaning over a treadle sewing machine, Alma reminded me of my mother as a young woman. She rocked back and forth, pumping a wide pedal with both feet while guiding a piece of red cloth under the needle. Suddenly she stopped and looked up at me with pleading eyes that seemed to say, *See me.* Her expression, which suggested that she felt judged by us foreigners who had invaded her classroom, filled me with empathy and compassion. I put my arm across her narrow shoulders and held her gaze, observing her dignity and grace, wanting to communicate the respect that I genuinely felt for her.

Alma suddenly stood up, took my hand, and led me out the door to a bare dirt courtyard, where a dozen or so children sat eating mangoes. She pointed to two toddlers, a girl and boy, and then to her heart. I understood the gesture to mean that these were her children, and she loved them, loved them enough to leave her life of prostitution for their sake. She would earn less money but be safer and more available to them as a mother. It seemed a courageous decision to change her course in life.

As the children bit into the fleshy orange fruit, juice dripped onto their bare chests in sticky stripes that dried quickly in the sun. The obvious pride in Alma's face touched me, and I showed her photographs of my three teenaged children, two daughters and a son. Then, I impulsively took off the necklace I had been wearing throughout the trip and fastened its chain around her neck.

A golden sun charm now hung beneath Alma's chin. I had worn the sun as a symbol of my astrological sign, Leo, but on her it signified the light of hope. It seemed appropriate, because Alma herself carried so much light.

That night, feeling that the day had surprised me with this human connection in the midst of hands-off political meetings, I wrote in my journal that Alma and I had, in a brief encounter, shared a deeply human kinship. I hoped that she understood my appreciation of the strength she demonstrated by choosing a better life for her children. I wrote: "I will never forget Alma's hazel green eyes, her heart-shaped face, and the way she spoke to me without words. Our hearts connected despite the great differences in our life circumstances, and I felt genuine love for her. Perhaps I have more to contribute to our mission than my reporting and photography skills. I must remember not to give in to judgment or fear."

Before departing Nicaragua, we met with Comandante Tomás Borge, the sole surviving guerilla leader of the original junta. He now served as Minister of the Interior, managing the police, security, the military, immigration, and the prison system. I had been wary about meeting him, because I had heard stories from Nicaraguan refugees about his brutal acts against critics of the Sandinista revolution. A female journalist had told me that she and her entire family had been threatened with imprisonment because of an article she'd written in a student newspaper.

When I met Tomás Borge, a small man with big responsibilities, his piercing dark eyes disarmed me. He seemed to be measuring us and the purpose of our visit. I knew he had been imprisoned and hung from his thumbs by former president Somoza's militia; they had also beaten and murdered his wife. Borge explained that he had recently met and forgiven the individuals who tortured him and murdered his wife. I wondered whether he allowed torture, now that he was in charge of Nicaragua's prison system, but something about his apparent vulnerability made me ask a different question: "How did you find the strength to forgive?" After a long pause, he answered that he did not blame men for following orders. "My forgiveness," he said, "may heal the pain of guilt that they surely must have felt." In that response, I saw his humanity.

(Many years later, I remembered Borge's powerful words when I had the privilege of meeting Chile's president Michelle Bachelet in Santiago during a visit to her palace with Human Rights Watch. She and her mother had been arrested and tortured during the brutal military dictatorship of Gen. Augusto Pinochet. After her election, Bachelet went on national television to announce that she forgave the torturers. "They were only following orders," she said. "I do not blame them, but they blamed themselves. We must start to heal the nation with forgiveness." Both Tomás Borge and Michelle Bachelet understood that those who had ordered torture were the true war criminals, not those who carried out the orders.)

In Borge's office, above his desk, I had noticed a colored poster—the image of a bright sun above an orange field. This was the same image I had photographed earlier on a roadside billboard, before police took the film from my camera. Obviously, it held meaning for Borge. I couldn't help wondering whether the sun was rising or setting for Nicaragua.

I met many people on this journey, from the very poor to the powerful, but the people I remember most vividly are a prostitute named Alma and a revolutionary leader, Tomás Borge. Both had touched my heart with their humility and their positive focus on creating a better future for themselves and their country. Clearly love, the most powerful energy in the universe, had fueled their resilience.

A last word. During this trip, as I mentioned, I had worried about leaving my daughter Kristin at the end of her senior year in high school. Coincidentally, after graduating from college and earning a master's degree in Latin American studies, Kristin accepted a job at the World Bank in its Central America division. Ten years after my journey, my daughter became the World Bank's country head for Nicaragua, traveling there monthly from Washington, D.C., and dispensing hundreds of millions of dollars to fund reconstruction and other aid projects. One of her programs brought American farmers, including Iowa farmers, to advise Nicaraguans on land use and how to produce crops that could be sold in the United States.

In 1988, the New York–based organization Human Rights Watch (HRW) asked me for help in creating a support group in Los Angeles, and I eventually joined the board of trustees. Exactly twenty years after my first international mission to Nicaragua, I was elected to chair the International Board of Human Rights Watch (2004–10). After witnessing many humanitarian disasters, I wanted to support HRW's work to prevent war by criticizing governments who abused their citizens and shaming them into complying with the Universal Declaration of Human Rights.

After our youngest child, Amy, left for college in 1989, I could travel more freely, and I certainly did! Coincidentally, the USSR began to implode the same year, 1989. Conflicts broke out among countries aligned with the former Soviet Union and the Cold War puppet states. I renewed my passport, bought a new camera, and emboldened my heart.

Another billboard celebrated Sandinista leaders

ABOVE: With fellow travelers from All Saints Church Pasadena, I met with Tomás Borge, center, and learned his heroic story of survival and forgiveness; OPPOSITE: Two children in Nicaragua captured my attention and my heart.

This woman in Zaporozhye, Ukraine, eyed me with curiosity, the first American she had ever seen.

CHAPTER FOUR

CRUISING WITH "THE ENEMY"

*The warmth of Iowa roots helps
to melt Cold War tension*

THE SOVIET UNION, AUGUST 1989

My father loved to surprise us with big gifts. One summer during my child-hood, we discovered a large houseboat in our driveway. Yellow and white to match our Ford station wagon, it looked like a regular house trailer, except that it sported fins and an outboard motor in the rear. We could tow the houseboat to a lake and back it down a boat ramp. Once in the water, we would crank up its wheels like an airplane's landing gear and float away. The houseboat opened up a new world for us. Dad, a Navy sailor who could not swim, loved to be on open water. During his childhood in Nebraska, the only waves he ever saw were those created by summer heat mirages or by autumn winds blowing through wheat fields.

My sisters and I often got to bring girlfriends along for weekend trips to Spirit Lake in northern Iowa. Unless it was raining, we would sleep between guardrails on the top deck, surrounded by a heavenly black sky dotted with trillions of stars, an inspirational setting for us girls to discuss matters of the universe, large and small.

My involvement in the 1980s with Cold War issues awakened in me a strong desire to visit the Soviet Union, a goal I managed to achieve in August 1989, when I traveled on a very large houseboat that had a profile similar to our family trailer. Along with a hundred other U.S. "citizen diplomats" from fifteen states, and a similar number from Europe and the Soviet Union, I cruised down the Dnieper River, from Kiev to Odessa (as they were known in 1989–90; Ukrainian cities' names have since been changed back from the Russian spellings).

The trip grew out of a unique peace initiative created and co-sponsored by the Ukrainian Peace Committee and an American organization called Promoting Enduring Peace, which was based in Connecticut. The amazing initiative introduced people from the outside world to Ukrainian cities that had been closed during the Cold War, shut off and protected because of the large defense industry located in the region.

I had been intrigued by the invitation, which said we would be meeting Soviet people who for decades had not been allowed to leave their home cities or see any outsiders. I wondered what they had heard about the United States. Some of the Soviet visitors we hosted through the Interfaith Center to Reverse the Arms Race told us about the negative propaganda they were taught about Americans and confessed they had believed it. During the long flight to Moscow, the responsibility of representing America, the "enemy," weighed on my mind.

There is never an easy time for a mother to leave her family, but this invitation came at a particularly difficult time for me, because I would have to miss taking our youngest daughter Amy to college for her first semester. I had served as Amy's Girl Scout leader, her Sunday school teacher, soccer team mother, and so much more, savoring the joys of motherhood, but now she and I would go our separate ways, both to great adventures. Taking a child to college is a major rite of passage, one that I wished to share. I had hoped to meet her roommate and make up her bed, as I had for Steven three years earlier. I wanted to speak with her head resident, a role that I once played, and take photos of Amy in various campus settings. Ron encouraged me to go and offered to escort Amy to college, an experience that gave them wonderful memories.

And so, with some trepidation and occasional tears, I flew to Moscow along with several other Southern Californians. We stayed for two nights at the Rossiya Hotel, because all foreign visitors were required to lodge at that or another enormous "intourist" hotel, where stout matrons monitored every corridor. We suspected that all three thousand rooms at the Rossiya were bugged with microphones we could not see, in addition to the other bugs, very visible cockroaches, but the Rossiya's convenient location near Red Square made up for discomforts. Even in driving rain and chilly fog, Moscow lived up to the magnificent descriptions of Tolstoy and Dostoevsky.

The second day, we took an overnight train to Kiev and a bus to the dock the next morning, where we boarded our large houseboat, the *Marshal Koshevoy*. I found my cabin and met my roommate, a friendly woman from Chicago, who carefully guarded her own small storage space after seeing my luggage, two enormous duffle bags filled with gifts that I had brought from home. I did not blame her. Remembering all the American products that had intrigued our Soviet visitors, I had gotten carried away buying gifts for those I hoped to meet.

While the crew pushed off for our journey down the Dnieper River, all passengers met in the dining room for introductions. Among the Soviet participants were two ecologists, a Russian Orthodox archbishop, an army officer, and a young man who spoke such perfect colloquial English that I pegged him as a KGB spy. Except for him and perhaps one or two others, we were all ordinary citizens, and that is how change happens.

I met a woman from Arizona named Mary who shared my passion for jogging. We agreed to go running together at every port, starting at our first stop, Cherkassy. Wearing shorts and sneakers, Mary and I exited the boat at 6:30 a.m. and ran through deserted streets, making detours around piles of trash and getting lost, such a "me" thing to do in those days before GPS and Waze.

During breakfast, our leaders warned that since this city had been largely sealed off for many decades, we might encounter animosity as well as curiosity. Even though Mary and I had met no one on our early morning jog, this warning made me feel a little apprehensive. I dressed in cheerful colors, filled a backpack with small gifts, and sucked up my courage. This would be our first encounter with Ukrainians, who might be expecting us to have horns on our heads. But as we walked down the gangplank, all anxiety vanished immediately with the sight of a plaza that was filled with people dressed in folk costumes and waiting to greet us—not as enemies, but as honored guests. Women sang and danced, and children handed out flowers.

What really caught my eye were the elderly World War II veterans wearing uniforms and standing at attention in a formal line off to the right. Seeing a photo opportunity, I walked right over to them. One of the men came up and asked me in a deep accent, "Where have you been all of my life? I have been waiting to meet you." Startled and amused, I asked, "So you speak some English?" He shook his head. I guessed that an Allied soldier had taught him that pickup line, and he must have been practicing it for many decades! Just the thought of that made me smile wider. I gave him and each of the other veterans a 1984 Los Angeles Olympics pin and watched as each proudly placed them beside the many war medals and faded ribbons on their uniform jackets. I wondered if they had any idea what the five Olympic rings meant, and if not, if they might invent a story about a battlefield it represented.

An older woman read my nametag and surprised me by saying, "Welcome, Jane Olson. Welcome to Cherkassy." Fedora, age sixty-seven, wore a wreath of artificial flowers and flashed a radiant smile that displayed brass-capped front teeth. Apparently, she had no embarrassment about the primitive dental repair, which I soon realized was common there with older people. (The brass caps looked better than ones made of tin that I saw later on other smiling faces.) I gave Fedora a silver JFK fifty-cent piece, and she clapped as if she recognized the profile of the late president John F. Kennedy. She seemed to be a bright and educated woman, and I wondered about her life history. Perhaps they had not all been as completely shut off from global news as we had been told.

Cherkassy, founded more than seven hundred years before, was surrounded by some of the richest farming land in the USSR. Thus, it had twenty-nine sugar refineries to process sugar beets, the region's primary crop. Other crops, such as wheat, sunflowers, corn, cherries, plums, and red currants, also grew abundantly in the region's rich soil. Most of Cherkassy's three hundred thousand people were involved with agriculture in some way, as was true of my home town.

A bus transported us to a model collective farm at Lozovatka, where we received a greeting from a second group of costumed singers and musicians, who were playing handmade instruments, including a washboard. Teenaged girls held beautiful loaves of braided bread as a symbol of welcome. I dropped perfume and eye shadow into their apron pockets, wishing I could see their faces when they discovered them.

Then the manager of a large "collective" farm, agronomist Mikhail Borozngak, welcomed us in a booming voice, cheerfully announcing "I love America!" An interpreter helped him explain that he had visited the state of Iowa the previous summer to study land management and farming practices. I clapped my hands and asked the interpreter to tell Mikhail that I grew up in rural Iowa. That news caused him to crush me in a two-armed bear hug, demonstrating how much he loved the people of Iowa, a heartwarming surprise.

Mikhail invited me, along with Iowa state senator Jean Lloyd-Jones and her husband, Richard, who were part of our delegation, to visit his home and meet his wife, Olga, and their teenaged children. While we drank strong black tea with too much sugar, Mikhail showed us photographs of the voyage he had taken on the Mississippi River bordering Iowa. With dramatic hand motions, he described the powerful river and the historic paddleboat steamer. The translator struggled to keep up as Mikhail explained how the steamer's captain had taken him into the wheelhouse and allowed him to steer the paddleboat.

"We should have paddleboats like that on the Dnieper!" Mikhail exclaimed. I thought about the thick fluorescent green polluted water we had just cruised through, and I could not picture Mark Twain on the Dnieper.

I learned that the Lloyd-Joneses and Mikhail had been together in Iowa and had made plans for a student exchange program, the first phase of which was already playing out. Six Iowa kids had recently come here to spend two weeks with Ukrainian families. They planned for Ukrainian children to travel to Iowa in 1990.

"Trusting others to care for our children is the highest form of trust," Olga said. I smiled my agreement. My own children would have enjoyed staying on this farm with this family. Olga took my hand and guided me into her kitchen, where she proudly opened a cupboard and displayed rows of quart jars filled with colorful canned produce. Then she took me out the back door and showed off a huge vegetable garden growing in black dirt that could rival Iowa's fertile topsoil. I felt glad that she intuited how much I would appreciate her efforts and share her pride in the beautiful garden. If I had found an interpreter, I would have told her that in Pasadena, California, I had a small greenhouse, a potting bench where I started flowers and vegetables from seeds, and a deep compost pit, which I shoveled and turned myself. Just thinking about my own garden generated a bond with this strong farm woman, a kinship that could help to melt the Cold War.

Back on the boat, we gathered to share our experiences and to hear a Russian economics professor explain glasnost and perestroika, policies recently initiated by USSR president Mikhail Gorbachev. Glasnost means openness, such as we had been experiencing all day. Perestroika, more complex and controversial, referred to economic issues, such as the need to increase wages, food production, and alternatives to state ownership. That sounded like a step toward capitalism. We were told that it was now possible for families to lease or own plots of land and to engage in small enterprises, but before profiting, the families first had to sell their products to the government, based on a quota system. He explained the Soviet five-year planning system, whereby all agricultural and industrial programs were given quotas.

"No one wants to meet or exceed the quota," the professor explained, "because it would then be increased for the next five years." He admitted that it would take a long time to transform the rigid system controlled by Moscow into an open market economy. Meanwhile, people had to stand in long lines every day to purchase scarce consumer goods, a situation we had noticed in Moscow. I greatly admired these hardy farmers who seemed to till, plant, grow, and harvest without any idea whether they could fill their own grain bins and feed their families and communities. Midwestern farmers face similar great unknowns, I realized. They buy seeds and other resources at retail prices and sell their crops wholesale, gambling that the market price will yield a profit. And then there is the constant threat of drought, floods, wind, and hail.

As we cruised down the Dnieper River between cities, we discussed social problems, such as the high rates of divorce, infant mortality, and abortion in the USSR. I certainly understood the difficulties of raising children, even in an affluent country, and could see why Soviet women would want to limit the size of their families. The tragedy of infant mortality no doubt arose from poor diets and the lack of prenatal care within a limited health care system. (A few days later, after we had established a friendship, a woman from Moscow told me that abortion had become the primary method of birth control for young women in Russia, a shocking confession that she stated nonchalantly.) Soviet passengers argued openly about these economic initiatives, but most of them claimed to support Gorbachev and his efforts to raise standards of living and increase global trade.

During the night, our boat docked at Zaporozhye, an industrial town of nearly a million people, and the next morning, August 16, Mary and I went out for an early run. We jogged from the boat straight to the train station and then explored several side streets. After an hour, we got hopelessly lost. I stopped a woman and asked, "Where is Lenin?" standing on my tiptoes and raising my arms to indicate the tall statue of Lenin near the dock. She understood and gave us directions back to the boat, but we missed breakfast and had to settle for granola bars from my backpack.

When we all disembarked, we again received a hearty welcome. One woman, hearing that it was my birthday, gave me a small bouquet of roses, and I found a lip gloss in the same shade of pink to give her. We toured a museum with interesting dioramas of Cossack history, and then we visited the pride of Zaporozhye, an enormous hydroelectric plant built in the 1930s. The city looked rather prosperous, but the mood here seemed less cheerful than on the previous stop. Along the way, people talked about World War II as if it had happened very recently. They said that the German army killed some forty-three thousand people here, destroyed 80 percent of the city, and took away sixty-eight thousand as slaves for their labor camps. Those astounding numbers were chilling. These traumas they had experienced more than forty years ago were still raw. I was shaken to learn that such a tragic history continued to haunt these people, perhaps because of the region's isolation from the world.

The next day we arrived at Kherson and toured a cotton factory that employed eighteen thousand people in two shifts. Although exhausted from the long day, Mary and I decided to skip dinner and go jogging at 7 p.m. Paying greater attention to directions, we ran through torn-up streets with open sewers.

Cooking fires contributed to the stench, which made breathing difficult. We passed many shabby homes with crumbling exterior walls and with windows covered by cardboard or plywood, quite a contrast to the guided tour we had been given earlier through a neighborhood of colorful homes and gardens. I realized that the same contrast could be found in any American city, where poverty often remains hidden, far from tourist sites.

At our next stop, Odessa, where the Dnieper River flowed into the Black Sea, a huge crowd greeted us on the dock, and "Young Pioneers," members of the communist youth group, passed out red bandanas. I tied one bandana around my neck and wore another on my head. That, plus my bright yellow jumpsuit and long-lens camera, attracted the attention of two local women, Nina and Maya, and a young man named Roman. The three approached me, saying they belonged to the English-Speaking Club (ESC) and had come to pick out two Americans and invite them for a guided tour of Odessa. Roman chose another American, a man named Bill, a fellow passenger I had not met, who happened also to be from Southern California. Nina introduced us to a group of women and teenagers, to whom she had been teaching English for two years, a dangerous activity for Soviet citizens during the Cold War. I was astounded to hear that she had learned to speak English on her own from tapes she found at the college where she taught. The tapes had been recorded in a British accent, she said, and neither she nor any of her students had ever met a native English speaker or heard an American accent.

As the ESC proudly led us on a tour of Odessa landmarks, each student described a different site, reading from notes on cards that they held. I watched Nina's lips moving while they spoke, like a choir director who had memorized all of the lyrics. She smiled with her whole face, crinkling her eyes above an open-mouthed grin. We climbed the famous Potemkin Stairs and toured Odessa's beautiful Opera House, a World War II memorial, a promenade lined with chestnut trees, and the House of Scientists. Then they invited Bill and me into a small apartment, where we shared food and drink, sang American pop music, and exchanged addresses. Nina made sure that each name and address had been written clearly in Cyrillic, so that I could copy them when I wrote letters from California. I passed around several copies of my most recent annual

Christmas card, which featured family photos and a parody of Mother Goose nursery rhymes that I had written. Roman immediately gave me the nickname "Mother Goose," and all the teenagers asked whether they could be my goslings. And so began my informal adoption of "goslings" all around the world. I needed to grow wide wings.

Leaving the warmth and enthusiasm of the English-Speaking Club was the hardest departure of the trip, but Bill and I reluctantly left to board the *Marshal Koshevoy*, which would soon head back north. During our passage to the next port, a few passengers presented a talent show, and I led a discussion on peace movements, with panelists from five different countries. Most of the peace initiatives dealt with easing the super power confrontation that was causing distress everywhere. As I listened to the presentations of Soviet and European panelists, I realized we all had come on this journey in hopes of playing some small role in easing global tension. This common desire brought us together as a community of peacemakers.

Before disembarking at Dnepropetrovsk, we were reminded that no visitors had been allowed to come here for decades. Again, I braced myself for hostility, but I immediately found myself surrounded by joyful and curious teenaged boys. They did not beg for cigarettes or blue jeans like the aggressive young men I had encountered in Moscow, but they seemed just as eager to communicate. Girls and older adults seemed more hesitant, but eventually they also came forward and posed for photographs. While I changed film cartridges, I asked the subjects of my photos to enter their contact information in my journal, under which I wrote descriptive notes, such as "orange and green scarf."

Some of the boys tried out English phrases they had memorized from books and pirated tapes. "Christ in Heaven!" exclaimed a tall skinny teen named Alex. I grabbed an interpreter to ask what he meant. "Don't all Americans say that?" Alex asked. "It's from John Steinbeck." I loved sharing that story on the boat, and I made a mental note to bring classic books and tapes of folk and rock music, if I ever returned.

After dinner, I left the boat to take a brisk walk alone before dark—just to process my emotions—and was startled to discover Alex, the "Christ in Heaven" boy, his sister, and two other boys standing on the ramp below. I wondered how long they had been waiting there, holding gifts for me of postcards and painted wooden plates. I led them onto the boat to find an interpreter, and they all followed me to my cabin. Luckily, I still had a few T-shirts in my shrinking duffle bags. As I escorted the teens down the gangplank, they proudly modeled shirts with baseball logos and peace slogans, symbols that they did not understand. I was so happy to meet Alex's parents, who were waiting on the dock. His mother called me her "first American," and I returned her hug with gratitude, neither of us wanting to let go.

Soon after I returned to my cabin, the *Marshal Koshevoy* pushed off from the dock. Looking out the porthole, I saw a black sky dotted by a trillion stars, which took me back to Spirit Lake, Iowa. The upper rim of a nearly full moon began rising above the horizon, and I hurried out to the deck to watch its growing brilliance dim and then put out most of the star lights. As always, its majesty made me blink back tears. Among passengers who had gathered on the deck under the moonlight, I greeted new friends from many countries, and we discussed matters of the universe, large and small.

We spent our last night on the boat in Kiev. After dinner, I presented a summary from the panel on global peace movements (and later distributed printed copies to several peace organizations in the U.S.). It concluded with my personal opinions:

> *"We are often asked, 'How can we achieve peace without strength?'*
> *I believe that we must redefine 'strength.' NATO and the Warsaw Pact count nuclear warheads like so many bows and arrows. Could we not compete instead for healthy economies and a clean environment? A nation demonstrates real strength by providing, even for its weakest citizens, the basic rights of food, shelter, work, quality education, and health care."*

(Because of the coronavirus pandemic, I would now list health care first.)

Back home, I wrote letters to all the people recorded in my journal and carefully copied their addresses in Cyrillic. I put photos into each envelope along with a personal letter to each, which thanked my new friends for their warm hospitality. As I looked at the names and photos, I realized how truly impactful this journey had been. Each of these people had enriched my life enormously through their open-hearted outreach. The deep connections I had made with so many Soviet people gave me hope that individuals can indeed make a difference. At the end of each letter, I wrote that I would return on the *Marshal Koshevoy* the following summer and hoped to see them again. When I had received the invitation to return, I knew immediately that I would go. This time I wanted to bring members of my own family along to meet new "family" in Ukraine.

Map of Ukraine, 1990

ABOVE: Across Ukraine, it seemed that World War II had ended only recently. Victory over the Nazis was celebrated in every town square; OPPOSITE: In every port along the Dnieper River, Ukrainian people turned out in their finest to meet "the enemy."

ABOVE: The bright colors I wore and cameras I carried attracted the attention of Young Pioneers, who gave me red bandanas; OPPOSITE, TOP: Someone with a revolutionary spirit painted this map portraying an independent Ukraine long before the movement burst open; OPPOSITE, BOTTOM LEFT: A World War II veteran proudly wearing his war medals asked, "Where have you been all of my life?"; OPPOSITE, BOTTOM RIGHT: In Odessa, I met a teacher of English, Nina Bondarenko, who became my sister for life.

УКРАЇНСЬКО-РАДЯНСЬКА ДРУЖБА

By coincidence, we arrived in Kiev (now spelled Kyiv) on the day a revolution broke out. After the hammer and sickle flag of the Soviet Union was torn down, I photographed the very moment that Ukraine's blue and yellow flag ascended the flag pole in Independence Square.

CHAPTER FIVE

THE REVOLUTIONARY DRESS

Dressed in a flag, I take my daughter
to ground zero of a revolution

UKRAINE, AUGUST 1990

The atmosphere in Kiev seemed radically different when I arrived in August 1990 for the second "citizen diplomat" cruise down the Dnieper River from Kiev to Odessa. For this trip, I had invited my brother Jack Tenhulzen and my daughter Kristin, who had just completed a year of graduate studies in international relations in Bologna, Italy. Jack, a home-remodeling contractor in Seattle and a Vietnam veteran, had never been to this part of the world, and I felt excited about sharing this adventure with the little brother I had cared for in early childhood. He did not remember the time I rescued him after he got lost and stuck in the mud. I told him the story and joked that our roles might reverse on this trip, because I always got lost while jogging in foreign cities. At my request, Jack brought his guitar. With his fluency in American pop and folk music, he no doubt would serve as a Pied Piper in the Ukrainian cities along the Dnieper River that had been slowly opening to the outside world.

Instead of taking the train, we flew from Moscow to Kiev and went directly to the *Marshal Koshevoy*. It made me happy that Jack remarked about the similarity of its outline to our small family houseboat. We found our cabins, stowed our luggage, and then left the boat and walked to the October Revolution Square, the center of Kiev's history and Ukraine's government.

I immediately sensed a more vibrant and open atmosphere in the streets than had been present the previous summer. Scores of people hawked independent newspapers, and political posters decorated city buildings and walls. What a difference a year made! I knew that Ukraine had been rocked by recent strikes and demonstrations, but these public displays of nationalism in Kiev surprised me and inspired hope that restrictions on freedom of speech had eased. Throughout the square, people stood in clusters, talking and arguing. I tried out a few phrases in my limited Russian with a man standing next to me, and he corrected me. Our interpreter explained that he wanted me to speak Ukrainian instead of Russian. Having spent the past year studying conversational Russian, I felt deflated, but at the same time glad that someone in Kiev felt comfortable enough to talk to me.

At dinner we met our fellow passengers: ninety Americans, sixty Ukrainians, sixty French, fifteen British, two Dutch, and ten German "citizen diplomats." I noted the absence of Russians, a significant change from the previous year, when there had been about twenty Russians, including at least one KGB spy. The strain in Ukraine's relationship with Russia must have influenced our hosts, the Ukrainian Peace Committee, but I wondered whether they would face reprisals. After dinner, we were told that the Ukrainian flag would be raised in the square the following day for the first time. I wanted to clap with joy and amazement at the good luck of timing. The previous summer, I had felt the separatist movement gaining momentum, but this seemed to be a very bold move and an important event for us to witness.

Along with nearly all the passengers and crew, we went out early the next afternoon and watched a procession of men in dark suits, as they solemnly carried a large blue and yellow flag from St. Sophia Cathedral, where it had been consecrated, down Kreschatik Street to the Republic government building. Kristin, Jack, and I held hands to prevent our being separated in the crowd of five thousand or more people who were clapping and cheering as the red hammer and sickle flag of the USSR fell to the ground. I held my breath, fearing a reaction to this show of disrespect to the Soviet flag and knowing there must be Russian officials nearby. The entire crowd seemed to hush, as if feeling the same concern, but then erupted with cheers as the Ukrainian banner ascended the pole. With great gusto and emotion, people started singing the Ukrainian national anthem in several discordant keys while waving small blue and yellow flags.

Kristin, who had a great facility for languages, picked up the refrain and sang along. It was a truly memorable time for us—being swept up in the national anthem that was so meaningful to the citizens of this troubled republic, as it struggled to become a new nation state. We had come to embody peace and offer solidarity to people who had been cut off during the divisive politics of the Cold War, and now they were giving us a lesson in the importance of freedom, reminiscent of 1776 in Philadelphia.

Suddenly, as we were swept up in the sea of people, I realized that by coincidence, I was wearing a cotton-knit dress in the same shades of blue and yellow as the flag. We had stumbled into the center of a revolution, and I happened to be wearing the national flag considered sacred by Ukraine, and treasonous by the USSR. Perhaps for that reason, several men pushed Kristin and me through the crowd to the platform in front. As we climbed the steps and stood above the crowd, I could see excitement in Kristin's eyes. Someone handed a small flag to each of us, and we waved them in rhythm with the music from the stage above the crowd. Writing about this scene years later, I can still hear the music rising from the Ukrainian people, who had endured so much suffering, and I shiver at the coincidence of our participation.

Wearing the blue and yellow flag dress at dinner on the boat that evening, I received a lot of attention. The leader of the Ukrainian Peace Committee told us that hundreds of Soviet troops had been standing behind the government buildings that faced the square, armed and waiting for any provocation to rush in and break up the crowd. I realized my naivety and remembered that when Ron expressed concern about the revolutionary climate in the USSR, I had promised him I would protect Kristin from danger. So, you can imagine my fear the next day, when I saw Kiev's leading newspaper with a front-page picture of Kristin and me standing on the platform holding our flags. Of all the photo opportunities, what was the chance that we would be featured? Jack laughed, but I started to worry that Soviet spies might come looking for us on the boat. I hid the flag dress under my mattress.

I could hardly believe how heightened the tensions had become in just one year, at least in Kiev. We got news that a coalition of political parties had just called for a general labor strike and also published demands that the nuclear power reactors still operating at the devastated Chernobyl plant be shut down. Both of these actions demonstrated the growing strength and courage of the separatists. I was especially interested in what action would be taken in Chernobyl. After that horrendous nuclear explosion, international scientists and environmentalists had called for a complete shutdown of the remaining Chernobyl reactors and all similar nuclear power plants that still operated in the USSR, but there had been no response.

During dinner, we learned that the nuclear explosion, which had taken place near Kiev four years earlier, would be the topic of our evening program, to be addressed by actual survivors of Chernobyl who were traveling with us. Since I had worked on the nuclear weapons issue for the past ten years, my ears perked up when I learned that we would be hearing personal stories, a special privilege.

But before the evening program began, Jack, a boating enthusiast, led Kristin and me out to the deck to watch the crew sweep the decks and check the ropes. I could see the excitement in his eyes and feel his spirit of adventure, which made me smile. The dining room had been cleared and nearly every seat filled when we returned, just in time to hear a tall, lanky man introduce himself as having been a control room engineer at the Chernobyl plant, saying that for safety he would use a false name, "Oleg."

Oleg told us that he had been ordered to report for duty early on the morning of April 26, 1986. When he arrived, he said, superiors announced that the explosion heard throughout the city had blown a thousand-ton steel lid off one of the reactors. They ordered him and other several other operators to contain the emissions, which had already formed a large and growing cloud.

"We were not given protective clothing or even warned about danger," he said. "A supervisor told two workmen wearing normal street clothes to go outside and perform the usual morning ritual of hoisting the Soviet hammer and sickle flag. Meanwhile, pilots were flying helicopters back and forth above a rising plume of steam, dropping water in an effort to cool the reactor core," he continued. "They did not admit it, but I felt certain that a core meltdown had begun. My colleagues and I stayed all day and night working to limit the catastrophe as much as possible, but we understood the futility of our efforts."

Then, speaking slowly and in English, Oleg confessed that he was now dying of cancer, a stunning admission. This intelligent and courageous young man said he wanted the world to know how Soviet authorities had covered up the seriousness of the explosion and failed to protect tens of thousands of people in the region.

"They lied to us!" he declared. Feeling his outrage and his pain, our eyes filled with tears, a contagious condition throughout the room. The full story has finally come out, and the human tragedy still makes me cry. Ground zero had been Pripyat, a city of fifty thousand people, located one hundred miles north of Kiev. Radioactive contamination spread from Pripyat to large parts of neighboring Belarus and Russia as well as Ukraine.

"Many of the 250 people involved with immediate on-site cleanup died within months," Oleg said, bowing his head slightly. "I will not see the new year. And many thousands of civilians will suffer and die for years to come."

After dinner, Kristin, Jack, and I invited Oleg to share a bottle of wine with us. He seemed glad to talk about his childhood, his wife, and their children, whom he would not raise to adulthood. We really bonded, and, over his second glass of wine, Oleg repeated some of the traumatic details he had shared during the program. We listened quietly, as if hearing them for the first time, because it seemed that the telling helped to ease his trauma in some small way. I would have sat with him all evening if he had continued with a third telling, but the bottle had been emptied, and so, it seemed, had his need to talk. But before we departed to our cabins, Oleg invited us to go with him the next morning to meet some of his friends from Chernobyl who were living in Kiev. I accepted his generous invitation at once, knowing the rare opportunity this presented, and assured Kristin and Jack that we could miss the official tour of Kiev. And so, the following morning, with a precious four hours before we departed Kiev for our cruise down the Dnieper River, Oleg escorted us to a high-rise concrete block apartment building that sheltered Chernobyl survivors.

"Families are being housed here to make it convenient for doctors and scientists to document the progression of diseases caused by acute radiation syndrome," he said, disgustedly. "This building is nothing more than a high-rise research laboratory with human guinea pigs."

His statement jolted me. While Oleg's description of the explosion and the criminal coverup by authorities had made me feel physically ill, the callousness that this building represented sounded absolutely inhumane. And frightening. With a sense of dread, we followed Oleg into the building to visit the apartments of several families known to Oleg, friends who courageously welcomed us and openly shared their suffering.

Among the most difficult cases were the many children we met, small victims who showed us their visible symptoms, such as skin lesions and cancers of the mouth, throat, and thyroid. Out of respect, and because I felt overwhelmed with sadness, I kept my camera in my backpack. But I do not need photographs to remind me of those horrors committed against innocent families. At the time, I could not have imagined that Kristin and I would be meeting Chernobyl families in Cuba three years later.

Anatoly, a fellow engineer and friend of Oleg's, showed us a scrapbook he had been creating ever since the Chernobyl accident. It held photos taken at the plant, both during and after the core meltdown, and many subsequent newspaper clippings, which he said contained lies and disinformation. I felt his fury and realized that my clenched jaw was causing me physical pain.

Many of the survivors we visited in the apartment building told us they had secretly gone back to their homes near Chernobyl to retrieve clothing and furniture. They clearly did not understand the danger or the duration of radiation contamination. As we sat in their small apartments, I speculated about the level of radiation exposure that we might be receiving, and wondered whether Kristin was pondering the same question. I watched her face closely, and I noticed that she stayed close to her uncle Jack, but I could not be sure whether she was supporting him or drawing on his strength.

When Oleg took us back to the dock, a goodbye had never seemed so final. Our hearts felt heavy for him and the other survivors we met. Only later, as the boat left Kiev to head south, did Kristin and I discuss the experience. In the privacy of our cabin, I encouraged my daughter to express her feelings about the people we had met and their heart-bruising stories. With tears sparkling in her blue eyes, she said it had been very difficult, but through the pain, she had appreciated the extraordinary opportunity to touch raw human suffering. When she mentioned how much she admired Oleg and understood the courage it took for him to expose such terrible truths, I decided to hang my flag dress back in the closet.

Kristin and I agreed that, because we now knew so much about the Chernobyl tragedy, we carried a special responsibility to share the information. I would not have slept that night except for the rhythm of boat engines, the lapping of water beneath our portholes, and the pride I felt in my daughter. She balanced her capacity to feel deep compassion with her wisdom not to take in too much pain from others. Or perhaps, like her mother, she could cover her deepest feelings.

The next day, as we motored down the Dnieper River, I wondered whether I would see any of the people I had met the previous summer. The answer soon came in the form of delightful but embarrassing demonstrations. At each stop, where crowds again gathered to greet us, we saw people waving signs that said, "Jane Olson." I confessed that I had sent letters to all of the people who gave me their addresses, but I never anticipated this kind of response. Can you even imagine? I honestly felt humbled, and I hoped that none of the fellow passengers would think I was some kind of celebrity.

In Cherkassy, we gathered together three groups that were holding signs with my name and went together to a park, where we created a picnic by combining our food. The locals had brought bread, ham, tomatoes, cucumbers, and apples. I pulled peanut butter, nuts, granola bars, and cans of tuna and sardines out of my backpack. More importantly, Jack opened his guitar case. At every stop, he created a party by playing and teaching classic American folk songs, several of which the locals knew, despite their years of isolation. Jack often started with the simple song that fit our journey, "Row, row, row your boat, gently down the stream," an easy lyric and rhythm that often prompted the locals to join in on the third or fourth repetition.

After we arrived in Zaporozhye, Kristin and I disembarked for an early morning run. I noticed that a few painted buildings brightened the gray landscape of my memory, and the city looked a bit more cheerful. By the time we returned to the boat for breakfast, a welcoming crowd had already gathered on the dock. I spotted two signs bearing my name, one held by a young blond woman, a teacher named Julia Sobol, who stood with her husband, Yure. Having bonded with Julia on the first trip, I had kept her photo on my desk. She looked like she could be Kristin's older sister. Julia and I had corresponded a few times, and her English was excellent. Not remembering the other people's names, I asked that they introduce themselves to each other and please make a plan for the day while Kristin and I showered and found my brother.

Because they had a larger apartment, Julia and Yure offered to host us, and we drove to their home in two cars. Julia prepared tea while translating a lively discussion about Ukraine's independence revolution. When I told them about the flag ceremony in Kiev and the newspaper photo, Julia expressed concern for our safety.

"Russia needs Ukraine, and it is watching," she said. "Ukraine grows grain for the whole Soviet Union, and the bear will not release the land that feeds him."

Yure said he felt certain that violence between Russia and Ukraine would break out before too long, and he added that many people across the Soviet Union had become dissatisfied with Gorbachev and supportive of a rising populist politician named Boris Yeltsin. That surprised me, because Western nations continued to laud Gorbachev as a progressive leader, and I had assumed he enjoyed the same popularity in the USSR.

The four Ukrainians talked about the recent return of thousands of Soviet soldiers from the war they had been fighting in Afghanistan, a conflict they called "the Soviet Union's Vietnam War." Julia, a high school teacher, said, "Veterans are sitting on the floor in every classroom. They want to finish high school or go to college, but there is no room for them. Veterans cannot find jobs or housing, and they are creating stress on local economies."

We moved on to the port of Odessa, where we found a dozen members of the English Speaking Club waiting at the dock to welcome us. Nina's daughter, Natasha, jumped up and down with excitement when she met Kristin, whom she immediately nicknamed "Butterfly." My "gosling" Nick took Kristin's hand, and Roman guided Jack. As we toured Odessa's cultural sites, Nina and I walked behind the group with our arms around each other, beaming like proud mother geese. Having exchanged several letters over the past year, we had created a strong feeling of sisterhood.

Nick's family hosted us in their apartment, the largest I had seen in the USSR, as was the spread of food and drinks. Nina told me that everyone had donated food ration cards, and I understood what a sacrifice this festive spread represented. The goslings delighted me by reciting nursery rhymes in English. Alexey (another Alex), who had grown up in Siberia, recited the entire preamble of the U.S. Declaration of Independence—from memory! His voice broke when he explained how much those words inspired him and how he yearned to see America. We nodded in silence, too moved to speak. I wanted to take them all home to California.

Again, it was difficult to leave Nina and the goslings. I had never been very good at goodbyes: Ron once told me that I had no "terminal facility." So true, but at least I felt certain that Nina and I would meet again. I had already hatched a plan to bring her to California. And as for my Ukrainian goslings, the internet has allowed us to stay in frequent contact. When Russia invaded Crimea, for instance, several of them reached out to me for information and to share their fear and anger. I commiserated and forwarded reports from Human Rights Watch and other resources. I longed to wave a blue and yellow flag in Kiev's municipal square to protest Russia's annexation of Crimea, an outrageous act of war against Ukraine.

On the return trip north, I anticipated meeting Alex and his friends. I had told Kristin about Alex and his sister, but I had heard nothing from them and could not be sure they received my letters. Wearing my blue and yellow dress, I stood on the front deck as the *Marshal Koshevoy* approached Dnepropetrovsk, searching for the other Alex among a large crowd of greeters. When I spotted him and his sister, I realized I had been holding my breath. Kristin and Jack followed me down the ramp as I ran to greet him and several other teenagers I recognized. They noticed my dress and laughed at its colors.

I did not immediately share the story about the flag raising in Kiev, wanting to gauge whether the revolutionary spirit had reached this city, but I told them later when Alex asked about Kiev. He responded that voices promoting independence could speak only in whispers here. I remembered that over the years: when confronted with hateful and divisive speech in the U.S., Americans are allowed the right of free speech under the First Amendment, even when it leads directly to violence.

I told Kristin and Jack that we would have more fun with these kids than we would on the scheduled tour of Dnepropetrovsk, which I had already seen. Alex led us to a small café, where he said we could speak safely. Seated at a large round table, I passed out letters from teenaged pen pals whom I had recruited in Pasadena and laid paperback books and pop music tapes in the center of the table for them to share. Expressing delight with the gifts, the Ukrainian teens practiced using short English phrases they had learned. During the past year, they had been studying about California and wanted to know more. Jack described Seattle and the Pacific Northwest, and Kristin gave them a geography lesson by drawing a map of the USA on a brown paper tablecloth.

When the kids questioned Kristin about the life styles of American youth and asked about applying to American colleges, she offered guidance and hope, especially to Alex's sister. Jack taught them a few simple songs, including "Twinkle, Twinkle Little Star." Then he played a popular folk song, one that had special meaning for me. Everyone sang along when he repeated the refrain very slowly, "Did he ever return, no he never returned, and his fate is still unlearned." I felt so happy that I had returned and brought my daughter and younger brother. I was also glad that I had brought my flag dress, and I decided to wear it in Kiev the next day. Kristin would be proud of my courage, and people in Kiev might see it as a sign of solidarity with their yearning for freedom.

That blue and yellow dress still hangs in my travel closet as a symbol of my personal revolution and the trips that changed my life and gave me purpose. I could not bear to part with that dress. It took so many journeys with me, *it* could write a book.

In 1992, Nina flew from Odessa to California to live at our home and teach Russian language to high school students in Pasadena. She arrived on New Year's Eve, just in time to attend Pasadena's Rose Parade the next morning, which she described as giving her a "culture shock of pure joy."

During the spring of 1992, riots erupted in Los Angeles following the Rodney King criminal trial. Nina and I watched televised news of the chaos and violence taking place in LA, with people looting stores and burning buildings. We could hear police and ambulance sirens, as ashes rained down on our lawn and swimming pool. Not believing my assurances that the police and government officials would control the situation and keep us safe, Nina shook with fear. In the Soviet Union, police officers more often perpetrated violence.

Nina and her husband now live in Texas with their daughter, Natasha, who got a good job and became a U.S. citizen. Natasha still calls me "Mother Goose" and her American sister, Kristin, "Butterfly."

In Kiev, it was a time for celebration and a time for reflection on future challenges

OPPOSITE: Dressed by coincidence in the colors of the Ukrainian flag, I posed under a very tall statue of Vladimir Lenin; TOP: An old man played traditional music on a beautiful lute; BOTTOM: My brother Jack used his western guitar to teach American folk songs.

OPPOSITE: Everywhere I pointed my camera, a photo of exuberant joy, pride, and celebration appeared; ABOVE: Thousands of Ukrainians filled Independence Square that day in August 1990, waving their national flag with vigor, already tasting freedom.

During an attempted coup d'etat, Muscovites built barricades to protect the White House, home of Russia's parliament.

CHAPTER SIX

COMFORT FOOD

———————

Women stop a coup attempt with love and macaroni

MOSCOW, RUSSIA, AUGUST 1991

When I arrived in Moscow in August 1991, a year after my second Dnieper River cruise, I got to see in person what I recently had been viewing with great trepidation on television—disturbing remnants of a very recent coup attempt. An enormous jumble of barriers surrounded the White House, home of Russia's Parliament, evidence of a scenario that still confounds both military and political experts. In the heart of Moscow, military tanks filled Red Square, and I could see broken up pavement in the square and on surrounding streets. A dozen or more tanks, all of them idle and empty, faced the Kremlin, with others near beautiful St. Basil's Cathedral, which is known as the "Cathedral of the Intercession of the Virgin." The irony of that name occurred to me after I learned how Russian women had helped save their city, but I don't want to get ahead of a great story.

For me, personally, the entire journey to Moscow in August 1991 had been a bumpy road. It began with an invitation to join a small delegation from Human Rights Watch (HRW) on a trip to Moscow, to serve as a public delegate to the first human rights conference held behind the Iron Curtain. The landmark event was sponsored by the Conference on Security and Cooperation in Europe (CSCE), which changed its name in 1995 to the Organization for Security and Co-operation in Europe.

A week prior to the scheduled meeting, a few Soviet leaders and military generals startled the world by attempting a coup d'état. On August 19, coup plotters invaded the vacation villa of Soviet president Mikhail Gorbachev in the Crimea, forcibly deposed him, and held him under house arrest for several days. Meanwhile, scores of army tanks invaded Moscow's city center from a base near the municipal airport. The generals had planned to seize government buildings in Moscow and take over leadership of Russia and the entire Soviet Union.

At home in Pasadena, I stayed glued to news coverage of the chaos and worried about Russian friends I had met the previous summers, several of whom lived in Moscow. I looked for them among the throngs of people shown on CNN demonstrating in the streets—and worried about their safety amid the chaos. I flew from Los Angeles to Washington, D.C., to join the HRW delegation and other American participants, and we all stood by, watching the crisis unfold on television—better to be stranded in Washington than in Moscow. After a couple of tense days, which we spent discussing important human rights issues on the conference agenda, we were relieved to learn that the coup attempt had been put down. Gorbachev returned to Moscow and resumed control of the government, and the CSCE conference would proceed.

I kept thinking about my Russian friends during the flight to Moscow, eager to learn the inside story from them. After I got to my hotel room and unpacked, I opened a new journal with a red leather cover. When I found the book many years later, I read these words: "For 48 hours on August 19th and 20th, I barely slept. I watched CNN and prayed for the courage and triumph of the Soviet people and for the safety of Mikhail Gorbachev, who had shined for them a beacon of hope. I prayed this challenge to his leadership would not develop into a bloody civil war. It is thrilling for me to come to Moscow at this threshold moment, and I share the joy and hope of the Russian people, as I shared the pain of their oppression, fear, and despair."

We soon learned that not only columns of tanks had rolled into Moscow, but also armored personnel carriers and trucks filled with soldiers, men who had been told they were being sent to maintain order in the city. But once they arrived, they never received orders about what to do next. It seems that some of the coup plotters got drunk in their dachas (summer homes). Apparently, those holding Gorbachev in the Crimea also surrendered to vodka and let down their guard.

Eight men with powerful positions in Russia and the USSR tried to turn back the clock and "restore order" through heavy-handed rule, but they had misjudged the people. During my visits the previous summers, I had formed the impression that President Gorbachev popularity had slipped, but it seemed that his reform initiatives, such as perestroika, were gaining acceptance and support. Somehow the coup plotters did not understand that Gorbachev reforms inspired hope for greater freedom in that vast communist country, where human rights had long been suppressed. Once the lid of freedom opened even a crack, and once people experienced freedoms they had never known, it would take more than tanks to reclose the lid.

The closest friend I made on the "citizen diplomat" cruise trips, a woman named Natasha, lived in an apartment building directly across the Moskva River from the White House, seat of the Russian government, with her husband, Tolya, a noted cinematographer. When I called to ask about their experiences during the coup fiasco, Natasha invited me over for dinner. Having grown up as the daughter of a celebrity movie actor, she had a very sharp mind and projected an air of refinement. On previous visits, Natasha gave me lessons in cooking blinis and borscht in her small kitchen, and Tolya taught me how to judge caviar.

Looking across the river from a window of their apartment, I could see an impressive barricade still standing in front of the White House. Natasha and Tolya had joined scores of other Muscovites in building it, and both said they felt proud to have played a small role in protecting the Russian government. That surprised me, because they privately had criticized its authoritarian rule. Then, over tea and pryaniks, my favorite Russian cookies made with honey and ginger spice, Natasha delighted in telling me about an even more impressive role she played during the coup, a story that I had not learned in news sources. Her warm brown eyes lit up the minute she began talking.

"Many of the young men who drove the tanks into Moscow came from far reaches of the Soviet Union and did not know the city," she said. "They had no maps or communication devices, so they couldn't receive orders from commanders or even talk to each other. As they drove down the highway from the airport, the tank drivers asked local people how to get to Red Square. Imagine that!" she said, laughing at the absurdity. "Muscovites, outraged at seeing tanks on their city streets, gave them incorrect directions on purpose and caused them to drive hours out of the way." Natasha's eyes crinkled with glee as she continued, "When tanks arrived at the Kremlin late at night, I called my friends and suggested that we should feed those boys." It seems other women had the same idea, and many took food and drinks to the soldiers in Red Square that night.

"I took a pot of macaroni," Natasha said. "We called to the tank drivers and told them that we are their sisters and mothers. They should come out of the tanks so we could feed them and take care of them." She told me that most of the soldiers climbed out of their tanks and accepted the food gratefully, and then after eating, many of them joined the barricade.

"It seems that they had no orders about what to do once they got here," she added, laughing. "They had no idea of the purpose for their wild ride."

The story was both humorous and deeply moving. As Natasha spoke, two thoughts went through my mind. One, a memory of being frightened during the 1968 Poor People's March on Washington. Hunkered down in a small apartment with our first two babies, I actually had feared that democracy could be ending in the United States. And the second, warm memories of helping my mother deliver macaroni and cheese casseroles to friends and neighbors in need. I shared both stories with Natasha, hoping that I was not diminishing her much more dramatic experience. Sometimes I speak when I should just listen, but friendships are built on this kind of give and take.

I greatly admired Natasha's courage and her ingenuity. Instead of seeing the tank drivers as invading enemies, she had realized they were just ordinary boys like her own son Andrew, and they probably were hungry and frightened. Her humanitarian response helped to defuse a potentially explosive situation. Women throughout history have played an important role by showing up with food, a powerful tool of diplomacy.

In fact, the coup attempt came very close to succeeding, we later learned from Russian prime minister Valentin Pavlov, one of the core group of plotters. He blamed the generals for its failure. Trained as an economist, Pavlov had turned against Gorbachev because he disagreed with his economic policies. He later told Russian television that the plan had been perfect except for one flaw:

"If we had followed the original plan and convened the Supreme Soviet, and everyone had signed the papers there," he said, "it would have been very simple. If someone had not been so stupid and introduced combat vehicles into the city, nothing would have gone wrong." A scary thought! We may never know, but I will forever give credit to the women of Moscow for stopping the overthrow of Russia's government with their pots of food, and I couldn't wait to tell my mother how macaroni had served as so much more than "comfort food" during the 1991 coup attempt in the USSR.

Despite the uncertainty, thirty-five countries sent delegations to participate in the Moscow conference, which promised to focus on the human dimension of conflict between nation states. I realized what perfect timing this had been for the first conference on human rights to be held behind the Iron Curtain, an invisible barrier that was shredding and thinning even as we gathered. In many ways, the extraordinary gathering marked the end of an era for the Soviet Union. The conference produced a document laying out the obligations of each nation to its citizens, and it included a "Moscow Mechanism," which enabled states to hold each other accountable, a remarkable achievement.

The Hon. Max Kampelman, who headed the U.S. delegation, said he knew the USSR was weakening, but that no one could predict how quickly the old Soviet bear would die or how many violent conflicts would erupt in the process of its dismemberment. Would the fifteen republics of the USSR, distinct lands and populations who had been held together for seventy-four years through force and fear, break off into fifteen separate nations? Or would they form regional unions or federations of some sort? Only time would tell.

As we listened to revelations about the massive suppression and forced dislocation of people throughout the USSR and Eastern Europe, one thing became clear in my mind: the great potential for violence. Full-out wars could soon break out in various regions because of ethnic conflict and border disputes.

Whatever the future held, I wanted to participate actively, as an advocate for human rights, as a humanitarian, as a peacemaker, and as a mother goose.

On my last night in Moscow, Natasha cooked a special dinner for me. She prepared my favorite foods early in the day and then picked me up at my hotel, asking whether I would like to stop by a bakery . . . I said "yes to that!" A new experience. We parked the car and joined a long line of people waiting to enter the bakery. I had seen many long queues outside stores in Russia and Ukraine, but I had no idea that there would be three more lines inside the store—one to select the bread, a second to pay for it, and a third to pick it up. The last line took the longest, because the clerk could not find Natasha's name on any of the paper-wrapped loaves waiting on shelves to be picked up. When we finally left, I checked my watch and told Natasha that the process of buying a loaf of bread had taken a full hour. She smiled and replied that we were lucky to get through so quickly.

Over our delicious dinner, Natasha and Tolya joked about the queues, which they referred to as boot camps for training Russians to be patient, "a major achievement of communism." Tolya said that wealthy people often hired someone to stand in lines for them. As a guest in their home, I did not express my opinions about the ridiculous waste of time caused by gross inefficiency. It had not seemed worth the wait, but when Natasha warmed and sliced that bread, its fabulous aroma took me back to the kitchens of my mother and grandmothers and to the wheat fields of Nebraska and Ukraine. When it comes to comfort food, I decided, nothing beats freshly baked bread.

TOP: When these two Russian soldiers greeted me with friendly curiosity, I realized that they were, after all, just boys; BOTTOM: My friend Nina cooking in the kitchen of her Moscow apartment.

Both the people and the architecture of Havana, Cuba, fascinated me.

CHAPTER SEVEN

WIND BENEATH WINGS

Stuck in a 1950s movie, Cuba delivers
dramatic scenes, clearly not black and white

CUBA, MARCH 1993

Before our daughter Kristin was two years old, she had journeyed through most of Western Europe with Ron and me in our Volkswagen camper, collecting countries like my sisters and I had collected states during family vacations in the 1950s. We bought costumed dolls from each country for baby Kristin, a collection that may have inspired her interest in studying world history and international relations in college and graduate school.

Kristin had already traveled throughout Western and Eastern Europe and parts of the Soviet Union before the Iron Curtain fell. For her twenty-seventh birthday in March 1993, I gave her another gift of travel, a trip to Cuba to investigate the Cold War's impact on that country, an island nation so near to the United States. The organization Promoting Enduring Peace, with whom we had traveled to Ukraine, sponsored this trip. It would take American "citizen diplomats" to Cuba, which had not seen visitors from the United States in many years—in this case because the U.S. had established an embargo and banned travel to Cuba some thirty years earlier.

Again, Kristin and I joined one of the first delegations of Americans allowed to travel to an "enemy" country. Since our trip to Ukraine, she had earned her master's degree in international studies with a focus on Latin America and was working at the World Bank in Washington, D.C., serving as country director for Nicaragua. But this trip would not be an official visit for her in that capacity.

The United States had imposed strict sanctions on Cuba in 1961 and made travel there nearly impossible until recently. Travel restrictions were now softening for special groups, such as environmentalists and artists. Our delegation of thirty-four Americans from seventeen states secured legitimate visas as "environmentalists," an expertise I could not claim, but our leaders and several others in the group had strong credentials.

Since no American airline went to Cuba, we flew from Miami to Havana on Haitian Airlines. The plane we boarded looked as if it had more than thirty years of flight time under its wings. Most likely, an American company had sold it cheaply to Haiti, along with assurances that duct tape and baling wire would hold the plane together for a few more years. Once in the air, I feared it would break apart during our ninety-mile flight. The shaking reminded me of my first DC 10 Braniff Airways flight from Omaha to New Orleans at age twelve, and my stomach once again rebelled.

On our drive from the airport to the city center of Havana, we passed only a few cars on the highway. Instead of automobiles, the streets were lined with horse-drawn carts, bicycles, and a few rusty trucks. I noticed billboards picturing children above slogans in Spanish that read *ninos primeros*, meaning children first. One billboard promised that all Cuban children would receive a liter of milk every day. It struck me that in our country we see a lot of advertising in support of senior citizens, but children, especially poor children, had few advocates, perhaps because children do not vote. Cuba, which had no democratic elections, seemed to put children first. I pulled myself back from this cynical line of thinking and did not share it with Kristin.

Along the route, American automobiles from the 1950s littered the streets, as if auditioning for roles in a documentary film. The cars, we learned, had been abandoned after it became impossible to secure spare parts from the USA or oil from Russia, which recently had cut off the trade practice of Russian oil in exchange for Cuban sugar. I spotted a 1956 black Chevy sedan, and I told Kristin that it looked identical to the car I bought during college. Teenaged Cuban boys were peering under the Chevy's raised hood—as if frozen in a James Dean movie.

After arriving at the Inglaterra Hotel and admiring its marble floors and colorfully tiled walls, Kristin and I quickly unpacked and went out to explore Old Havana on foot. We immediately attracted curious young men, as we had in the Soviet Union, and Kristin answered all their preguntas. I had anticipated hostility, given the many hardships caused by the U.S. blockade, but people on the streets greeted us with great enthusiasm, expressing pleasure at meeting Americans and delight that Kristin spoke such fluent Spanish. I felt pride, watching my daughter interact with foreigners in their language, on their turf, with curiosity bathed in kindness. Many others in our delegation soon recognized her skills and called on her constantly to translate for them.

From Human Rights Watch, I knew a lot about President Fidel Castro's brutal dictatorship, especially its practice of censorship and the imprisonment of political dissidents, common traits in authoritarian regimes. But I hoped to learn about living conditions, and especially to determine whether the quality of life had deteriorated recently, since the collapse of the Soviet Union ended its support of Cuba. Our itinerary included visits with officials in governmental agencies and tours of schools, hospitals, churches, and scientific institutes. I felt certain that we would also learn a lot by talking to ordinary Cuban people, as we had in Russia and Ukraine.

Cuba's ministers of education and agriculture invited Kristin to meet with them after they learned about her role at the World Bank. As it turned out, they asked her a lot of questions about Central America's recovery from the contra wars, but they did not share much about their own programs. That was frustrating and disappointing, because she had hoped to learn more about economic and political conditions, important insights from government officials that she could have shared with our group and taken back to the World Bank.

Back to the story. The first night, March 12, Kristin and I got to sleep rather late, because a disco band was playing in a bar on the floor above us. To block out the noise, I wore earplugs and put a pillow over my head. In the middle of the night, Kristin shook me awake. Even through earplugs, I could hear deafening sounds, but I somehow had incorporated them into my dreams. We looked out our window and watched a car flying down the street and slamming into the side of a building. Kristin shouted, "Hurricane!" She had been awake long enough to fill the bathtub and every container she could find with water. I admired her survival instincts but realized that I had once again brought her into a dangerous situation.

The next morning, we discovered that we had survived a major hurricane and also a tornado, which had hit parts of Havana. Perhaps the locals had known that it was coming, but we had no television sets in our rooms, and we received no warning. After returning home weeks later, we learned that this hurricane was part of a vast weather catastrophe, which meteorologists dubbed the "Storm of the Century." In addition to Cuba, winds of hurricane intensity had hit Florida's Gulf Coast and caused an enormous blizzard all along the East Coast from Alabama to Canada.

Our group, all of us quite shaken, met in the hotel lobby and decided to cancel our planned morning schedule (as if we had a choice), leaving us free to investigate how the hurricane had impacted the city. Leaning into strong winds, Kristin and I walked toward the harbor, where we saw huge waves splashing over the tops of seawalls and continuing with full force to the base of several important buildings, nearly reaching the United States Embassy, which still had minimal operations. Kristin learned from speaking with locals that Cuba's northern coast had been inundated by gusts up to one hundred miles an hour, pushing forty-five-foot waves. Either from ignorance, hubris, or because it was the American way, we decided by a bare majority vote to follow our planned itinerary for the afternoon, despite a warning and strong resistance from our bus driver.

When we reached our first destination, a botanical garden, a guard at the entrance told us that the grounds had been closed because of an accident two hours earlier. A flying coconut had hit and killed a European tourist! That got our attention, but we continued to drive along the coast to Tarara, a beautiful beach resort that wealthy Cubans had abandoned when they fled the revolution. Through blowing sand, we could see the outlines of palm trees arching over small white stucco cottages. This resort, now called the José Martí Pioneer Camp, had been transformed into a school and recreation center for Cuba's Young Pioneers youth organization. The director proudly told us that when Pioneer youth leaders learned about the Chernobyl nuclear power plant disaster that had devastated Ukraine in 1986, they generously offered their camp to be used as a refuge for Chernobyl children who needed medical treatments.

Kristin and I exchanged startled glances, remembering Oleg, whom we met on the Dnieper River cruise in 1990, and our visits in Kiev with families from the Chernobyl region. The director told us, "We set up a medical clinic, and more than ten thousand Soviet children have come here for treatment, most suffering from leukemia, lymphoma, and thyroid conditions caused by radiation poisoning. Four hundred kids are in residence now." In Spanish, Kristin told him about the apartment building in Kiev filled with Chernobyl survivors. As they conversed, I watched my daughter tear up, and I wondered whether I had exposed her compassionate heart to too much suffering. But this felt like a very meaningful coincidence. My heart filled not just with worry about the impact on her soul, but with pride that my child could feel so deeply.

We learned that Ukrainian children younger than eight, and those requiring surgery, had been allowed to come here with one parent or guardian and could stay as long as necessary, under the care of skilled medical personnel trained in Cuba's free "education through college" program. The fact that Cuba provided everything except transportation impressed me greatly. The conversion of this beautiful camp, from its previous life as a popular resort for wealthy Cubans into a medical clinic for children, challenged my assumptions about the nature of Fidel Castro's authoritarian dictatorship.

After visiting with Ukrainian families, Kristin and I joined the rest of our group, touring a small clinic that treated Cuban children who suffered from diabetes. Once again, a surprise awaited us—this time, one that lifted my spirit. A young woman in our delegation told the doctor she had been diabetic since childhood, and had found out about this diabetes clinic. I soon understood her eagerness to follow our itinerary that morning despite the hurricane. She explained that she had brought from home a special gift for the clinic, a large suitcase containing several hundred insulin-filled syringes layered in cold packs.

She said that the insulin had to be kept cold, and it may have been wasted if we had not come on this intrepid journey the first day. She started to apologize that she had not been able to bring more, but the doctor held up his hand in a universal "stop" sign. He took her to a small refrigerator that held only a few small bottles, and then to a closet, which was the clinic's pharmacy. It really shook us to see that less than a dozen syringes sat on a shelf, and that was their entire supply. The doctor continued to explain that they had been sterilizing and reusing those syringes. I greatly admired this thoughtful gift from one who understood the vital importance of insulin.

"We are very handicapped," the doctor said, "because the blockade has stopped the delivery of drugs and medical supplies from the U.S." I made a mental note to bring more over-the-counter medical supplies on future trips to poor countries, and I later wrote in my journal that U.S. lawmakers should be made to come and witness the human consequences of their policies.

Kristin and I left the clinic, and, shielding our eyes from blowing sand, walked among cottages to visit with young Ukrainian patients and their parents. With the help of a translator, Kristin told them about our experiences with Chernobyl victims in Kiev; they expressed surprise and appreciation that we understood their plight. Many of the Ukrainians clutched their hearts, as if they understood the English words, and it was clear that sharing personal traumas helped to relieve some of their pain and anxiety. Even the sickest patients demonstrated optimism that they would recover and return home. They expressed admiration for the skills of Cuban doctors and nurses and gratitude for the kindness and generosity they had found there.

Given their situation, such optimism would have seemed unlikely, but Kristin and I understood. We had toured that apartment building in Kiev, where Chernobyl survivors were being treated like "guinea pigs" for Soviet research studying the effects of radiation on the human body. Even though they were far from home and very ill, these children were being treated here by qualified Cuban doctors. No wonder they felt grateful. I shared their gratitude. Perhaps just coming here gave them hope, and hope can serve as a powerful medicine to strengthen the immune system and nurture a will to live.

Before we departed, the director told us that Nelson Mandela had visited this camp in 1991, when he came to thank the Cuban people for supporting South Africa's fight against apartheid and colonialism. In the director's office, Kristin read a framed newspaper article and translated its quote from Mandela calling Cuba the most generous country on earth. "What other country has such a history of selfless behavior? Many countries benefit from Cuban health care professionals and educators," Mandela had declared.

All of this surprised and amazed me. I had never heard that Mandela had come here, because American media covered very little news about Cuba. Nelson Mandela had endured twenty-seven years in a horrendous prison on Robben Island. When he was finally released in 1990, Mandela forgave his prison guards for their cruelty and torture. I remember hearing his words at the time and thinking, those years in prison must have taught him a lot about human character. His words moved me and stayed with me. Five years later, in 1998, I took my daughter Amy to South Africa following her law school graduation. While in Cape Town, we toured Mandela's cell on Robben Island, and I told Amy about his visit to Cuba and shared his wisdom about the importance of forgiveness.

Back in Havana, with calmer winds, Kristin and I walked the streets and asked random people what they thought about the United States. Many said they liked American people but not the government, because it did not allow ships to come here. They were right—the Cuban Democracy Act of 1992 banned travel to Cuba by U.S. citizens and stopped family remittances to Cuba. A brutal and vindictive law, it also declared that if any ship, no matter the nationality, took supplies to Cuba, it could not enter a U.S. port for six months,.

In 1959, during the Cold War, a revolution led by Fidel Castro overthrew the Batista regime, which had been supported by the U.S., and created a socialist government allied with the Soviet Union. The following year, the U.S. imposed an embargo that banned trade, commerce, and financial relationships with Cuba. The ban on U.S. exports to Cuba had continued for more than six decades, longer than the U.S. had sanctioned any other country. President Barack Obama eased relationships with Cuba substantially, but President Trump later labeled Cuba a terrorist country, along with Nicaragua and Venezuela, and imposed significant new sanctions.

We visited several small grocery stores in Havana and noticed that the shelves held only a few canned goods. Labels identified products as having come from Canada, Germany, and other European countries that clearly had resisted pressure from the United States. No doubt the Cuban government and elites lived well, but most Cuban people had to stand in line to receive ration cards and then queue up again to buy food, like the long food lines I saw in Russia and the Ukraine.

We entered a small drug store, where an elderly woman "pharmacist" showed us jars of dried medicinal herbs and baskets of fresh herbs. "Indigenous Cubans have used these remedies for hundreds of years," she explained. "They are needed now, because people are suffering from beri-beri and other diseases caused by malnutrition." I recognized wisdom in her deeply lined face and wished we could have stayed to learn about her indigenous heritage, knowledge needed now. Why, we wondered, had this government failed to set up an agricultural program sufficient to feed its people? Cuba's rich soil and ample sunshine should have allowed sustainable food production. Through the World Bank, Kristin had created a program for Nicaragua that brought American farmers, including Iowa farmers, to advise on agricultural procedures. The current travel restrictions here would prevent that from happening, as would politics.

The next morning, although strong winds were still blowing, our leaders decided to stick to the plans and fly south to the Isle of Youth. Authorities at the airport, however, used better judgment and made us wait for several hours until the winds died down. While Kristin and I walked around the small terminal building to stretch our legs, we searched the tarmac for a plane large enough to accommodate our group, and we saw only a fat-bellied cargo plane that looked like a relic from World War II. Later, we boarded that relic, entering through a hatch in the rear end, and sat on wooden folding chairs that faced inward, our backs against the windowless exterior.

As we fastened flimsy seat belts, I secured a white-knuckled death grip on my seat, and cursed myself for going along with this dangerous plan. While the plane bounced and lurched south in hurricane tail winds, I regretted, too late, my lunch of Cajun-style sausage with spicy red beans and rice. But we bounced down safely on the Isle of Youth, the comma-shaped island off Cuba's southwest coast, and took a bus to the Colony Hotel. The hotel manager, who looked like Desi Arnaz, greeted us enthusiastically, saying we were the first group of Americans ever to visit his resort.

Fidel Castro had been imprisoned from 1953 to 1955 on this small island, which at that time was called the "Isle of Pines." In 1978, Castro changed its name to the Isle of Youth (Isla de la Juventud) and created a network of schools for youth from other countries, including from Latin America, Africa, and Asia. He ordered sixty-one schools, each with a capacity of about five hundred students, to be built on plantations and resorts that had been abandoned by wealthy owners after the revolution. We were told that Cuba sent thousands of its soldiers to support various poor countries, mostly in the Southern Hemisphere, that were fighting revolutionary wars against European colonial powers. And Castro invited children from those nations to come here for protection and free education, a less than altruistic exchange of soldiers for children. More than ten thousand teenagers had studied here and then returned to countries like Sudan, Ethiopia, and Namibia as teachers and leaders. But by 1993, only fourteen of the sixty-one schools remained. We got to tour several of them.

I couldn't have hoped for a better itinerary for Kristin. She had spent a summer in Lima, Peru, as an exchange student during her junior year of high school, and I knew she would love meeting these students. We first went to a large grapefruit plantation that had several four-story buildings that collectively housed 450 students from what was referred to as the Arab Republic of West Sahara. The students were allowed to stay there for four years or longer to study agriculture, education, technology, and other skills. To support their tuition, we were told, they worked in the orchards every afternoon. My ears perked up at that, because it sounded like a form of child labor, but I could not learn more about the length or severity of the work requirement.

We then toured a mosque, which had been built to help Muslim students retain their religion and culture. That impressed me as an enlightened idea. And then, just as I was praising Cuba's thoughtfulness, I noticed murals painted on dormitory walls depicting Lenin, Che Guevara, and other revolutionary leaders, a colorful and bold endorsement of communism. The confluence of the mosque and the murals confounded me. Nothing about Cuba's benevolence seemed straightforward. This was not a judgment call, just an observation of fact.

On Kristin's actual birthdate, the Ides of March, she and I visited a school for girls from Angola, an oil-rich southwest African country that had been embroiled in civil war since gaining its independence from Portugal in 1975. The girls greeted Kristin with delight, as my goslings had done in Odessa. They led us on a tour of their classrooms and then took us into an outdoor patio room, where we sat on folding chairs while they combed Kristin's blond hair and took turns trying on her cute straw hat. She talked and giggled with them, fitting comfortably into their school-girl conversation. What a memorable experience that was, seeing my child interacting with girls from another continent, embracing their culture, sharing her warmth, kindness, and humor. I knew these girls would remember that forever. She would represent "America" to them, and she would never forget their sisterhood.

I told the Angolan girls that Kristin's nickname was "Butterfly," and she translated, "Mariposa." Then I whispered to the girls, while pointing at Kristin, "Es su cumpleaños." At that, the girls joyfully sang "Happy Birthday" to her in three languages. They called me "Momma," and, obviously missing their Angolan mothers, soaked up hugs and kisses. We handed out postcards from California along with cosmetics and costume jewelry.

Then I pulled a wrapped present for Kristin out of my backpack, a small butterfly kite. I could not have chosen a more perfect setting for this gift, which I had purchased in Pasadena. We went outside to a grassy lawn, and the girls took turns learning to fly the kite. Finally, Kristin took the strings, and the butterfly bounced and dipped, then soared aloft on a gust of wind, where its colorful wings, still visible high above the tallest pine trees, flapped exuberantly.

Every second of the time we spent with those beautiful Angolan girls still lives in my heart, especially watching those children, so far from their homes, singing "Happy Birthday" to my child. It makes everything in my life feel worthy of my goals, of our goals. I couldn't wait to tell my goslings in Ukraine how their "Butterfly" flew that kite in Cuba. Parents throughout the world seek joyful freedom for their children.

Back in California, I visited Direct Relief International, an international humanitarian relief organization in Santa Barbara, California, to request medical supplies for the José Martí center, but was disappointed to learn that, due to the blockade, even they could not send shipments to Cuba. I felt strongly that because of the blockade, the U.S. government served as a scapegoat for many failures of Castro's government and its socialist economy. Cuban people blamed the blockade for their shortages of food, clothing, machinery, and supplies. Even Direct Relief could not get around the blockade, and that just broke my heart.

Moreover, just one year later, in 1994, economic conditions forced the closure of all schools on the Isle of Youth. More than a decade later, in 2008, Hurricane Gustav decimated the island and destroyed what remained of the international school buildings that Fidel Castro had created. When I read about that tragedy, I pictured those girls from Angola, and I could not stop crying.

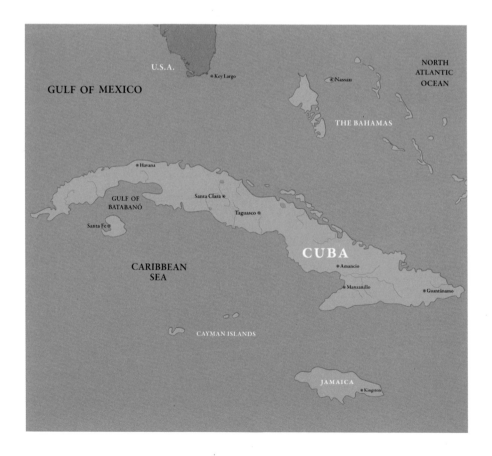

OPPOSITE: Cuban heroes appeared larger than life on billboards and buildings; ABOVE: American cars from the 1950s, in need of repair and gasoline, littered the streets of Havana.

TOP: In every café, we found Cuban musicians strumming classic guitars; BOTTOM: The signs of revolution could not be missed; OPPOSITE, TOP: Boy power replaced horse power; OPPOSITE, BOTTOM: Teenaged girls from Angola, who were being educated in Cuba, helped Kristin to celebrate her birthday.

THE BALKANS

Map of the former Yugoslavia

men in concentratn
made to sodomize
other in a row, Shot
not do it.
os of men having to
rotums off other men
s. True?
in video of trays
e organs,

Ma...
Zep...
shot — scores of bodies on road
3rd US airdrop completed. Being
suspended now & truck convoys
readied to go.
Shld send trucks to escort
evacuees
Cerska was target for airdrops.
Report this am that Cerska was
overrun by the Serbs.

Taking
Local woma...
reports of s...

By MONICA PRINZ...
Life staff writer

A Bosnian Musl...
physician's life a...
same...

2 kids put in mental instil.
father drunk — beat kids, still
800 kids here on coast
w/o parents all
not orphans all
HC takes care of them
reunite families

3 kids all wounded, 17, 14,
father killed in war
mother slaughtered in Vites
lost ?t — Croat family
girls arm dead — schrapnel
boys wounded in stomach
walked out 2t
boys don't hate
Psychiatrist

After war will have generath
of lost kids —

VIZA - VISA

za jedan - ~~neograničen~~ izlazak - ulazak - tranzit
for a single - ~~unlimited~~ exit - entry - transit
pour un (e) seul (e) - un nombre illimité de sorties - entrées - transits
br./No _02/3-448/95_
Vrijedi od/It is valid from/Valable du _22.03.95_
do/until/jusqu'à _20.05.95_

U svrhu/For the purpose of/Dans le but de _turist_

Voditelj grupe
Group leader
Chef de groupe _22 osoba_

ZAGREB
ul. 29.III.95

de of those without a voice

n second trip to Bosnia with
umiliation and shining spirit

> possible to exaggerate the level of
> ity. While some people say rape
> r, this is the first
> has been
> strategy in war.'

—Jane Olson

...d to the fact that help is
...ning.
...y are depressed, frustrat-
... angry. Many of them
...elling at me, saying peo-
...'t need to keep asking
...ons, the world already
...what's happening. They
...nebody to do something.
...onscionable to do noth-

...while, Olson said the
...continue.
...possible to exaggerate
...l of brutality," said
...she recalled some of
...grisly stories regarding
...of sexual mutilation,
..., rape, forced incest,
... and sickness.
...some people say rape
...urs during war, this is
...ime in history when
... been specifically
...s a strategy in war,
...re being raped and
...any where from age

The new stories being heard
were the rapes involving men. It
is not about sex, but about
...home purchased a year ago.   ...humiliation and an effort to
Concerned about the plight of the

MEDICINSKI CENTAR
SLAVONSKI BROD

Jane Olson reflects on her latest trip to war-torn
struggle to keep hope alive.

place there. Many are having
abortions because they don't
want the stigma ... and many
have the babies then leave them
at the hospital."

Another Bosnian who made a
noticeable impression on Olson
...iona herself, Olson could
...ticularly identify with him.

high lev...
explained...
...ble." "...
...tle, but...
...give O...
drink...
littl...
cloth...

HANDBOOK OF FACTS ON:
THE BREAK-UP OF YUGOSLAVIA,
INTERNATIONAL POLICY,
AND THE WAR IN
BOSNIA-HERCEGOVINA

...nst was 7 mon. pregnant
...ld only stand — held
...90 days at priests house
...7 days at sch
...es took them to forest to
...em — shot some
...en came from village + help
...took to Brussa   the
...other-in-law + son who ha
...sch friends arrested + abus

...has 10 named Semir
son   called Senco
Fasilo - sociologist

Elma +
E

...
b... fun f...
estaf
making 10 loth
goal 950 i...
IRC is only org
grp here
mandate only
+ water distrib
but doing mu
Problems #1 shelt
20% have no
15 pple in some
food —
every day brea
ICRC says 22T
(imp to 25T

Children's art reflected their frightening experiences of war.

CHAPTER EIGHT

THE ART OF WAR

*Refugee children's faces mask horrors
needing to be expressed*

YUGOSLAVIA, SEPTEMBER 1992

In August 1992, Ron planned and hosted a big surprise party to celebrate my fiftieth birthday, one of the rare times he really surprised me. I am much more comfortable with the planning and giving side of life, but this event absolutely delighted me, especially the mix of guests he invited, family members and friends from all parts of our lives. None of them will ever forget the spectacular setting of that celebratory dinner, a long tent with an open roof set on a south-facing beach in Santa Barbara, decorated with long stripes of white cloth and strings of sparkling lights that allowed a full view of the night sky and a rising full moon. As a child in Iowa, I had always wished to see the Pacific Ocean, and I felt such gratitude and joy.

Another wish came true during the delicious surf and turf dinner. One of the guests, Catherine O'Neill, invited me to travel to a war zone and witness the needs of refugee women. A few words about Catherine will explain why this was such an intriguing invitation. As a lifelong advocate for women's rights and vulnerable people, Catherine had traveled through refugee camps in Pakistan, Thailand, and elsewhere.

In that incongruously beautiful setting by the Pacific Ocean, Catherine and I spoke of a war of "ethnic cleansing" brewing among three of the six Yugoslav republics, Serbia, Croatia, and Bosnia-Herzegovina (hereafter referred to as "Bosnia"). American journalists had been reporting accounts of rape being used as a weapon of war—an insidious strategy meant to destroy Muslim families and communities in Bosnia. When I told Catherine that the use of an innocuous term like "cleansing" in reference to violence and murder made my skin crawl, she suddenly suggested that we should go to Yugoslavia to investigate the situation on the ground.

At the time, I did not know Catherine O'Neill very well, although I admired her accomplishments. I had been touched when she hired me a few years earlier to photograph her wedding to the noted author and biographer Richard Reeves. I knew that she recently had co-founded an organization, then known as Women's Commission for Refugee Women and Children (now the Women's Refugee Commission, or WRC), under the auspices of the International Rescue Committee (IRC) in New York City.

For several years, I had been presiding over an empty nest, which gave me more time to do volunteer work for non-profit organizations, especially Human Rights Watch. I loved my trips to Central America and the USSR and had been hoping for more international travel to places of conflict growing out of human rights abuses. I secretly worried that I might be sidelined after turning fifty, a number that sounded old at the time. With this invitation, Catherine gave me a unique birthday gift, an opportunity to travel with protection from the IRC and learn more about the refugee crisis. Her invitation helped me avoid a crisis of confidence.

Even though my three trips to the Soviet Union had taught me about the growing tensions between Russia, Ukraine, and other USSR republics, I had not anticipated the epidemic of ethnic hatred that broke out across Iron Curtain countries when the Soviet Union split up in the early 1990s. Most of the conflicts involved two issues, challenges to borders and demands for freedom and basic human rights, issues that could be irreconcilable and intractable.

On this mission for the WRC, I could learn the full impact of violence on human beings by meeting victims, hearing their stories, and documenting the cruelty and destruction of a war that specifically targeted civilians. While anxious to go and see for myself, I felt a bit of trepidation. The war had just begun, and no one could predict how massive and devastating it would become.

On that beautiful evening of my birthday party, Catherine explained that 80 percent of refugees in nearly all situations are women and children. "Relief agencies are staffed by men," she said, "but women have special problems and needs that they will not share with men, especially in cultures such as the Muslim population being brutalized in Bosnia." Her explanation made perfect sense to me. Years ago, when I had served as head resident of the dormitory in Michigan, my students would come to our apartment in the dorm to share sensitive female issues, such as sexual assault and fear of pregnancies, but they would not talk in Ron's presence. We would have to find a private room to talk. During that year, I dealt with the near death of one of my students, who had gone to a back-alley abortionist, a horrendous experience that made me a lifelong advocate of reproductive health rights for all women and girls.

In September 1992, a month after my fiftieth birthday, I flew to Yugoslavia with Catherine and a female WRC staff member to investigate conditions for women and children in this fast-breaking war. When we arrived in Zagreb, Croatia, I was surprised to see that people on the streets seemed so normal, walking calmly, shopping, eating at cafés, and carrying on what looked like normal social life. The city did not appear as I had expected, as the capital of a republic that had already lost 20 percent of its land in an increasingly bloody conflict. The lobby of the Intercontinental Hotel, however, provided a more realistic picture. Young men wearing camouflage uniforms, with arm patches that indicated their countries of origin, stood in clustered groups, divided by languages. Among these newly arrived troops of the United Nations Protective Forces (UNPROFOR), I counted Argentinians, Canadians, Nepalese, Swedes, and Peruvians. In the dining room, soldiers mixed with each other at round tables and communicated in English, a UN universal language. I noticed men drawing maps on the white paper tablecloths, maps that I assumed designated battlefields. I cringed, realizing that we would soon be driving through the regions they were sketching.

I followed Catherine's lead and hoped that I could keep up with her bound-less energy, because truly, the woman never stopped. Without pausing to un-pack, we left the hotel and drove to a refugee camp near Zagreb, where we met the two female Croatian doctors, Dina and Sasha, who would serve as our interpreters. I asked about their medical practice, and they explained that the war had disrupted everything, and they now could earn more money translating for us than they could as physicians. I was astounded! Both of them specialized in obstetrics and gynecology, which I knew would be helpful for the sensitive interviews we needed to conduct.

That first camp, called Resnik, held more than 3,500 refugees in unheat-ed wooden barracks, which had been built to house around five hundred men for summer military training. Dina and Sasha asked questions and learned that these refugees, nearly all women and children, had recently fled from around Banja Luka in northwest Bosnia after Serbian troops shelled their homes and invaded their towns. Weeping and gesturing wildly, they explained that most of the men and older boys had been either captured or killed. Many of those who survived had stayed to fight with a minimally armed Bosnian resistance militia. Even as I write these words, that "most of the men and older boys had been either captured or killed," I ponder what that means and how accurately that raw statement described the circum-stances in this wretched place. Then, as I once again feel rage in my body, I must remember where I found seeds of hope.

Across the barren grounds outside the barracks, I saw children sitting on the bare ground in silence, alone, in pairs, and in trios, some of them back-to-back, but with no apparent awareness of each other; this was a scene I had nev-er witnessed on a school playground. I took shallow breaths in the cold autumn air, as apprehension suddenly gripped me, and I felt ashamed in the face of Catherine's buoyant spirit. When she suggested that we enter a building to meet the refugee women inside, I said I wanted to stay in the yard with the children. I was not yet ready to face traumatized women. I immediately felt drawn to the children, confident in my strong maternal instincts.

Left alone, I sat down on the ground beside the building, near a string of clotheslines and close to a dozen listless children, who were studying the ground as if it held secrets about why they were here. I watched a boy, who looked to be about eight years old, pick up a clothespin that had fallen to the ground. Clutching it in his left hand, he started slowly tracing in the dirt, first straight lines and then geometric shapes. That gave me an idea. I unzipped my backpack and pulled out a packet of paper and a jumbo box of crayons that I had brought. From a kneeling position, I drew straight lines on a piece of paper with a red crayon.

The boy with the clothespin took a few steps toward me, and soon other children followed, curious to see what I was doing. Some kids approached me from behind and looked over my back. A few others tentatively sat down beside me. I gave each child a piece of paper and two crayons, and they automatically formed a circle in front of me and watched as I drew a simple square house with a triangular roof, then a tree with branches that stretched up and out. That was about the limit of my artistic skills.

Then, a girl about eight years old picked up green and brown crayons and drew a green house. She looked at it for a minute and then added a skinny brown dog with short legs. This seemed to prompt a few others to bend over their papers and begin drawing cars, cows, and stick people on the uneven surface of the ground. At first, they worked slowly, uncertainly, as if doing this only to please me, but it warmed my heart to see the effort they made.

(I had a long history of working with children and art. In the 1970s, most public schools throughout California eliminated their arts programs, because they suffered serious revenue losses due to property tax cuts. Realizing the importance of art, I co-founded a non-profit art organization in Pasadena, which is now called the Armory Center for the Arts. We hired professional artists to teach classes at a program that served thousands of school children, who came on buses from throughout Los Angeles County. While not an artist myself, I knew that art could provide children with an alternative means of expression and enhance their self-esteem.)

Sitting on the bare ground, I picked up a sheet of paper, folded it into an airplane, and sent it gliding over the clotheslines. Art was supposed to be fun, but none of these children laughed. I could hardly imagine what they had experienced. At first they seemed to be locked up, lacking expression and energy. Trauma can do that. So can exhaustion and fear. Their initial lack of response made me feel a bit helpless.

Then a girl with stringy blond pigtails reached for my red crayon and used it to draw flames above the house she had made. I sat back and watched, stunned. Soon a taller boy wearing torn overalls, one who had not yet participated at all, picked up a black crayon and sketched a very good portrait of a bearded man holding a big gun. Trying not to show the shock that I felt, I handed out more paper and emptied the entire box of crayons. The image of a gun seemed to have motivated several children to add details to their drawings, images that I found to be appalling, scenes of violence that these children no doubt had witnessed.

Some of the pictures demonstrated real talent, and they also provided primitive but graphic imagery about the "ethnic cleansing" of Bosnia. My first instinct was to keep a few drawings for our report, but I realized that everything had been taken from these children. They had lost their homes, all their possessions, and even members of their families. In truth, they had lost their childhoods. So instead, I took photographs of their drawings. Then I had them write their names under their pictures, so they would have something colorful to keep in this dull and dismal place. After that, I folded another paper airplane, and soon they all were eager to learn how to make and fly planes.

I ran out of typing paper at that first camp, but I gained a lot of confidence and learned to trust my life lessons. My mother had taught more through example than words, but some of her advice came to me that day under the clotheslines: "Use what you have, dear. Do what you can." It occurred to me that I had followed both pieces of advice that day rather successfully. I felt my heart expanding as the children warmed to my presence.

When I saw Catherine and the others emerge from the barracks, I didn't want to leave. Instinctively, I opened my arms and gathered the children into one big group hug, consciously sending the contagious energy of love to each one. I hoped that because they had opened up a little bit by sharing some traumatic memories with each other, they would now begin to talk and play together, that they would support each other and try to recapture the innocence of childhood. I hated to leave them, but the warm memories of that afternoon with those amazing children continue to sustain me.

During our drive to the next settlement, Catherine talked about the women she had met and shared their stories about violent experiences. As I listened to Catherine, my admiration for her confidence and positive attitude grew. She did not doubt for a moment that we could make a difference here, but I still felt overwhelmed by the enormous tragedy we were just beginning to understand. Catherine talked louder and faster than I could listen, and what I really needed was some quiet time alone to process my experience of the art class. The children had taught me so much. When I first sat down with them, I had been somewhat afraid—of being in a war zone, of being with traumatized people, and of being inadequate. They had helped me not to overcome my fears, but to go beyond them.

When we arrived at the second refugee settlement, Gascinska Camp, we met a teenaged refugee named Mila, whose warm welcome perked me up. Her green eyes and the wavy black hair framing her heart-shaped face seemed familiar to me. Mila told us that her family had escaped Sarajevo in a long convoy of cars shortly before the capital city of Bosnia fell under a siege that would last a thousand days. "All roads closed behind us," she said. "At a checkpoint outside the city, Serb soldiers took my father away." Not wanting to abandon him, the family had stayed at the roadblock and slept in their car until he returned, bearing marks of a beating that he refused to discuss. Mila said she had been planning to enter college this month as an art major. "I am disappointed that I can't go to school," she confessed, "but at least I made it here safely. Most of my friends are stuck in Sarajevo. All the boys have to fight."

With the help of our interpreter Dina, I told Mila about my recent art experience at Resnik Camp, how children who had been listless and withdrawn had seemed to come to life a bit when I gave them a chance to draw. Dina, who had been inside the barracks, seemed surprised when I talked about the drawing experience. She wanted me to say more, but I asked her to suggest to Mila that perhaps, since she wanted to study art in college, she could teach art to children here at Gascinska. Mila nodded her head but pointed out that she had no art supplies here. I told her about the boy at Resnik who was drawing in the dirt with a clothespin, and how he had inspired me to distribute the crayons. She could begin with simple projects that did not require special materials, such as making collages and sculptures from found objects like rocks and sticks. I could see Mila's mind working and her interest growing. I promised to send out art supplies after we returned to Zagreb, and I put that on a growing list of requested items that the IRC later delivered for us.

While we toured the settlement, Mila stayed close to me, holding my arm. I noticed that she paid attention to some of the children, and I wondered whether she was already picturing them as her future art students. Suddenly, I realized that Mila's eyes and the shape of her face reminded me of Alma, a young woman I had met in Nicaragua during my first international humanitarian mission in 1984. I had connected emotionally with Alma, a former prostitute and the mother of pre-school children, because she was trying so hard to improve her life. Like Alma, Mila exuded a warmth and grace that belied her youth. I saw them both as inspiring women survivors, not victims of their circumstances. I probably would never see either of them again, neither Alma in Nicaragua nor Mila in Bosnia, but even so, they felt like daughters, and I would hold them in my prayers every day.

Driving between settlements, Catherine and I discussed the similarities we noticed among Croats, Serbs, and Bosnians. We wondered how they identified each other, since all shared Slavic roots. "Yugoslavia" means "south Slav." Although the practice of religion had been banned for many decades behind the Iron Curtain, the majority of Croats still identified as Catholic, and most Serbs remained Orthodox Christians, like the Russians. These Bosnian Muslims simply had ancestors who had converted to Islam during the Ottoman Empire in order to obtain jobs and education, but most had not practiced the Muslim religion for several generations.

From Zagreb, we went to Split, located on Croatia's beautiful Dalmatian Coast, and from there drove northeast on a narrow mountainous road. At the border dividing Croatia and Bosnia, we found a roadblock with armed guards who seemed curious about the direction of our travel. They were there to stop refugees trying to enter Croatia from Bosnia. No one went into Bosnia, they said, except for aid organizations carrying relief supplies in trucks. They could not imagine why a car full of women defied that norm, but after checking our passports they allowed us to continue.

Our first and most memorable stop was in a small hillside town named Posušje, where we found a settlement of people who had fled from central Bosnia but failed to reach Croatia before its border closed. In Posušje, the town's only school now held 1,400 refugees, again mostly women and children, who were sheltering in this unheated two-story school building, which already felt cold and damp in the early fall. The local people, we later learned, had been keeping conditions as uncomfortable as possible, hoping the refugees would leave.

As we walked through various classrooms, I looked for evidence of what school life had been before each room sheltered two hundred or more refugees, mostly women and children. In one room, I examined a bulletin board. Instead of a daily schedule or homework assignments, it held small scraps of paper with a few words written on them and also some small photographs. Above this collage of tacked-on paper scraps was a sign that Dina translated as saying, "Have you seen them?" My mouth dropped open. These were names and photos of missing people.

(A decade later, I happened to be in New York City the week of September 11, 2001, during the World Trade Center tragedy. New Yorkers did the same thing then. They taped names and photographs of their missing loved ones throughout lower Manhattan, on lamp posts, mailboxes, and store fronts. In this cold school, and later in New York, I felt devastated and bereft, as if each name and photograph represented a loss to my own life.)

In another room of this dimly lit building, I found a blackboard covered with chalk drawings. Bits of broken chalk lying in a wooden tray had enticed children to become creative. Simple sketches, presumably made by smaller children, covered the bottom half of the board. Higher on the blackboard, more detailed drawings reminded me of the children's work at Resnik. One picture really shocked me, a realistic drawing of a woman lying on her back, with a bearded man on top of her. When I pointed it out to Dina, she guessed that the artist had witnessed the rape of a mother or sister, a thought that nearly made me vomit.

At that school, I met a woman named Subha, a very special woman who remains in my heart as a heroine. Subha was a doctor who lived and practiced medicine in nearby Split. After visiting this school building, she said, she felt so much compassion for these helpless refugees that she decided to stay in Posušje, because there was no one else to provide medical care for them. When I told Subha about the drawing of a rape scene, she lowered her head for a moment, absorbing my unspoken question.

"Yes," she said, sadness in her voice, "several women here evidence symptoms of physical and emotional trauma, but no one has specifically reported rape. In fact," she added, "most of them barely speak at all, even to each other."

Subha took us into a small office room that she called her clinic and opened a closet to show us how few drugs and medical supplies occupied its shelves. "People will soon get sick in these cold and crowded conditions," she said. I asked her to make a list of necessary medical supplies and promised to have them shipped, a wish later fulfilled by Direct Relief International from Santa Barbara, California. (I later joined Direct Relief's Board of Trustees in gratitude for this and many other generous responses to my requests for aid to refugees.)

After we left Posušje, none of us could remember Subha's full name. I referred to her as "Dr. Angel" for the rest of the trip. The strength demonstrated by Dr. Angel made me feel ashamed that I had been afraid to cross the border into Bosnia. If she could leave her home and live in the midst of such devastation, I could at least muster the courage to witness the human cost of this senseless war.

When we returned to Split, we visited the office of the United Nations International Children's Emergency Fund (UNICEF) to report on conditions in Posušje. Staff members told us they had delivered more than a thousand mattresses and an equal number of blankets for refugees in that school, but town leaders had taken the desperately needed bedding and locked it all in a warehouse. "The town wants those refugees to leave so they can regain use of their school," a logistics officer said. Honestly, it is hard to describe my rage and frustration at this kind of news.

We headed to visit a tent settlement north of Split, one of the first shelters that had been set up in Croatia specifically for Bosnian refugees. During the drive, Dina and Sasha mentioned that people in Split had recognized us as

Americans and wanted to ask us how soon the U.S. Army was going to come and stop this war. Sasha laughed and said, "A man asked me whether you know John Wayne."

When we reached the camp, we found its director, a Croatian military officer, in his "office," a gray tent under a large oak tree. A lower branch of that beautiful tree had already dropped most of its leaves, and it was serving as a clothesline for the director's camouflage uniform, socks, and underwear. Trying not to smile too broadly about the laundry tree, I asked the director why tents were being used as shelters here, since freezing winter would arrive soon. His answer surprised me. "When thousands of refugees from Bosnia began fleeing all at once," he said, "the International Red Cross followed its policy protocols for 'Situations of Armed Conflicts,' and they sent hundreds of tents."

Dr. Mary Black of the World Health Organization in Zagreb later confirmed his statement and explained that this was the first big refugee crisis in a northern climate. "The International Red Cross sent us medicines for malaria and other diseases that are common in Africa, Thailand, Cambodia, and Pakistan," she told us, half smiling at the irony.

Behind the commander's camp table, I noticed that a mural of drawings on a long sheet of butcher paper had been pinned around half of the tent's interior. With poster paints, children had created colorful images of hospital and school buildings exploding in flames, portraits of bearded soldiers pointing guns, and gray tanks with big shells that had blasted out from the tanks and remained suspended in air. There were pictures of houses covered with fire, of tanks pointed at a playground, of wolf-like dogs attacking people, and many of bearded men pointing assault-style rifles—all painted, apparently, from personal witness. I kept staring at the mural, wondering how these child artists would ever recover from such an assault on their tender souls.

On our last night in Zagreb, Catherine and I stayed awake to compose a report and list the special needs of women and children in the settlements we had visited. Our advocacy report and my photographs soon circulated throughout international humanitarian and human rights organizations, United Nations relief agencies, and media outlets. In addition to many other requests, we urged social workers to set up therapeutic drawing programs for children in refugee settlements.

When I returned home, Ron took me out to dinner, as had become our custom. A consummate newspaper reader, he had been following developments in the former Yugoslavia, and he asked informed questions. As I described my experiences and the extraordinary people I encountered, Ron listened quietly for more than two hours, a generous gift of understanding that really helped me to process the suffering I had witnessed. Even as he expressed concern for my safety, Ron knew I would be going back, perhaps many times, to support victims of the hideous war of "ethnic cleansing."

A final word about Catherine. This accomplished advocate for refugees, who traveled constantly on behalf of vulnerable women and children, had been a challenging travel companion, with her frenetic energy and her manner of interviewing people to get important information, an interrogation style that could seem demanding and unfeeling. But I had learned so much from Catherine and knew that her manner came from a brilliant mind that worked too fast and a warm heart that cared so much. I hoped she had learned something from me also, my focus on being present in the moment, with compassionate warmth, providing a safe place for traumatized people. The presence of a mother.

Nearly twenty years later, Catherine fought a courageous battle but eventually died from cancer. She was seventy and a woman of valor. I felt honored to have worked with Catherine and glad that she had still been here a decade after this trip to see that Human Rights Watch submitted children's drawings from Darfur as evidence of war crimes. During a trial concerning the war in Darfur, the International Criminal Court accepted children's art as convincing evidence of war crimes and crimes against humanity that had been committed by Sudan. The children had drawn scenes of traumatic experiences that no child should ever witness. Their drawings accurately depicted the conduct of the war in Darfur, including types of weapons available only to the government of Sudan.

TOP: A child's painting of the ethnic cleansing of Bosnia depicted a cemetery; BOTTOM: Children expressed painful memories through art, painting horrors they had seen but could not speak.

ABOVE: As shelling intensified during the brutal war of ethnic cleansing in Bosnia, thousands of refugee women and children fled to safety. At Resnik Camp in Croatia, they carried out daily chores in challenging conditions; OPPOSITE: Women of three or four generations supported and consoled each other as they worried about the men and boys left behind to fight.

The exterior wall of a heavily shelled cathedral in Mostar, Bosnia, is propped to prevent its collapse.

CHAPTER NINE

SEPARATION

Population is torn asunder in the name of cleansing

BOSNIA, APRIL 1995

After several trips to the former Yugoslavia, I became obsessed with the war of ethnic cleansing in Bosnia, a brutal war that targeted innocent civilians. In 1995, I eagerly accepted an invitation to return to Bosnia with World Vision, whose international program was based near Pasadena. I would accompany a member of their staff from San Francisco, Angela Mason, on a mission to investigate living conditions for refugees in the central part of Bosnia, a region I had not visited on previous travels.

According to all reports, death and destruction had greatly intensified in Bosnia. After several years of heartbreaking butchery perpetrated primarily by the Serbian militia, many thousands of Bosnian Muslims had been pushed into this central region, except for those who were serving in the military or seeking asylum outside the country. Looking at a map of the former Yugoslavia, I find it ironic that Bosnia, the most central of the six republics, was shaped like the human heart, but the symbolism failed to sustain love in Bosnia. There was much more hatred than love in Bosnia.

World Vision had created projects to support and empower displaced and refugee women in this region, and they wanted Angela and me to evaluate the new programs. We would travel by car with two Bosnian men, a driver and a World Vision program officer. During our planning calls, I grew to love Angela's British accent and her irreverent sense of humor, which I knew would help to relieve stress in a war zone. This was Angela's first trip to Bosnia, and I wanted to prepare her for the emotional trauma she would experience.

Our journey began in Split, Croatia, on the beautiful Dalmatian Coast that Ron and I had enjoyed during our year at Oxford. I had fond memories of the shoreline, aqua waters, and medieval architecture, buildings now stained with blood. From there, we would drive to Mostar for a short visit and then continue north through a mountainous region, skirting the besieged capital city of Sarajevo, and on to Fojnica and Zenica, the main two cities in central Bosnia where World Vision programs served an enormous population of displaced people.

Before leaving Split, Angela and I visited a local humanitarian project called Help Children, which had been created in response to the mass invasion of refugees fleeing from Bosnia into Croatia. The program's volunteer leader, a woman named Theresa, who was about my age, told us that thousands of unaccompanied children, many so young they did not know their own names, had shown up here, refugee children without their parents. Theresa explained that families trapped in Bosnian towns, under constant shelling from the Serbian militia, were so desperate to get their children to safety that they threw them into cars, buses, and trucks, any vehicle heading south, not knowing if they would ever see them again.

The thought of children coming to a strange land, not even knowing their own names, knocked the wind out of my soul. Theresa said that nearly every vehicle crossing into Croatia arrived full of children, many of them in very bad shape. "The kids are exhausted and hungry, and often they are hysterical," she said. "We just hold them until they calm down a bit." She added that she and the other volunteers have no way of letting parents know that their children arrived safely. "We simply have to keep track of every one, knowing that some of them will be orphaned permanently," she said, tearing up. These words expressed the tragedy, pain, and simply unimaginable situations of parents who threw children into any vehicle to save them, children who escaped madness, alone and exhausted and scared. I couldn't imagine the desperation of a mother, the courage it took, nor the grief it caused—the never knowing.

Theresa's group had been working with the U.S.-based international organization Save the Children, which had, with great innovation and success, created a computer database to document all of the information they could glean, such as arrival dates, vehicle identifications, and drivers' names. They took photographs of each child and uploaded the images with individual records.

"After the war," Theresa said, "the database will help to link parents with their lost children. We can only hope that parents will come and find their children." This software solution impressed me, especially considering how new computer technology was in 1995. We learned that all the war orphans would be housed on an island off the coast of Split, sheltered and protected in places that had once been tourist resorts. At least they would be safe, I thought, and perhaps children from the same towns would find and comfort each other.

The longer I talked with Theresa, the more I admired her commitment. Before we left, I asked Theresa what kind of work she did when she was not volunteering her time to care for Bosnian orphans. "Oh," she said, "I'm just a mother." Being just a mother also, I gasped in realization that we both had the best credential for the work we were doing. Later, when I reflected on the grace that seemed so natural in Theresa and the love she gave to traumatized children—two arms and a lap, just what they needed—I vowed never again to apologize for being "just a mother."

I felt reluctant to leave Theresa, but I greatly anticipated our next destination, Mostar, my favorite city in Bosnia. On our drive north from Split, I told Angela about my previous two visits to this region and described the town of Mostar, with its famous Ottoman era bridge, and shared some vivid memories of the chaos I had witnessed there two years prior, when families were being separated, with masses of people fleeing on foot or in over-stuffed vehicles.

These three ethnic groups had lived together peacefully for decades under the leadership of Josip "Tito" Broz. Tito began as a "revolutionary" leader, but he became the architect of socialism, ruling Yugoslavia from 1943 until his death in 1980. Tito had been called both a benevolent dictator and a selfish and cruel leader. For instance, he downplayed religion and encouraged mixed marriages, because he wanted people to think of themselves first and foremost as Yugoslavians. But, like Stalin, he retained control by not allowing any religious or ethnic group to gain strength and unite against him.

During this war of "ethnic cleansing," people learned that their identity and fate depended on the religion and ethnicity of their fathers, a patriarchy. If women had a different ethnicity than their husbands, they either had to convert or leave their families, a cruel process followed by a traumatic division of the city's entire population. Muslims living on the west side were forced to relocate to the old city on the eastern side, while Croats and Serbs did the reverse. During the chaos of crisscrossing the river, a wide and distinctive dividing line, Muslim families moved into apartments recently vacated by Croats or Serbs, and vice versa, wherever they found a vacancy. Household goods that couldn't be transported had been left behind, and in some cases, laundry had been left hanging on clotheslines.

As we approached Mostar, I recognized what looked like the remains of a Catholic church that I had visited before, and I asked the driver to stop. I nearly cried when I realized the extent of its destruction. All that remained of this church, which had been an inspiration and respite for me in 1993, was a three-sided, empty shell. The tallest wall had been battered badly, but miraculously, a circular leaded-glass window, a six-petaled flower, remained intact, not a single pane broken. Sunlight streamed through that window as if urging the flower to bloom and shine. Above the window, at the peak of connected roof beams, stood a simple cross—a flower made of glass and a cross, two symbols that represented both strength and fragility.

The remains of a small chapel or baptistry were also pock-marked by shells. A three-letter word had been painted on that wall in black capital letters, *MIR*. I had seen *MIR* written on walls throughout Russia and Ukraine and knew that it means "peace." What a poignant and perfect symbol, a prayer for peace in this setting! The side roof beams remained connected, the cross and the leaded-glass window unbroken, and the only graffiti was a prayer for peace, a foundation upon which to base hope that humanity itself could be repaired and reconnected in this devastated city.

TOP: Remnants of the destroyed cathedral included a cross and a leaded-glass window, symbols of strength and fragility; BOTTOM: After leaving Mostar, we discovered another destroyed church with graffiti that said *MIR,* the Russian word for "peace."

After Mostar's eight bridges were destroyed, only a temporary bridge connected east and west, a "swinging" bridge that I crossed in both directions above the wide and swift Neretva River.

CHAPTER TEN

BRIDGING GREAT DIVIDES

Crossing a river on a swaying bridge and
meeting a mysterious guide

BOSNIA, APRIL 1995

As we drove into Mostar, my third visit in the past three years to this medieval city, I felt a familiarity with what had been such a beautiful river town. I rolled down the window to point out the Neretva River, explaining to Angela that eight bridges had spanned the river on my last trip, but all them reportedly had been destroyed. We reached the spot where we should have seen Stari Most,"the historic 16th Century Ottoman single-arch bridge, a UNESCO World Heritage site that had stood 427 years. It had survived both world wars, only to be destroyed by the Yugoslavs themselves. I had to accept with a heavy heart that the famous landmark referred to as "the rainbow bridge" was indeed gone.

Croats battered it down with heavy mortar shelling on November 9, 1993, effectively destroying the last link between east and west Mostar and leaving the region's Muslim population stranded on the eastern side, the old part of the city. I cried for the people, all the people; I cried for the bridge; I cried for the ignorant fools who had destroyed their own beautiful heritage. Bridges are symbols of connection, but in Mostar they had been used to separate people.

(I have always loved bridges, beginning with the old Mormon Bridge that crossed the Missouri River and linked Iowa and Nebraska, the span that my father's ancestors from the Netherlands had crossed before settling in Holland, Nebraska.)

As we drove slowly on a narrow road close to the river bank, we discovered that a wooden footbridge had been built across the Neretva River, a narrow pedestrian bridge near where the Stari Most Ottoman bridge once arched over the river. This wood-plank swinging bridge, anchored by metal scaffolding along the bank, had been positioned just a few feet above the river's swift currents. When Angela and I told our driver and guide that we wanted to walk across that pedestrian bridge to visit Muslims in the old city, they declared that we had lost our minds. As if confirming their judgment, we stubbornly insisted that we would go by ourselves. I loaded my camera, several rolls of film, and snacks into my backpack, and we started across the rickety bridge. It suddenly swayed in a sharp wind, and I had to clench my teeth tightly to tamp down a combination of acrophobia, motion sickness, and a secret fear of small bridges that began in my youth, when a horse had bucked me off on a wooden bridge near our Iowa farm.

We reached the other side of the river, climbed the bank, and walked past rows of narrow stone buildings, all of them scarred from shelling. Farther along the river bank, we could see rows of six-sided wooden stakes that I recognized as Muslim grave markers, and realized that this open strip of grass between the river's edge and a stone walkway had become a graveyard. For as far as we could see, there were mounds of dirt marked by wooden stakes and a few scattered crosses.

I had been in Mostar during an incomprehensibly tragic period of its recent history and witnessed the forced separation of ethnic groups, an experience still etched in my soul, but I had only read about the disaster that followed. After forcing Muslims to resettle here, on the east side, Croat forces began shelling this historic old city from across the river. At the same time, the Serb militia moved in behind the hills east of the old city and lobbed shells from that position, cooperating in a cruel crossfire that trapped and killed many people here, mostly displaced Muslims. This makeshift graveyard provided evidence of the death toll from this chapter in the war of "ethnic cleansing."

Even without active shelling, it felt terrifying to stand here and experience raw vulnerability. I had to remind myself that I lived a life of privilege, with access to powerful organizations dedicated to helping people. Even so, I felt scared and vulnerable, but I needed to stand in this place of horror and absorb the experience fully. Only then could I advocate for survivors, from a place of true knowing, and demand an end to this evil war.

As Angela and I walked quietly and solemnly past semi-destroyed buildings, our steps fell into unison, and our shoulders touched. When we passed another person, which was rare, we communicated with them in sign language, asking permission for me to take photographs. I noticed a rather distinguished elderly man, distinctive in a black beret and holding a cane with a bear's head carved on its handle. He stood beside a mound of dirt near the river's edge. When we made eye contact, he pointed with his cane first to a shell-pocked building and then to that new grave. I walked over to meet him. "Pierre," he said, answering my quizzical expression. A French name? Though a bit hunched by age, he stood more than six feet tall, a height more typical of an ethnic Serbian man. I wondered about his history and whether he had fought in World War II, and if so, on what side.

I suddenly smiled, remembering a line that an elderly World War II veteran in Ukraine had spoken to me in 1989, the only English words that he seemed to know: "Where have you been all of my life?" Pierre, not understanding the reason for my broad smile, took my hand and led me down a long row of stakes, some with names written in black paint and others bearing dates but no names. At a grave marked by a cross with no name, Pierre stopped, bent lower, and pushed his hands out in front of his knees, pantomiming the act of digging with a shovel, as if he had helped to bury this body. His palpable compassion touched me, and the dignity expressed in his posture stopped me from taking a photograph of him. He wanted to communicate something about this grave, and I wanted to understand. I wanted to give him my respect, to know his loss and to share his pain.

Angela came up behind and tapped my shoulder, then pointed to her watch. It was time to return. But I needed to stay with Pierre a bit longer. He posed a mystery to me. With the sound of river currents in the background, I suddenly thought of Virgil, the guide in Dante's *Inferno*, the verses of which I had read many times. Pierre was serving as our "Virgil," our guide between the living and the dead.

I followed Pierre's lead down another block, where he stopped and pointed to a small bronze medal hanging on a black ribbon from a wooden cross, another dead Christian. Was that a military medal? Did this mound hold a comrade, or was this a wife, a friend, brother, child? Whoever it was, I felt Pierre's deep sadness and wanted to hug him, but I remembered being on the receiving side of an uninvited bear hug in Ukraine, so I just gave him an apple and a granola bar, which he probably appreciated more. I hoped he had seen the compassion and respect that my eyes surely reflected.

As Angela and I crossed the narrow wooden bridge to return to the car, I felt like screaming into the currents below, not from fear, as this fragile rope bridge swayed in the wind, but because I felt helpless and overwhelmed by grief. Not wanting to alarm Angela in this precarious situation, I simply bowed my head, willed my feet to step from plank to plank, and silently asked God to protect our "Virgil" and all those whom he guarded, the living and the dead.

When I returned to Mostar in 1998 with Landmine Survivors Network, people traveled freely across a solid new bridge that connected the east and west sides of the city. Many remained displaced in temporary apartments and shelters. I found more evidence of healing and humanity but, though I looked hard, I could not find Pierre.

After the war ended, and with funding from UNESCO, engineers began the task of replicating Stari Most. A beautiful new "rainbow span" opened on July 23, 2004, a modern miracle. Engineers and builders had constructed the new bridge very rapidly, by 16th Century standards, using cement as mortar. The workers who created the Ottoman era arch in 1566 had relied on an adhesive mixture made with egg whites. How I wished I could have told my deceased father, the poultry man, that "egg white glue" had held a magnificent bridge together for nearly five hundred years.

The 16th Century Stari Most bridge, a UNESCO World Heritage site, stood 427 years and survived both world wars, only to be destroyed by Yugoslavs themselves.

We discovered massive destruction all along the journey from Mostar to Fojnica in central Bosnia.

A tank operated by Canadian soldiers of the United Nations Protective Forces blocked the road on "sniper alley" while an overturned truck was cleared.

CHAPTER ELEVEN

UNITED NATIONS PEACEKEEPERS

Vulnerable children abandoned by doctors
teach the meaning of courage

BOSNIA, APRIL 1995

When we departed Mostar, I carried with me a deep sadness that was hard to shake. Emotional pain had sapped my energy and quashed my usually optimistic spirit. Because Angela and the two men understood and shared my somber mood, we drove out of town without speaking. But a few miles down the road, I broke the silence and scared everyone by spitting out three words that seemed to sum up our feelings and relieve the tension: "Shit! Shit! Shit!!!"

We planned to drive from Mostar to Fojnica, spend a couple of days there, and then continue on to Zenica, the heart of the refugee crisis in Bosnia. This central region of Bosnia, which now served as the only relatively safe haven for hundreds of thousands of displaced people (mostly Bosnian Muslims and ethnic Croats) was being guarded by United Nations Protective Forces (the UNPROFOR). We drove through mountains and valleys that no doubt, with the advent of spring, would soon be beautiful, but winter seemed to be hanging on tenaciously in the higher elevations.

Spring was always my favorite season in Iowa and also my mother's. As soon as the grass turned from brown to green, she would go out to her small herb garden near the kitchen door, where she had planted herbs between the lawn and her beloved rose garden. Every year, grass invaded the little herb plot as if trying to expand its rightful territory. I loved to watch through a plate-glass window in the living room while my mother performed her hilarious annual spring ritual. She would get down on her hands and knees to search for her favorite herb, chives, which looked a lot like grass. I couldn't tell the difference, but Mother would patiently break off blades of grass, taste them, and spit them out, until she discovered the unique, peppery taste of chives, which she loved to sprinkle on scrambled eggs and baked potatoes. Then, triumphantly, she would banish invading grass with a hoe.

Shades of green, the primary palette of spring, evoke hope for new life, and hope was exactly what Bosnia needed at this time. For now, however, everything looked monochromatic and bleak. We passed farmhouses and barns that had been destroyed by shelling, and drove through villages in which houses seemed to have been targeted randomly. On one street, for instance, the second, third, and seventh houses had been hit. We speculated those must have been the houses owned by Muslims.

World Vision had set up humanitarian programs in both Fojnica and Zenica, and Angela and I wanted to spend however much time we needed in each town in order to evaluate their effectiveness for rehabilitating refugee women. I looked forward to spending time with women survivors, but getting there was not easy. I did not relish our drive through the "triangle road" in the hills west of Sarajevo, the capital city of Bosnia that was still being held under siege. I had read terrifying reports about Serbian snipers who guarded these mountain roads with orders to "shoot anything that moves," the same command that snipers stationed in the hills above Sarajevo were following. That order alone defined savagery and barbarity. "Anything that moved" included young children who stepped outdoors to catch a ray of sunlight, mothers who risked their lives to buy milk or bread for their children, and elderly men and women too grief-stricken to understand the real and present danger and too tired or lame to run.

By the time we reached a narrow dirt road that wound up steeper hills, a late spring snowfall had created slippery conditions with poor visibility. Driving conditions seemed nearly as dangerous as the sniper threat, and I felt increasingly uncomfortable and unsafe. This road, we later learned, had been constructed hastily as a route for trucks carrying essential supplies to the displaced and cut-off people in this region, a vastly growing population.

I remembered country roads in Iowa, where I learned to drive in winter conditions like this. After I got my learner's permit at age fourteen, my intrepid mother took me out on icy country roads to teach survival lessons, such as how to turn into a spin rather than fight it, and how to accelerate slowly in order to keep traction on rear tires that tend to spin on ice. Her lessons had served me well during the years Ron and I lived in Michigan, when I often had to drive ten miles to my newspaper job through two or three feet of snow at 6 o'clock in the morning. Our current driver clearly had not been taught by my mother! I wanted to take the wheel—or at least sit in the front seat, which would have eased the motion sickness caused by the car's fish-tailing rear end.

We reached Konjic, ten miles from the border of Serb-controlled territory, and decided to stop for some fresh air, parking on a river bank and stepping out into a bracingly cold wind that made my eyes water. Further up the river, we saw the remains of a substantial bridge that had been bombed and broken into three sections, and a mangled UN helicopter resting on frozen ground, its tail dangling in the ice-patched river. The bridge and the downed helicopter broke the monotony of the landscape with a startling reminder that this, indeed, was the heart of a war zone.

Angela and I decided it was time to don the flak jackets we had brought from California. As we were zipping on the puffy vests over our parkas, Angela looked into my eyes as if she wanted to say something profound. I waited, thinking she might be about to confess fear, which would have allowed me to do the same, but instead, she told me that my vest was the same color as my blue eyes, and she asked whether I thought hers made her look fat. As usual, Angela's humor eased the stress we were both feeling. It was a small joke by her standards, but it was just what we needed at the time, a chance to laugh and to brace ourselves for the unknowns of our immediate future. The men, our driver and guide, again looked at us like we had lost our minds. I asked them to please turn their heads so we women could pee behind the car. The yellow snow Angela and I created on the road struck us both as hilarious, and we nearly toppled over from laughing while squatting precariously. Throughout my travels, I have learned that laughter is the best reliever of fear, but it can be dangerous to laugh while relieving oneself.

After driving several more miles through continuously accumulating snow, we reached a long line of stopped cars and trucks. People standing outside their idled automobiles said they had been stranded here for several hours behind a roadblock being guarded by United Nations troops. Angela and I decided to walk up the road and assess the problem. We navigated the slick, rutty trail in our hiking boots, passing dozens of cars and trucks before reaching the very effective roadblock, a large World War II–style military tank that made me feel nervous until I saw *UN* painted in blue on its side. I smiled, thinking at once about my role model, Eleanor Roosevelt, and her diligent work to establish the United Nations. I had often asked the spirit of Eleanor to join me on journeys into war zones, and I felt her presence.

Several soldiers wearing blue UN helmets stood next to the tank, near a large gray canvas tent. We approached the soldiers and introduced ourselves as humanitarians from California. To our delight, the men guarding this roadblock were English-speaking Canadians. They explained that a lorry had flipped over up the road, and a crew had been working for several hours to move it and reopen the passage.

A soldier named Mike wearing a blue beret opened the tent flap and invited us to enter and meet several young Canadians in camouflage uniforms gathered around a table with a propane lantern illuminating their faces. As Mike made introductions, I tried to keep track of the names, but a large copper teakettle steaming nearby on a wood-burning stove captured my attention. Still chilled from the walk, Angela and I moved closer to the fire to warm our hands before joining the men around the table, where we sat on tripod stools and talked for more than two hours. We drank their tea and hot chocolate, and we shared from our backpacks some apples, peanuts, and granola bars.

Angela and I had talked about the complicated role of UN peacekeeping soldiers. When a major conflict breaks out anywhere in the world, the UN Secretary General can set up a peacekeeping mission to protect civilians and international aid workers; UN member countries would be asked to supply soldiers. I knew from past encounters that Canada had sent excellent troops to this mission in the former Yugoslavia, called UNPROFOR.

Before answering my question about impressions, Mike told us that he had trained with U.S. Special Forces, which gave more credence to his reply. "Insane!" Mike said. "These people all look the same, but they are killing and torturing each other. I don't understand what it's all about." I took a notebook and pen out of my backpack and started recording the soldier's words, guessing at their names. Shawn expressed his frustration and outrage at having to witness horrendous violence against civilians while not being allowed to intervene. In their mandate to protect civilians, he explained, they could not fight back unless they personally were targeted. I wondered what Eleanor Roosevelt would have thought about this paradoxical rule and guessed that Eleanor, champion of the innocent, would have shared Shawn's feelings.

I suddenly remembered a newspaper article I had read more than a year before, a report about the intervention of Canadian UNPROFOR soldiers at a hospital in Fojnica, the town we hoped to reach that day, a story about how soldiers had rescued abandoned children. I had clipped the article for my files and reread it in preparation for this trip.

John Burns, a British journalist, one of my favorite war correspondents, wrote an eyewitness account for *The New York Times* in July 1993 in which he described visiting a hospital for handicapped children in Fojnica. When the town was being shelled, he reported, the medical staff fled and left helpless children to fend for themselves. I was stunned and horrified by the account. Burns wrote about meeting some Canadian soldiers who had discovered the horrendous situation and taken care of the children. When I first read the article, nearly two years before, I had no idea that I would soon be visiting that very hospital, called Drin.

Wanting to know whether any of the men in this tent knew what had happened at Drin Hospital, I interrupted a conversation about the relative qualities of regional beers to ask whether these soldiers knew anything about a hospital for disabled children in Fojnica. "Well, yeah. That was a bloody nightmare!" Shawn exclaimed. "How do you know about that?" Without waiting for an answer, he continued, "Oh, I know; a newspaper reporter was there."

Shawn looked at each of the men around the table, then over his shoulder, to see if anyone else wanted to talk. As if given permission, several started speaking at once, interrupting each other to add details. Startled by this outpouring, I realized that these men knew about the abandoned hospital, and that some of them had actually participated in the heroic rescue. What luck! I wrote rapidly, leaving blanks for names that I hoped Angela could fill in later, and trying not to convulse over the dreadful stories I was hearing, firsthand accounts of an unimaginable experience, one so shocking that it made the front page of *The New York Times*.

Some background is needed here to give history and context to the behaviors of people from diverse ethnicities in this region. The town of Fojnica, with a primary population of ethnic Croats and a minority of Muslims, was located in the mountains of Bosnia-Herzegovina west of Sarajevo. Fojnica had a wealth of natural mineral hot springs that for hundreds of years had attracted visitors to its healing pools. Because of these health benefits and its central location, Yugoslavia established two institutions in Fojnica to house mentally and physically disabled people from all over the country. One hospital, called Drin, served physically and mentally disabled children and also a few adults. The other hospital held mentally and physically handicapped adults.

The Serbian militia began its war of ethnic cleansing with a goal of expanding Serbia's territory and eliminating non-Serbs, especially Muslims. As the war progressed, towns fell and civilians fled by the hundreds of thousands. Eventually, all three sides fought against each other. In this region of central Bosnia, the Croatian nationalist army and the Muslim-led Bosnian army battled each other for control of a shrinking territory. But because of the hospitals and healing centers in Fojnica, the two sides agreed to set up a peace zone around the town, a kind of "king's X" agreement that kept the war at bay there until the summer of 1993. Then suddenly the Muslim-led Bosnian army, wanting to set up a safe zone for thousands of displaced Muslims, began shelling Fojnica to chase out its majority Croat population. Under constant shelling, about five thousand of Fojnica's 6,500 inhabitants fled, including Croatian troops and nearly all the doctors and nurses from both hospitals, who abandoned their patients. I read the NYT report several times, and the shock effect never lessened. In fact, I still puzzle over the confusing facts—the behavior of those health care workers was antithetical to their vocation.

John Burns reported that when troops defending the city left, the Croatian commander ordered the medical staff to flee and to leave the patients behind, but these Canadian soldiers were not certain of that fact. Owen thought they fled to save themselves when fierce fighting in the surrounding hills got closer. His Canadian patrol, he said, had difficulty getting through because of the fighting, which he described as a battle between Croat and Muslim forces, separate ethnic militias that initially had fought together against the Serbs, but later fought each other in a scramble to secure land not already seized by the Serbs.

I interrupted Owen to make a comment: "This war of ethnic cleansing is demonstrating the truth that *violence begets violence*. All three ethnic groups are now fighting each other." He nodded in agreement, then gave us some grisly facts about how his patrol had arrived in Fojnica three days after the exodus and discovered the two hospitals.

"So, I guess there were more than two hundred patients who were left alone, just at Drin, most of them children," Owen said. Dave broke in, adding, "It was very hot and filthy, smelled worse than a pig pen. All those helpless kids. There were two dead babies in an upstairs room. And we found another six babies who seemed barely alive. Heat and dehydration."

"Kids were trapped in locked rooms and in cribs with bars. Bare naked crippled children had excrement all over their bodies and their beds," Owen added. "Some of them kept banging their heads against railings because they could not get out. We found windows that had been broken from the inside, and some kids were bleeding."

I set down my pen, closed my eyes, and listened intently, barely breathing. I would never, ever forget this story or the word pictures the men painted from vivid memories. Angela placed her hand over mine, as Shawn picked up the story.

"We bathed babies. We boiled water and mixed it with powdered milk so we could feed them from bottles," Shawn said, "and we made soup for the older kids with canned food that we found in a closet. All of the bedding and clothes had to be washed, floors and walls scoured," Shawn added. "We worked like housemaids."

Shawn now spoke faster, in a kind of rush, as if this would somehow ease the pain of the story he had to tell. "Finally, more help arrived, including some doctors," Shawn said. (Later we learned that, during a pause in the fighting, more UNPROFOR troops had gotten through and reached Drin Hospital, some of them Dutch and Scandinavian.)

Owen broke in to add that they also fed the disabled adult patients at Drin. "After the adults came from their wards to eat, some of the men picked up mops and helped," he said. In my mind, I pictured soldiers in army uniforms working beside patients in pajamas, doing the work that had to be done, tasks considered to be women's work, the stuff of survival.

A tall redheaded soldier entered the tent to announce that the road would be open soon. Wanting the stories to continue, I felt disappointed, but we had to get back to the car. Before leaving, Angela and I asked whether we could take photos with the men around the tank. After such an emotional conversation, I felt a special bond with these young soldiers. It is never easy to leave after such an intimate conversation. If these men had been American, I would have written the White House and suggested that they receive special honors for their courage and valor.

I asked each man to write his name in my journal and also the names and address of his parents in Canada. When I returned home to California, I wrote personal letters to all the parents, complimenting them on what wonderful sons they had raised and enclosing photographs. It was important for me to make contact with these parents, and I received letters of gratitude from several. I wished I could have sent a letter to Eleanor Roosevelt telling her how these fine men embodied the spirit she had envisioned for the United Nations.

When we got to Fojnica, Angela and I went straight to Drin Hospital, even though we had arrived mid-afternoon, hours later than anticipated. We were greeted warmly by staff members, who expressed appreciation for World Vision's support in suppling fresh food, medicine, and clothing every week to both hospitals. Then, before we asked any questions, two nurses told us they had come back to the hospital as soon as possible; they must have felt guilty about leaving. They also wanted us to know that the staff had not been paid during the war, although they did get food and other supplies as "gifts-in-kind." That saddened me. I could imagine their fear and guilt, but not the decision to abandon such vulnerable children. I wanted to believe I would have stayed, but in truth, it required courage to be here even now.

Rather than considering the blame for actions taken literally "under fire," I chose to focus on the patients and their current conditions, which we found to be appalling! Overcrowding in every room made the wards look more like cattle pens than hospital rooms—but I feared this might be "normal" for this institution. In both the boys' and the girls' wards, beds nearly touched each other, making it practically impossible to pass between them. How, I wondered, did staff members feed and clean these patients or change their bedding? Many children lay curled up in metal cribs too short for them to stretch their legs. To get out, they would have to crawl across the other beds. I turned away to hide my sadness and rage, and my body just shook with overwhelming despair.

On the ground floor, mobile boys and girls in wheelchairs caught our attention, with their curious glances and endearing smiles. Both the wheels and the long hallways gave these children a touch of freedom, an escape to a world beyond their cribs and cramped rooms. A teenaged boy named Dario, the most disabled-looking child I had seen in the facility, or anywhere, reached out a deformed hand and touched my arm. Then he rocked his wheelchair back and forth and tipped his head forward, inviting me to follow as he joyfully cruised down a hallway, yelling a Serbo-Croatian version of *wheeee*!

Dario had me at that first touch. Despite being terribly crippled, he exuded the courageous spirit and energy that I so admired, that of a survivor, the art of living in the moment. And in this moment, Dario took off down the hallway to show off for me. I had to jog to keep up with him, grateful that I had exchanged my heavy hiking boots for tennis shoes. When the hall came to a dead end, Dario spun a wheelie, and I clapped in praise of his impressive trick. I wanted to tell him that a president of the United States led our nation from a wheelchair throughout World War II, but I could not find an interpreter.

I doubt that he could have imagined such a thing anyway. Dario led me down another hall, and we passed an industrial-looking kitchen, where I saw four men, wearing the gray cotton uniforms of patients, washing dishes and sweeping floors. Later, a doctor explained that the Canadian UNPROFOR soldiers had praised these patients for their assistance during the crisis, and now they got paid to work.

Later, when Angela and I were speaking with the hospital administrator, I could not pay attention. My mind and my heart remained with Dario. Before leaving, I returned to the children's wards to take photographs. In the last room, where Dario lay curled up in his too-small bed, I paused at the door and waved goodbye. Some of the boys smiled, others stared as if I were some strange zoo animal, but Dario struggled to raise his deformed arm and return my wave. In his eyes I could see intense determination and sadness, as if he knew that I would be leaving. I wanted to go to his bedside, but stayed in the doorway, fearing that he and I had already become too attached in that brief time. A social worker had told me that Dario's family dropped him here as an infant and never returned, a common practice, she said, with obvious disgust.

As I stood in that doorway, I remembered newsreels of Eleanor Roosevelt visiting children in orphanages. No doubt her heart hurt every time she departed. Eleanor once said, "You gain strength, courage, and confidence by every experience in which you really stop to look fear in the face." The opposite of FEAR, I know for certain, is LOVE, and I felt an abundance of love for these children. Pulling myself away from Drin Hospital was one of the saddest and most difficult moments of this journey. Everyone Dario loved had left him, and so did I.

I think about Dario every day, because I keep his photo on my desk as part of my "gosling gallery." That deformed child, frozen in a moment of gladness, had never seemed disabled to me, because he shared so much love and light, and I treasured those qualities in him. When I look at him now, his body so twisted in that wheelchair, I realize what a teacher he had been. He embodied the wisdom of living in the moment, with no expectations, and celebrating the warmth of human connection.

I had to leave him, but he never left me.

TOP: Angela Mason of World Vision and I spent several hours in a tent with Canadian UNPROFOR soldiers, enjoying their hot chocolate and their amazing stories; BOTTOM: I posed like GI Jane beside a United Nations tank being operated by Canadian peacekeeping soldiers.

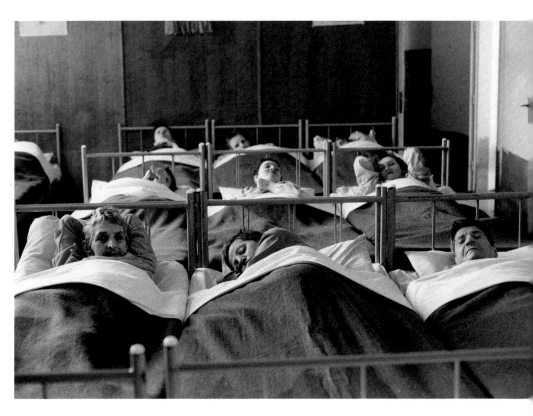

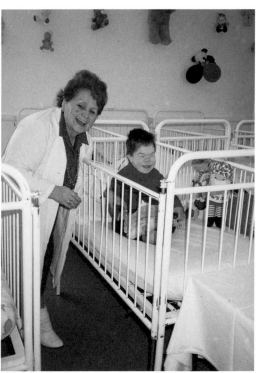

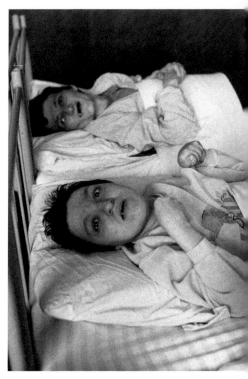

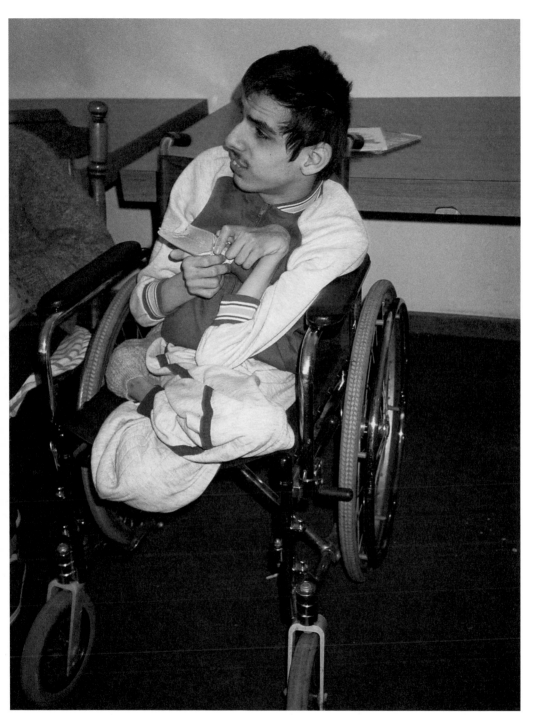

OPPOSITE: In Fojnica, we found crowded but clean conditions at Drin Hospital, the institution for mentally and physically disabled children that had been abandoned during heavy shelling of the town; ABOVE: The children at Drin Hospital broke my heart, but one patient, Dario, taught me about human resilience, with his joyful spirit. How I loved that boy!

Yasna Mandic, an internally displaced woman from Sarajevo who happened to be a fashion designer, used her talents to teach and uplift battered girls as part of the healing program designed by the Society for Women Survivors of War Crimes in central Bosnia.

CHAPTER TWELVE

BORN AGAIN BURLAP

Recycling becomes a creative instrument for healing
a community of wounded women

BOSNIA, APRIL 1995

After our powerfully emotional experience at Drin Hospital, Angela and I debriefed in the car, sharing our conflicted feelings about the children—devastated about their living conditions, but amazed by their resilience. We hoped to return to Drin the following day, if time allowed, after our scheduled meeting with an organization called the Society for Women Survivors of War Crimes. But for now, I felt exhausted from emotional overload. After a light dinner, we retired to our sparse room in a small resort hotel that had been converted into a refuge for international aid workers. By now, I had given up hope for a hot shower and felt grateful that the rust-stained sink had running water and a rubber stopper.

The next morning, we showed up at a complex that may have served as a resort in another time, but it now bore a facade that looked as tired as we felt. We had come to meet with the Society for Women Survivors of War Crimes. The name intrigued me, but I had no idea what it meant or what to expect. The bright-eyed young woman named Mensi who greeted us warmly at the door was wearing a light green wool jacket with a brooch on its lapel and matching earrings. Her outgoing personality cheered me up. I assumed Mensi was a social worker, but she had the confident look of a leader, a school principal, or perhaps even a business executive. We soon learned the startling truth of her identity. After serving tea, Mensi began to tell us her personal story, and I soon realized that her confident manner came from being a super survivor. Her story made me sit a bit straighter. I began writing in my spiral notebook, but soon could not see the words through tears.

"I am thirty-two years old," Mensi said, "and I worked as an economist in Belgrade and Kosovo before the war. Serb soldiers surrounded my village in eastern Bosnia, near Srebrenica. For several days, they lobbed shells and held our village under siege. Then they entered the town and drove us all out of our homes, street by street."

I set down my pen and gripped the metal seat of my chair. Having heard similar openings many times, I guessed where the story was heading. But Angela kept smiling at Mensi nodding with encouragement. I knew that her heart would soon break. Lowering her voice, Mensi told us she had been several months pregnant when the shelling began. She and her son Semin, age ten, were in their front yard, she said, when "a small man with a big gun" shot and killed her husband, Semin's father. Then two soldiers threw his dead body back into their house, where her invalid father remained in his bed, and set the house on fire.

"I'll never forget my father's horrible screams," Mensi whispered, covering her ears with both hands. "The Serb militia herded everyone into the town square and separated the men and older boys from women and children," she continued. "They shot many men on the spot and took others away in trucks." Our interpreter interjected that she knew they had taken many men to labor or "concentration" camps in that region. The soldiers loaded Mensi and her son, along with other young women and children, into a truck, and drove them to another town.

"We all were held in a priest's house for about three weeks before being taken to a school near Garazdne," she said. "Five hundred women and children were held at that school, thirty-three in each of the nine square meter classrooms," she said. "It was so crowded that most of us had to stand all day and take turns lying down."

Mensi paused in her narration and glanced from Angela to me. We both must have looked horrified, because no matter how many such shocking stories we heard, their effect always shook us to the core. But we both held her gaze in wordless expressions of understanding. Finding compassion in our eyes, Mensi confessed that she and other young women had frequently been pulled out of classrooms and raped brutally on the grounds outside, sometimes by several Serbian soldiers in a row.

"If any men in the militia showed reluctance, they would be ordered at gunpoint to rape us," she said. I wondered how a man who had any grain of compassion or humanity could accomplish the act of rape against his own will. This sounded like the behavior of mad dogs.

I asked about the baby, and Mensi made a downward sweeping motion with her hands from her waist to her knees, indicating that the violent rapes had ended her pregnancy. Angela and I, both mothers, understood the gesture and the magnitude of her loss. My whole body shivered, and I struggled to hold back tears until finally, unable to match Mensi's dignified strength, I dug for a tissue in my pocket. Horrendous stories like hers are never easy to hear, but this chain of events nearly overwhelmed my capacity to listen. I found myself staring at Mensi with awe. She held the collective violence against Bosnian women in her own slim body, but somehow she seemed to have made peace with the pain.

What about her son, Angela asked Mensi. She paused before answering. Semin, whom she called "Senco," had not spoken a word since his father died, she told us. "He clung to me in that crowded school room. He saw the men rape and beat us. Thankfully they left him alone," she said, slumping and finally giving in to sadness, "but he had seen too much. He forgot how to be a child. He has lost his picture of himself." Angela and I exchanged looks that promised each other a long talk and cry session.

We held the space in silence until Mensi could continue. She told us that two men from a nearby village eventually managed to come and rescue her and other women and children, load them in trucks, and bring them here to Fojnica, where refugee and displaced people had more than tripled the town's normal population. We asked the identities of the men who rescued her, curious about their ethnicity, but she did not know, nor did she know how they had found the school, but she told us she hoped someday to thank them. "All of us women and girls," she said, "arrived here half dead, starving and barely able to stand. If not for Senco," she added, "I would surely have given in to death. I stayed alive for him."

Mensi's next revelation stunned us; it taught a huge lesson about the capacity of human resilience. Shortly after arriving here in September 1994 as a devastated rape-camp survivor, Mensi told us, she realized that many other women and girls had experienced similar abuse. She gathered other traumatized and injured women and built a community of grieving females, who helped her create an organization that she called the Society for Women Survivors of War Crimes.

"At first," Mensi said, "I had to keep living for my son, but soon I gathered a whole family of sisters and daughters, and I had to be strong for them as well." She explained that many survivors, especially the young girls, seemed to be separated from their own bodies. It took time for them to open up and reveal some of what they had experienced.

"Some of the girls talked about torture they had suffered in addition to rape. They had been burned by cigarettes, beaten, and choked nearly to death," Mensi added. Seeing our startled expressions, she said, "Yes. All of that, and also terrible verbal abuse." I listened intently, unable to take notes.

"Their stories brought back my own terrible memories," Mensi said. "I wanted to help them reconnect body and soul. I am older, and I had a loving husband, and I have a wonderful son. I don't want them to hate and fear all men." Reading these words in my journal many years later, I thought about my loving husband, son, and eight grandsons. I also could not classify people as good or bad because of their gender. I'm sure Mensi would agree with me that we had a duty to raise boys who loved and honored females.

Stunned by Mensi's revelation of goodness in the midst of horror, we followed her into an adjoining room, where a dozen young women sat around a table that held another tea service and plates of cookies. She introduced us to Mona, age thirty, who had been shot by a neighbor, paralyzing half of her face. Both Raza, a textile engineer, and Vessna, a journalist, had suffered gunshot wounds to their limbs, which still held shrapnel. We met several teenaged girls, whom Mensi said had also been held in rape camps, where they experienced torture and near starvation. She introduced us to one young woman, a trained nurse, whose name I could not catch, who told us that while she was at a detention camp, she had been raped by a doctor she knew. "We worked at the same hospital," she said, "and I worked with him in the surgery room. He knew me and my family. How could he?" Indeed!

I took Angela's hand, needing to feel her strength. I had heard reports like this many times, but stories of such egregious inhumanity never failed to shake me, physically as well as emotionally. We asked Mensi to tell us more about the community of survivors she founded.

"More than eight hundred women and girls have joined," she proudly announced. "I named it the Society for Women Survivors of War Crimes. *Survivors*, not *victims*," she emphasized. "We refuse to be victims! As long as we don't surrender to hate, we are still human beings. If we turn to hatred or revenge, then we truly will have lost everything."

The older women survivors, Mensi explained, had helped the teenagers to reconnect with their bodies by giving them beauty treatments, hair styling, and massages. She then introduced a slim blond woman named Yasna Mandic, an ethnic Serbian woman, who had been a fashion designer in Sarajevo. "Yasna came up with a great idea for helping these girls," Mensi said. "She taught them fashion design, sewing, and modeling." While that news was being translated for us, Yasna smiled broadly and then curtsied in anticipation of the admiration we expressed.

An explanation is needed here. Before the war, Fojnica's primary industrial center had been a textile factory, which employed many people in the manufacture of clothing. Although shelled and burned, the factory building still stood, and a few industrial sewing machines were recovered from the ashes in decent working order. Refugee men cleaned and repaired the partially burned machines, and they also cleaned the shears and other important tools found in the ashes. Just imagine Yasna teaching fashion design in conditions like these. Honestly, all these years later, I look at my photos of these amazing females and marvel at the mix of horror and goodness and perseverance. Small anecdotes keep coming, simple but unforgettable.

The lack of material posed a big problem, because fire had reduced the supply of fabrics to ashes. Yasna had another inventive idea. She suggested that they use a fabric they had in abundance—burlap. The UN World Food Program delivered basic food supplies, such as potatoes, rice, and beans, in large burlap bags stamped with colorful symbols of the contents and the names of donor countries. Many empty burlap bags lay stacked in piles, ready to be recycled into clothing after being softened by repeated washing. Yasna created paper patterns for various articles of women's clothing and showed the girls how to place the patterns on top of the burlap and cut around them.

And then came a moment that seems extraordinary and heartwarming even now, one that reminds me how much these human moments matter, both the ugly and the beautiful. That evening, over a dinner of fried pork and boiled potatoes, a feast provided by World Vision, Angela and I watched a truly re-markable fashion show. A fashion show! Courageous teenaged girls, survivors of imprisonment and rape, circled the room in confident catwalk strides, pivoting proudly, as they modeled jumpers, skirts, jackets, overalls, pants, and vests, all created from burlap. Their joy was a miracle, given the circumstances, and shar-ing in their joy—well, nothing could be more gratifying. I flashed on the feed sack dresses that my mother made for her three daughters during World War II, a very different war.

Mensi allowed Angela and me to buy some of the burlap fashions, using the German marks I had brought, and we took home a dozen pieces in a va-riety of styles. The skirts and pants were much too small, but I often wore a burlap jacket or vest when I spoke to schools and women's groups, hoping to portray victims of war as resilient survivors and thereby inspiring audiences with hope.

On a sub-freezing day in February 2011, I gave a keynote luncheon speech in Bozeman, Montana, at the state's annual conference for high school girls, which they called Girls for Change. My daughter Amy drove to Bozeman from Missoula with her young twin sons, Win and Jack, two of my eight grandsons. They joined me at the conference, which brought together some two hundred teenaged girls from all across Montana. During my speech, I talked about Mensi's organization. At the end of the story, I surprised the girls by turning around to show off the burlap jacket that I was wearing, which had bright-colored printing on the back and sleeves.

After the question-and-answer period, I told the girls that I wanted to give my jacket to the girl who found a gold star under her saucer. A fifteen-year-old indigenous girl jumped to her feet and waved her arms excitedly. I walked across the dining room and took off my beloved jacket, which had traveled many miles with me. It had kept me calm during countless public speeches, because it reminded me of Mensi, a truly courageous heroine and leader. I guided the girl's arms into the sleeves and smoothed the burlap across her shoulders. A green leaf decorated the left sleeve, and Arabic words now ran diagonally down the back of this beautiful teenager, who was the same age as the models I had met in Central Bosnia. I felt delighted that the burlap jacket would go home with her to a Native American reservation in northern Montana. I hoped that, if she ever faced adversity, the story of the jacket's creation would give her the resilience to overcome fear, the courage to forgive, and the wisdom to create a community of support, an inclusive community that embraced diversity.

Under Mensi's policy of inclusion, the Society for Women Survivors of War Crimes had admitted all women of any ethnicity or background, requiring that they sign a pledge promising not to hate their perpetrators or seek revenge. "We all promised to teach our children not to hate, label, or judge anyone based on ethnicity or religion," Mensi had explained. "Only through forgiveness can we break the cycle of violence and war."

ABOVE: Women and girls modeled fashions that they made by using what they had—burlap bags from the United Nations World Food Program—showing confidence and pride in their faces and their runway gait; OPPOSITE, TOP: Young women who had experienced brutal abuse in captivity now modeled the difference between "victim" and "survivor"; OPPOSITE, BOTTOM: Mensi, left, founded the Society for Women Survivors of War Crimes to help victims of torture and rape recover their sense of self. Nearly a thousand members all promised not to hate their abusers or seek revenge in order to stop the cycle of violence.

Along the drive through central Bosnia, we may have passed places where Bosniak fighters hid out and plotted revenge on Serbian forces. For many years, I blocked memories of a terrifying nocturnal meeting.

CHAPTER THIRTEEN

A RUDE AWAKENING

Coming face to face with evidence of brutal torture

BOSNIA, APRIL 1995

Angela and I spent a full day with the Society for Women Survivors of War Crimes, another powerful day that gave us a lot to digest over dinner. We retired early, hoping that the stories we heard from Mensi and the other survivors would not play out in our dreams. Sometime during the night, a loud knock on the door jolted me out of bed. Since my twin bed was closer to the door, I walked barefoot across the cold linoleum floor and opened the door just wide enough to see two scruffy-looking men standing under a light in the hallway. I should have slammed the door shut, but my dream state and curiosity prevented that rational response. Angela soon joined me and opened the door wider, both of us now visible in our flannel pajamas. One of the men said in understandable English that they wanted to take us somewhere to show us important evidence of war crimes. They would wait outside in a car.

I should have known better. I was older and more experienced than Angela, but I admit that my journalistic nose for a story overcame my better judgment. Perhaps I hoped to discover something that I could take back to researchers at Human Rights Watch, something they could use as evidence of war crimes. But honestly, I just reacted without thinking. When Angela looked at me, wide eyed and obviously scared, as I should have been, I told her to get dressed. That was my first mistake. I have never told this story to anyone, in part because there is nothing of hope or resilience in what happened next, just some good luck. All's well that ends well, but this could have ended very badly.

Dressed in parkas, jeans, and boots, Angela and I stepped into the cold night air and entered the back seat of a small sedan for what turned out to be a short drive to a cabin in a nearby wooded area. Three or four other men were waiting for us in that cabin. When I entered and saw them, I felt an adrenaline shot of fear and foreboding. Barely visible in the dim light, the men sat on chairs, a bench, a table, and the wood-plank floor. The scene is a bit fuzzy in my memory, but I vividly recall the combined stench of body odor and cigarette smoke, which made me feel ill. I had never been in a more vulnerable situation!

The English speaker who had picked us up at the hotel directed us to sit on two empty chairs, facing a bearded man across the table, who then laid two pieces of white typing paper on the table in front of us. I did not look down at first, because his eyes held me transfixed. With irises as dark as pupils, one eye looked straight at me, and the other seemed to dart about the room, wild and unfocused, like a drunken person. When I did look at the papers, I saw that each page had been divided by black horizontal and vertical lines into four sections. Within each of the eight resultant squares, someone with artistic skills had drawn rather realistic scenes of people being tortured by bearded men. Rendered with sparse details, each scene portrayed a different method of torturing and killing people, men, women, and children. Eight separate and horribly grisly pictures.

One drawing showed a man whose legs had been tied to two different tractors, farm vehicles that seemed to be moving forward in a V pattern, about to separate his legs and body. There were scenes of rape, of hanging, a child being thrown down a well, and a baby being tossed like kindling into a bonfire. Angela bowed her head, but I, ever the reporter, took it all in, although my stomach revolted and my bones hurt.

In truth, I must have been in total shock. This experience seemed to be happening in another time and place. Maybe shock protected me at the time from fully realizing the danger. We were somewhere in a forest, in the middle of the night, surrounded by half-crazed men. I had no idea who they were, but they had to be Bosnian Muslims.

I felt inclined to believe what I saw in the pictures, because no one could make that stuff up. I realized that I had to pay attention and get us out of here and back to the hotel. Our translator must have read my mind. Speaking in a kinder tone, he explained they had heard we American women had come and thought we presented an opportunity to let the outside world know about the brutality and depravity of this war, hoping we would pass this information on to our leaders. He meant the president of the United States. The men felt certain that, if our president knew what was happening to Bosniaks, he would surely intervene to stop the war.

No wonder these men looked so wild, I thought. They most likely had seen or even survived torture. I asked whether I could take the papers with me, but they refused, saying these were their only copies. Of course, there are no copy machines in a war zone. I wished I had brought a camera to photograph the papers. The details of those eight images of torture were seared into my brain, but without evidence, who would believe this story without the identities of victims or witnesses?

After less than a half hour, the driver and translator drove us back to our room. Miraculously Angela and I were returned to the hotel, physically unharmed, but emotionally scarred. I suggested that we try to sleep and not discuss this experience until later, because I needed to process everything and decide what to do. In the end, I did nothing. I had not witnessed any torture. I had no names for the men we met, and no proof of specific perpetrators or victims, only the horrendous memory.

As I write this confession, I again experience a sense of failure. I failed to protect Angela. I failed to report what we had seen to someone who could investigate the torture allegations, and I failed to provide a lifeline for those Bosniak men, desperate men who invested hope and trust in us Americans that we would ring the bell of freedom. Angela must have shared some of the same regrets, because we never again talked about it.

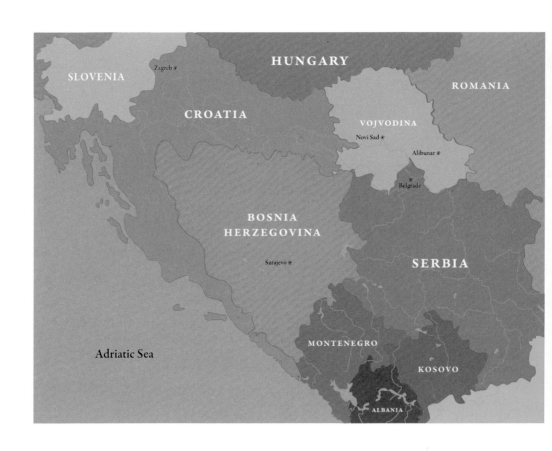

Map of the former Yugoslavia

CHAPTER FOURTEEN

HEALING HARMONY

A massacre, a courageous doctor, a displaced
choir, and a teapot

SERBIA, SEPTEMBER 1995

Occasionally, a person comes into our life who, through her very being, challenges our belief systems and reminds us of who we are. A woman named Dragana Vukotic, a doctor I met in Belgrade, Serbia, did that for me. Dr. Vukotic happened to belong to an ethnicity that I (and most humanitarians) had come to think of as "the enemy" during the ongoing war of "ethnic cleansing" in the former Yugoslavia. Like Mensi, Dragana was one of the most impressive women I ever met, and the fact that she was Serbian reminded me that stereotyping or labeling people or groups is always wrong.

After many trips to the former Yugoslavia, I went to the Republic of Serbia for the first time in September 1995, motivated by a surprising turning point in the war of ethnic cleansing, which had already been raging for three years. The war had taken place primarily in Bosnia, and its victims had mostly been Bosnians, with Croats placing second in the grim body count. All neutral observers agreed that Serbians were by far the primary perpetrators. And then the Republic of Croatia decided to accomplish its own "ethnic cleansing." During the summer of 1995, with little warning, the Croatian militia sought revenge against Serbia by forcibly evicting a large population of ethnic Serbs who had lived for generations in the Krajina region of eastern Croatia.

At home in Pasadena, I watched television news reports showing long columns of Serbian people fleeing east from Croatia to Serbia, passing through a narrow corridor in northern Bosnia that the Serbian army controlled. I knew the names of towns and cities that flashed on the TV screen and felt a sad sense of familiarity with those desperate people in long caravans of cars and trucks, wondering whether I had ever met any of them.

Through its dominance over the course of this violent war, Serbia had incorporated much of northern and eastern Bosnia into its growing "Republica Serbska" and eliminated most non-Serb inhabitants, especially Muslims. But these refugees from the Krajina region of Croatia were Serbs, and more than fifty thousand of them were seeking refuge in Serbia. A question formed in my mind. Would these refugees, 70 percent of them women and children, be welcomed as fellow Serbs or branded as foreigners?

To answer that question and to assess the needs of these newly displaced refugees, the Women's Refugee Commission (WRC) decided to send a delegation to Belgrade. At the time, I was serving as co-chair of the WRC and a board member of Human Rights Watch (HRW), both located in New York City. I reached out to HRW researchers for advice as I prepared to participate in this first WRC mission to Serbia, promising to report back when I returned.

I flew from Los Angeles to Vienna and got a direct connection to Belgrade, planning to meet two WRC colleagues from New York at the airport in Belgrade. Their itinerary included a stop in Tuzla, Bosnia, and a transfer flight from Tuzla to Belgrade. But when I landed in Belgrade, I received the surprising news that the others would not be joining me. During my flight, news of a shocking event had been leaking out, the massacre by Serbian forces of some eight thousand Bosnian Muslim men and boys who had been held in a settlement camp near the town of Srebrenica in eastern Bosnia, the worst single event of the entire war.

This horrendous humanitarian catastrophe shook the whole world, and it also impacted my immediate plans by causing the closure of Tuzla's airport. The airport facilities there were going to be used to shelter thousands of Bosnian

Muslim women and girls who were being transported to Tuzla from Srebrenica, traumatized females who would arrive without their husbands, sons, fathers, brothers, uncles, or grandfathers. I received a message from New York advising me that my WRC colleagues would be staying in Tuzla to help these women document personal stories amid the mass hysteria.

News of this massacre, of families being ripped apart, of boys and men, thousands of them, buried in mass graves—it was more than I could absorb. The numbers just didn't seem possible, so many helpless men and boys being hauled off and slaughtered like cattle. In my mind, I saw the faces of hysterical women and girls, waiting for news. I suddenly realized that I was in Serbia by myself, alone in what I had come to think of as "enemy territory," a frightening thought. My colleagues would not be coming here, but now the purpose of both our separate missions seemed even more important.

In Serbia, we had planned to meet with several international and local non-governmental relief organizations, including the Serbian Red Cross, which was controlled by the government. We had made appointments at the U.S. Embassy in Belgrade and the United Nations High Commissioner for Refugees office, substantial sources of insight about the surge of Serbian refugees from Croatia and also about the massacre in Srebrenica.

As I rode in a taxi from the airport to a dreary hotel in downtown Belgrade, I noted that the city sat at the confluence of two major rivers, the Danube and the Sava. Where the rivers came together, they formed a lake with an island in its center. Belgrade's buildings looked drab, like all the cities I had visited in the USSR, with 1950s concrete buildings that lacked any architectural detail or effort to soften their cold, straight lines, walls stained by smoke and soot over decades of existence behind the Iron Curtain.

The lobby of my hotel reminded me of the soulless "intourist" hotels in Moscow. In fact, of the six republics that made up the "former Yugoslavia," Serbia most resembled Russia, with its Orthodox Christianity and Cyrillic alphabet. So even though no matrons guarded the hallways here, I fully expected that my room was bugged and that my luggage would be searched during my absence.

I usually felt happy in hotel rooms. Having gone from sharing bedrooms with my two sisters, to college roommates, and then my husband, I relished having a room of my own for brief periods. But as I unpacked in this mildew-scented pea green room, a feeling of loneliness overcame me. Since I had made many trips to Croatia and Bosnia, I felt moderately confident that I could manage alone, but a rising sense of fear made me feel a bit faint. Whenever that happened, I often turned to music, and music, once again, calmed me. I started humming "I Whistle a Happy Tune" from *The King and I*. Right away the music lifted my spirits and helped me to stay calm and centered, especially when I sang: "You may be as brave as you make believe you are."

(I actually knew all the lyrics from many popular Broadway musicals from years of singing with my family around our mother's piano, which got my sisters and me through a lot of teenaged angst. Music had the power to open hearts and heal emotions. I could sing, but I had never quite mastered the art of whistling, something every child should learn in kindergarten.)

After a shower and change of clothes, I felt much better by the time the International Rescue Committee (IRC), our host in Serbia, sent a driver to take me to their office for a meeting. In the back seat of the gray sedan, I loaded fresh film, then opened my new spiral notebook and wrote the date: September 21, 1995, the Autumnal Equinox, an auspicious day.

Richard Delaney, the Belgrade director of the International Rescue Committee, introduced the staff and invited me to join their brown bag lunch briefing, an IRC tradition. It began with a discussion about the scarcity of international relief organizations in Serbia. Some sixty-five international NGOs were currently operating in Bosnia, compared to fewer than twenty here in Serbia. I commented that it was difficult to raise sympathy, and therefore funding, to benefit Serbs, who were widely believed to have caused this war and perpetrated the majority of human rights abuses and war crimes. Richard said there were other factors to consider—Serbia's tight controls, red tape, and obvious resistance to taking in refugees.

I could see that his words had an emotional impact on a woman seated directly across the table from me, who had been introduced as Dr. Dragana Vukotic, a recently resettled Serbian refugee from Sarajevo, the capital of Bosnia. When Dr. Vukotic first greeted me, I had noticed her outgoing personality and fluency in English, and I liked her immediately. To help the group understand the situation for refugees here in Belgrade, she bravely shared her own experiences.

"Instead of being welcomed here as an ethnic Serb," she told us, "I have faced resentment and rejection from my own people." Surprised, I looked at her more closely and made eye contact, which she held until I looked away first. A flood of thoughts came over me in that moment. I realized that for several years I had been holding negative feelings about all Serbs because of their conduct during this war. I privately scolded myself and made a mental note to think of all people as individuals, not just members of a group, because stereotypes always have many exceptions, and this woman, I could see at once, was an extraordinary exception.

After the meeting, Dragana (as she asked me to call her) surprised and delighted me by offering to drive me around the city of Belgrade in the afternoon and to Serbia's northern region, called Vojvodina, the following day. With Richard's approval, I dismissed the driver and interpreter he had assigned to me, both of whom seemed delighted to receive my gifts of apology, tapes of American pop music and red packs of Marlboro cigarettes, highly prized gifts, as I had learned in Russia and Ukraine. True to her word, Dragana led me to her car, gave me a quick tour of Belgrade's city center, and then drove to two refugee shelters within the city limits to deliver medical supplies.

Out of curiosity, I asked Dragana how long she had been in Sarajevo during the siege. She started to answer me while driving but, after becoming emotional, she turned into a parking lot and stopped the car in order to give me a long and thoughtful response, a personal story that truly surprised me.

"I was working as a physician at a cancer hospital when the siege began," Dragana said. "I am an oncological physician, but I had to operate on bullet wounds and broken bones. Eventually, a Danish doctor helped me to escape, still wearing hospital scrubs." When Dragana mentioned escaping in hospital scrubs, I remembered seeing a woman doctor being interviewed on CNN and asked whether that had been her. She nodded, with a shy smile that revealed her humility, a trait I'd seen in many strong and heroic women. She added a few details about how her home and work conditions changed when war arrived in Sarajevo. Then she got to the heart of her story, and I soon understood why she had stopped the car. She said that Bosnian Serb military officers had entered the hospital where she worked, captured her, and held her there for months, forcing her to perform surgeries on their wounded soldiers.

"I was born in Sarajevo and never thought I'd leave there," Dragana continued. "Every night now, before I fall asleep, I walk through the streets, so I will not forget my city," she said. She told me that in Sarajevo her friends had included Croats and Muslims, and that many of her friends had intermarried. "Now they are scattered all over the world, in New Zealand, Norway, Germany, Canada, and London. I try to keep track of them, but they all have moved on to new lives," she added, sighing with resignation.

Dragana said she felt grateful to the IRC for employing her as a medical health advisor to refugees in Serbia. She knew six languages, she added, but her accent in her native language had caused trouble in Belgrade. She recalled how an elderly Serbian woman, a welfare case that the IRC had assigned to Dragana, heard her accent and screamed at her, "There is nothing you can do to help me, you Bosnian bitch! We don't want you people here!"

I felt faint and realized that I had barely been breathing while Dragana shared this intimate story, wanting neither to interrupt her nor to steam up the windshield, which happened anyway. When she finished talking, we found ourselves sitting in a kind of bubble, suspended in time and space within fogged windows that shut out the world. I knew that my face, however, visible to Dragana, said everything about the compassion and love I felt for her. After a long silence, she checked the time and asked whether I wanted to join her for dinner at a restaurant with some of her friends, women who were also refugees here in Belgrade.

En route to the restaurant, Dragana described the three women I would meet, ethnic Serbians who had been driven out of their homes in Croatia the previous month. All three of them, she said, were members of a Serbian Orthodox church choir in Knin, a town in the Krajina region of Croatia that had been "cleansed" by the Croatian army in early August. My heart leapt! I told her that I had watched that exodus on television with great sadness, and I explained that my main mission in Serbia was to assess how these Croatian Serb refugees were faring. This sounded like a great opportunity to find out.

When we arrived at the modest restaurant, three women were waiting for us at a rectangular table covered with brown butcher paper. Dragana introduced me as her "friend from America," and that endorsement seemed enough for them to enfold me in their confidence. After we ordered our meals, the three women began speaking at once, forgetting that I was a foreigner, even as Dragana translated for me. They chain-smoked cigarettes and drank sweet red wine between bites of Serbska chropska safand (salad with cheese) and coarse dark bread. I ordered strong coffee, coffee I could almost chew, to counter the jetlag threatening to put me under the table.

As Dragana translated the conversation, I realized that this day, which started very badly, had taken quite a lucky turn. I held my journal in my lap and took notes about the riveting stories the women were sharing, descriptions of difficult, life-changing experiences, starting with the destruction of their homes in Croatia.

When I asked about their lives in Knin, all three said they had enjoyed professional careers and earned good salaries. And how were they living here? I asked. The woman who had spoken the least over dinner held up her hand, as if seeking permission and full attention, which she received. The day after they crossed the border into Serbia, she told us, her husband and oldest son were sent back and ordered to join the Serbian army in Croatia. She had not yet found a place to live in Belgrade, she added. She and her four younger children had been sleeping in their car, trying to avoid policemen and soldiers for fear they would catch her fourteen-year-old son, tall for his age, and draft him into the army. Whenever she could get fuel, she said, they moved around the city to different locations near public toilet facilities. (Having experienced several such public facilities in the Soviet Union and Eastern Europe, I gagged, imagining their filth and stink.)

All of us sat quietly, imagining what it must be like for five people to live in a car, especially now that cooler fall weather was in the air. Dragana promised to find a safe shelter that would take them in and to bring blankets and warm clothing from the IRC. She later told me that she was helping all of these women and their children with relief supplies.

"They cannot receive governmental assistance," Dragana explained, "because they have no relatives here. They have lived in Croatia for generations.

Actually," she said, "they are 'illegal aliens,' the same as I am." I wrote down that term, "illegal aliens," and underlined it three times in my journal. I had often heard that vile phrase in the United States, two words that objectified and dehumanized people. I thought about the vulnerable immigrants from Mexico and Central America who came to California seeking shelter and work, vulnerable people whose labor benefitted many corporate enterprises, especially agriculture.

The mood remained somber while the waiter cleared our table and served tea and hard candy. I wanted to do something to raise the spirits of these women, who had so recently survived the devastating loss of their homes and life they had known as normal, but I had brought no gifts. Then on a crazy impulse, I picked up the teapot, stood, and began singing "I'm a Little Teapot." The women looked startled; I sang it a second time.

This impromptu performance grew out of a deep childhood imprint. When I was four years old, as my mother had told me many times, I participated in a summer festival at Denison Park's band shell, performing a pantomime to this simple song. Short and stout myself, with dark brown hair cut in a Dutch bob, so the story goes, I curved my arm like a handle and leaned at the waist while singing, "Tip me over and pour me out." Mother swore that my "charming" performance stole the show, my only musical claim to fame.

Dragana laughed and clapped. She asked me to sing it again slowly so she could translate. The Serbo-Croatian words did not sound lyrical at all, but the women laughed and clapped. Then, as if the idea had just occurred to them, they invited Dragana and me to attend their choir practice that very evening. Dragana explained to me that the Lazarica Orthodox Church in Belgrade, located nearby, had been paying the Knin choir to sing at its liturgical services on Sunday mornings. Yes, I wanted to join them. Absolutely! I wanted to spend more time with them, to meet other choir members from Knin, and to hear their music.

We walked a few blocks along the narrow sidewalk, two-by-two, and entered a dimly lit room, where they said their choir had been meeting twice a week to practice and socialize. Several other women had already arrived and were busy settling their children on the floor to play. A short, red-haired woman wearing glasses organized the women by vocal ranges, then directed them in a warm up, *la la la la la.* I could speak the language of *do re mi.* I thought about my maternal grandfather, Frank Lister, a musician and piano tuner, who had traveled across Iowa during the Great Depression, tuning pianos in homes, churches, and dance halls. Sadly, my grandfather died when my mother was only ten, but she had told us how patiently he worked for tonal perfection.

When the rehearsal began, I focused on the rhythmic energy of the choir's hypnotic liturgical chants and refrains. I knew little about the Orthodox religion, but I felt the healing power of the music's vibration, and my mind traveled back to the choir loft in Denison's First Presbyterian Church. On the drive back to my hotel, Dragana promised to take me to the next church service.

By Sunday morning, after visiting refugee settlements that looked every bit as horrific as those I had seen in Bosnia and Croatia, I felt in great need of spiritual uplifting. Dragana and I drove to the Lazarica Orthodox Church and greeted members of the choir in a back room before the service started. I received such warm greetings, like a trusted girlfriend, that I almost cried in gratitude. Dragana and I wished the choir members good luck and then found our places, standing in the rear of the church. There were no pews or chairs, and only men could stand in the front, near the altar. Once again, I felt elevated by the blending of female voices. Anticipating refrains that I remembered from the rehearsal, I hummed softly in alto.

After the service, Dragana and I waited for the choir outside on the patio, where we made plans to meet later at a café. I would teach them to sing "Amazing Grace," and for dessert, we would all become teapots.

OPPOSITE: Alone in Belgrade, Serbia, I traveled with Dr. Dragana Vukotic, a social worker with the International Rescue Committee, who showed me that Belgrade, too, had suffered from the shelling of civilian neighborhoods; ABOVE: Dragana, second from left, supported women refugees from a church choir in Knin, Croatia, who sang at a Serbian Orthodox church but felt unwelcome in Belgrade.

Tens of thousands of ethnic Serbs from western Croatia found refuge wherever they could in Serbia. This father created "home" for his children inside a barn.

CHAPTER FIFTEEN

THE OTHER SIDE OF WAR

Making friends with "the enemy"

SERBIA, SEPTEMBER 1995

My second day in Belgrade, Dragana picked me up early in the morning and
took me along on her weekly visits to refugee collective centers in the Vojvodina region north of the city. I knew she was taking a risk by inviting me to join
her, because Serbian government authorities did not allow foreigners to visit any
settlements or meet refugees. Dragana ignored that rule but warned me to be
careful. Before we cleared the city perimeter, two soldiers stopped us at a roadblock and approached the driver's side. I looked straight ahead, while Dragana
showed them her driver's license and International Rescue Committee credentials. They just glanced at me before waving us on. As a middle-aged woman
wearing clothes from my war-zone travel closet, they mistook me for a local. I
hoped we would be this lucky at every roadblock. If my two colleagues from
New York had been with us, we no doubt would have been turned around,
because our shoes alone could give us away.

   As Dragana drove, I told her how, one month earlier, I had been glued to
television news and reading newspaper reports of Croatia's violent eviction of
more than two hundred thousand ethnic Serbs. Dragana said that when so many

refugees from Croatia crossed the border into Serbia, they more than doubled the number of displaced people in Belgrade and also the surrounding area that we would soon be visiting. She explained that this additional influx had ignited fear and anger throughout Serbia, because its citizens already suffered great hardships caused by the economic trade sanctions imposed by the international community to punish their aggressions in the war of ethnic cleansing.

Sensing sadness in Dragana's words and posture, I reminded myself that Serbs are her people, and that she wished she could lift them up, both to a higher standard of living and to kinder behavior toward one another. Because of the close bond we had formed during the previous evening, I felt an uncanny ability to sense her emotions. Wanting to comfort her, I started to sing "This Little Light of Mine." The lyrics contrasted with the bleak, monochromatic autumn landscape unfolding outside the car, and the song seemed to lighten her mood. On the third round, she joined me on the refrain, "Let it shine, let it shine, let it shine," which we sang over and over again.

By the time we reached the first refugee center, we felt reenergized and ready to face emotionally challenging experiences together. In fact, I had already adopted Dragana as a sister. I was lonely for my own sisters and the harmony we three had shared while growing up. Both Judy and Cynthia had beautiful soprano voices, and they tolerated my efforts to harmonize in alto. Singing with Dragana, I just let my voice go where it wanted, and, strangely, my vocal range seemed to expand.

In all the refugee centers we visited, Dragana and I received an open-armed welcome. The residents knew and loved her, and therefore they embraced me. Because no other foreigner had been allowed to visit, the women seemed especially eager to tell me their stories, which I carefully recorded with camera and journal. But their delight in meeting an American made me feel a need to manage the expectations they communicated through Dragana's translation. I had a tendency to promise more than I felt certain I could deliver, and in this case, I knew it would be very hard to fill requests. As was often the case, these refugee families expected the United States to stop this war, and they believed that generous American people would help them return to their former lives. Perhaps Hollywood was exporting too many movies about wars with heroic American saviors.

In a bold challenge to the rules forbidding foreign visitors, Dragana took me to the Kovilovo Center, which was operated by the Yugoslav Red Cross, and therefore risky because of its government control. The facility consisted of several wood-framed buildings, which reminded me of refugee camps I had visited in Croatia during the past three years. Many of the refugees Dragana and I met at Kovilovo complained about not being able to get jobs or earn money, and about not seeing any path toward gaining Serbian citizenship. I wrote down every story in my journal for the preliminary report I would fax from the hotel to the WRC.

Before we departed the camp, I jotted down a one-word impression: hypocrisy! A goal of this war, Serb leaders claimed, had been ethnic purity, similar to Nazi Germany's policy that led to the genocide of six million people during World War II. If that really were the goal, then why would Serbs from Croatia and Bosnia not be welcomed in Serbia? It seemed evident that the true goal of Serb leaders was to bolster their own political power and to expand the territory of Serbia; this war was a land grab, a brutal expansion of power.

Along the way, I learned that many refugee families were being relocated to Kosovo against their will. Kosovo, the region directly south of Serbia, was considered to be the cradle of Serbian culture and heritage. The historic root of Serbian animosity toward Bosnian Muslims is a battle fought in medieval Kosovo way back in 1389. An invading army of Turkish Ottomans defeated the defending Serbian army, a loss often referred to as "the fall of the Serbian Empire." The Ottomans captured a large territory that included Kosovo. Serbs have forever mourned that loss. Yes, memories and blame run long and deep there, transferred from one generation to the next.

In recent decades, Albanians had been moving into Kosovo in numbers so great that they now comprised 80 percent of its population. Serbia wanted to change that balance and reclaim Kosovo by forcing many thousands of refugee Serbs from Bosnia and Croatia to resettle there. I tried to imagine what would happen if France tried now to reclaim the Louisiana Purchase—which happened only three hundred years ago.

As Dragana and I drove from camp to camp, we saw some very unusual refugee housing sites. In the town of Temerin, 135 refugees occupied a bowling alley. The women said they laid out bedding at night, from side to side in the corridors and end-to-end along bowling lanes where, if anyone rolled over in her sleep, she became a gutter ball. The place had no ventilation or lighting, and many of the forty-six children, we were told, often became ill. The lack of light in the bowling alley made me feel claustrophobic. I think I would have gone mad in that place, a totally despairing thought.

In the same small town, we visited a school gymnasium that held nearly one hundred people. Stacks of blankets and sleeping bags stood against mold-infested walls. The place reeked of mold. Women had strung clotheslines from basketball hoops in order to hang up wet laundry, which we could see dripping water onto the varnished wood floor. It must have taken a long time for clothes to dry with so little air circulation. I was taken aback. I found the situation to be troubling on many levels.

On most WRC missions, we are asked to evaluate refugee settlements for access to food, water, shelter, and sanitation, but I don't remember being asked to examine laundry facilities, a primary chore for women everywhere. The rural collective centers that I saw in Serbia were a lot cleaner and less crowded than many I had visited in Croatia and Bosnia, but these women expressed the same lack of hope and similar fears for their children's safety and future. Truly—*a refugee camp is a refugee camp.* And war, I was learning, is an equal opportunity abuser, no matter who did the abusing, even one's "own people."

By the time we returned to Belgrade, my small hotel room seemed much brighter and more comfortable, and best of all, I had it to myself. I had encountered so many putrid smells all day that the fragrance of mildew seemed almost welcoming. As I worked on my report, writing it long-hand on a yellow legal pad, I reflected on all I had learned in just a few days. I had not yet visited the U.S. Embassy or offices of the United Nations High Commissioner for Refugees (UNHCR), which I knew would be interested in my impressions. I had a lot to share and many questions to ask.

First, however, I wrote a long letter to my husband, Ron, on my personal letterhead and faxed it to his office. The original letter is in my trip file. I did not tell Ron about the change of plans and the fact that WRC colleagues could not join me. That would have worried him unnecessarily, and I always tried to protect Ron from worry, in part so he would not object to future travels I hoped to take. After catching up on paperwork, I suddenly and surprisingly felt lonely, and glad that Dragana would pick me up the next morning for visits to apartments in Belgrade to see our mutual friends from Knin.

When I visited the U.S. Embassy in Belgrade, it was another auspicious day. I learned that U.S. Ambassador Richard Holbrooke was flying in and would come straight to the embassy that evening to negotiate with Slobodan Milošević, president of Serbia. (I could scarcely hear the name Milošević without feeling absolute fury. Together with Radovan Karadžić, the Bosnian Serb leader, he destroyed the former Yugoslavia. I celebrated when the UN International Criminal Tribunal for Yugoslavia indicted the two heinous butchers and charged them with genocide, crimes against humanity, and war crimes.)

The embassy staff gave me a brief interview before apologizing that they had to cut short my planned meeting in order to prepare for Ambassador Holbrooke's visit. They confessed to being very nervous about the upcoming bilateral peace discussions; I told them I understood, and that I'd also be frightened to meet Milošević, a butcher and war criminal.

"Actually," a young staffer said, "Holbrooke also scares us. Whenever he comes here, we have to be up all night following his orders. He never stops!" When I expressed my surprise, he continued, "I've never seen anyone work so hard or be better prepared than Holbrooke."

I laughed, remembering Catherine O'Neill and my first trip to Zagreb with her. Despite being exhausted, she and I had stayed up all night drafting our reports for the WRC and IRC, listing our recommendations with long explanations. I told the embassy staff that they had my sympathy, because I had no doubt that Holbrooke would make them work all night, if that's what it took to turn the tide of this devastating war. Holbrooke understood that peace in the region depended in large part on his ability to out-bully the Serbian bully. European allies had shown little resolve to end the war, perhaps for reasons that dated back to the Ottoman Empire. I told embassy staff members that on one of my trips to Bosnia, a refugee man had asked me whether I knew John Wayne. "I didn't know John Wayne," I told the staffers. "However, I do know Richard Holbrooke, and I trust that he will get this war stopped!"

On the day I had planned to fly on Austrian Airlines from Belgrade to Zagreb, I discovered another scheduling calamity. My flight had been canceled. In fact, all flights between Serbia and Croatia were canceled, no doubt as a consequence of the massacre in Srebrenica. Understanding my dilemma, the IRC office suggested that I go to the UNHCR office and beg permission to fly on a cargo plane they were sending to northern Croatia, the very place my colleagues and I had planned to visit next, the Vojnic Camp, which was located in a narrow valley about three miles long near Croatia's border with Bosnia. The WRC itinerary described it as being swampy and unfit for human habitation, but some twenty-five thousand Bosnian Muslims had been trapped there between warring forces, in desperate need of potable water and supplies of all kinds. I was eager to complete the assignment of assessing their living conditions.

The IRC's letter gained me permission to join a sanitation team flying to Vojnic on a wide-bellied UNHCR cargo plane, and I felt relief when I boarded that plane through its rear, proudly wearing a plastic UNHCR credential (which I still have) clipped to my jacket. I wanted to call my daughter Kristin and tell her that this plane reminded me of the Russian one we flew in 1993, from Havana, Cuba, to the Isle of Youth, but this time I would not be flying in a hurricane. Kristin surely would understand both my relief and my interest in going to another challenging place. With that comforting thought, I loosened my grip on the wooden folding seat. It had no seat belt, but I trusted my guardian angels, who had served me well so far.

This may have been my first and last trip to Serbia, but it definitely would not be my last journey to Croatia or Bosnia. I now had a much broader perspective on the war of ethnic cleansing and a deeper understanding of the traumas it caused for people of all ethnicities. I cared deeply about people I had met on all sides, innocent victims of a complex war. Being in Serbia had deepened my commitment to bringing Serbian leaders and perpetrators to justice, so that all Serbs would not become pariahs.

Serb refugees crowded into farmhouses, barns, and sheds. School gymnasiums and bowling alleys were also used for shelter.

TOP AND BOTTOM: Wherever they landed, women refugees carried on the tasks of feeding and sheltering their children; OPPOSITE, TOP: Serbian refugee families made do with minimal shelters in fields and farmyards; OPPOSITE, BOTTOM: They also filled small apartments in the city of Belgrade.

A small red triangular marker reading *MINE* gives a barely visible warning that this forest in northern Bosnia contains landmines.

CHAPTER SIXTEEN

PERILOUS FOOTSTEPS

*Walking in Princess Diana's footsteps on
the minefields of Bosnia*

BOSNIA, FEBRUARY 1999

The war of ethnic cleansing ended in December 1995 with the Dayton Peace Agreement, which halted active fighting but did not stop violence and death in the former Yugoslavia. One million landmines planted during the war of "ethnic cleansing" in Bosnia continued to kill and maim innocent victims across the countryside. That one million represented only one-eightieth of the global problem, because approximately eighty million landmines still littered some eighty countries.

To call global attention to the landmine problem, Britain's Princess Diana traveled to Bosnia in 1997 and met with survivors of landmine accidents. When she returned to London, she declared that the journey had changed her life, and she announced that landmines would become a major focus of her future humanitarian work. As we all know, just three weeks later, Princess Diana died in a tragic car accident in Paris. In February 1999, I followed Princess Diana's itinerary in Bosnia and met many of the amputee victims of landmines whom she had visited. As I spent time with the survivors, sharing stories and feelings with them and their families, I learned about the healing effect of Diana's compassionate presence.

Along with 750 million other people in the world, I fell in love with Princess Diana during her fairytale wedding to the United Kingdom's Prince Charles. Ron and I had taken our three children to Europe during the summer of 1981. After touring several countries on the continent, we arrived in London on July 29, just in time to join masses of people near Buckingham Palace and witness the parade of royals in beautiful horse-drawn coaches along their route to St. Paul's Cathedral. When the golden coach carrying twenty-year-old Lady Diana Spencer came into view, we joined the deafening cheers that must have been heard all the way to Oxfordshire.

As Princess of Wales, Diana revealed her compassionate nature by becoming a champion of vulnerable people. Slipping out of the palace at night to avoid the paparazzi, she visited patients at London hospitals and listened to stories about their life challenges. Through many such selfless acts of caring, Princess Diana earned an affectionate nickname, "The People's Princess."

When Diana went to Bosnia, she traveled with two American amputee landmine survivors, Jerry White and Ken Rutherford, who had inspired her interest, taught her about the landmine issue, and taken her to Bosnia. Shortly after Princess Diana died, in the fall of 1997, Jerry White visited me in Los Angeles and asked whether I would chair the board of a new organization that he and Ken were creating, called Landmine Survivors Network (LSN). He captured my attention and commitment by describing landmines as "weapons of mass destruction in slow motion." Coincidentally, he and I both had worked, through different organizations, to stop the nuclear arms race, which involved weapons of instant mass destruction.

I agreed to spend one year helping Jerry put together a board of trustees, draft policies and a mission statement, and raise financial support—but in the end, I chaired the board of Landmine Survivors Network for more than twelve years, some of the most satisfying and impactful work of my life. Traveling with Jerry, I visited most of LSN's global programs in post-conflict countries with landmine problems, such as Colombia, El Salvador, Bosnia, Jordan, Vietnam, Ethiopia, and Mozambique—and later in Rwanda, Uganda, and Burundi. LSN hired and trained staff members, most of whom were amputee landmine survivors themselves, in an outreach methodology called "peer support." Since so many of our regional staff members had suffered limb loss, they could empathize with other survivors and assess their needs on a deeper level.

On the "Princess Diana journey" to Bosnia, my friend Howard Buffett, who shared my love of photography, came along. Howie's fascination with tanks and destroyed buildings, which he photographed even from moving vehicles, balanced my focus on the people. In Gracanica, Bosnia, we spent an afternoon with the Dulic sisters, Mirsada and Fahrija. Both women had worked at the local Fortuna Shoe Factory since graduating high school, and they lived together outside the village.

The sisters told us that on August 20, 1992, they heard gunshots in the town when they left work. In fear, they made an impulsive decision to avoid shelling by walking home on a longer route through the outskirts of town; but when they reached a bridge near their home, they heard more shots. Mirsada jumped off the road to hide under the bridge and landed on a landmine. As Fahrija rushed down to help her sister, she stepped on a second mine. Even in pain and shock, the two sisters had the presence of mind to take off their shirts and tie tourniquets around each other's legs. Neighbors later found them hiding in the river, and drove them to a local hospital, where a doctor explained that both women had lost a lot of blood and faced a high risk of infection. To save their lives, he had to amputate one leg from each of them.

When Jerry took us to meet the Dulic sisters on their small farm, they grabbed me, one on each side, arms around my waist, and held me tightly. I squeezed them back and told them I was accustomed to being in the middle of three sisters. Among my own sisters, however, I was the shortest, but here I stood taller than the Dulic sisters. I imagined that Diana must have towered over them. Before we entered the modest little farmhouse, they proudly showed off their large garden, now dormant under patches of snow. I could see stalks along what had been rows of corn, and vines remaining from a harvest of peas and beans. Inside, the sisters welcomed us with cookies and sweet tea. On a wall above their small pine table, I saw an eight-by-ten framed portrait of Princess Diana and asked them about her visit.

Fahrija, red hair framing her pale face, exclaimed, "She was so brave to come here. We were still at war, and not a day was safe. Can you imagine how excited we were that she came to our humble little farm?" Mirsada picked up the narrative in her softer voice. "When Diana spoke, we knew she cared so much. I could tell that she felt my sorrow from losing a leg and nearly losing my sister," Mirsada said. "It was my fault, you know, Fahrija's accident. She came to save me." The Bosnian LSN social worker interpreted to inform us that it had taken nine months for the sisters to receive prosthetic legs, a process facilitated by our staff.

"Until we received these new ones, one left leg and one right leg, we had only two legs between us," Fahrija said. "We could stand hip to hip and support each other only if our good legs were on the outside," she added. Then they did a little shuffle dance in the middle of the room, giggling, their arms around each other. "We did that dance for Princess Diana," Mirsada said. "And then we turned around, with our good legs on the inside, and we wobbled and fell," she chuckled. "Princess Diana really laughed, and she helped us get up."

As Fahrija and Mirsada continued to share memories of the visitor they called "Our Princess," it became clear that Diana's brief visit continued to give them strength and confidence, as did their obvious love for each other. Thinking of my sisters, I tried not to imagine our sharing such a traumatic fate. As was always the case with Judy and Cynthia, I had a tearful goodbye with Mirsada and Fahrija. I promised to write and send photographs of our time together. During my early travels in Ukraine, I had learned the lifelong reward of maintaining a connection through letters. No farewell had to be final.

We drove to a town called Klokotnica, just outside Tuzla, to meet fifteen-year-old landmine survivor Malic Bradnaric and his family. A Muslim family, they had come to the Tuzla region in northern Bosnia from Doboj, during the spring of 1993. They continued to live here as internally displaced people, occupying the home of an ethnic Serb family who had fled in the opposite direction.

I was photographing red plastic geraniums in a wooden tub on the front porch when Malic surprised us by opening the door. With a huge grin, he invited us to enter, adding that he had just returned from school. He set down a black book bag in order to give Jerry an enthusiastic hug, which I could see brought tears to Jerry's eyes. Without even asking us to sit down, Malic pointed to Jerry's leg and asked if he could see his prosthesis, recognizing that Jerry had a newer leg than the one he'd worn two years earlier, when he came with Princess Diana. Jerry understood the question. He sat down to roll up his pant-leg, remove the prosthesis, and hand it to Malic, who seemed fascinated by this tall American super hero's titanium leg, an enthusiasm that tickled me, as a mother and grandmother of boys.

Soon Malic's father, Fahir, his mother, Nevresa, and brother Habib, age twenty, came from a back room and greeted us warmly. Nevresa took my arm and led me to a wall that displayed several pictures of Princess Diana, exclaiming that these photographs were their proudest possessions. Diana's staff, Jerry explained, had sent framed photos to each of the Bosnian survivors whom the princess visited. Many of the families received them shortly after her death, a bittersweet gift, but one embraced with gratitude. One picture on the wall showed Jerry and the Bradnaric family standing beside the royal guest of honor. In another photo, Princess Diana sat on a log bench outdoors, beside Jerry, Malic, and all his family, a bench I had noticed on the front lawn. Noting my attention to that picture, Nevresa said, "That is our Diana Log." A solemn silence followed before she invited us to gather around the kitchen table for a cup of tea.

In what I hoped was a sensitive manner, I brought up the subject of Malic's landmine accident. "What is your date?" I asked the boy. "March 31, 1996," Malic replied. He knew what I meant, the date of his accident. I gently asked Malic whether he would talk about his accident. He bowed his head, in a kind of private grief, but said nothing, so Fahir took over. "When we arrived, war threatened all this area. In our home city of Doboj, we had seen how devastating war could be, so I volunteered to help the Bosnian army defend this area by planting landmines in fields all around Tuzla." Malic's father continued, "Those of us who laid the mines kept a map of where we buried them. Then later, after the fighting ended, we had to find and remove all the mines so that farmers could work in their fields."

Nevresa interrupted, "I made lunch every day for Fahir, and he would take it out to the fields. That day . . ." she began, then stopped, her voice choking, and covered her face with both hands. Fahir bravely explained, "I was on a hillside, using a screwdriver to poke in the ground in search of a mine." He picked up a spoon and demonstrated how he poked into the ground, holding the prod at a 45-degree angle, to locate the mine without setting it off. "I was focusing on that delicate and dangerous process when I suddenly heard Malic calling," Fahir continued. "I saw him coming up the hill toward me, the hill where I had just spent several weeks removing mines. Malic carried a basket with the lunch I had forgotten," he said. "He had been told to stay home."

Fahir glanced across the table at his son, and his stern look softened into one of compassion. Then he looked at me with a pleading expression, seeking understanding. "All of a sudden the ground exploded under my little boy," Fahir said. He lowered his voice and barely whispered these final words: "I'm afraid that mine was one that I buried myself in 1993."

I wondered how Princess Diana, the mother of two sons, had responded to this tragic story; no doubt she had embraced Malic. After a long silence, I intuitively put my arm around his father, and then his mother, while Jerry took the hands of both sons. Clearly this tragedy had impacted each member of this family deeply, and I knew that both parents felt responsible. In that silent recognition of tragedy, I gritted my teeth in an effort to hold back tears.

After a long pause, we all went outside so that Malic could point out the hill where the accident had taken place, a site visible from the house. The land looked so innocent, benign, but I couldn't help wondering whether any undiscovered landmines still remained on that hillside. Sadly, the easiest mine detector in the world is the boot of a farmer, the shoe of a woman, or the sandal of a child.

I asked whether I could take a group photograph by the front door, next to the red geraniums, but Malic insisted that everyone sit on the log bench in the same pose as the photographs from 1997. Jerry sat between father and son, the main characters in this tragic drama, on the Diana log.

TOP: I told the Dulic sisters, Mirsada and Fahrija, that I was used to standing between two sisters. Each had lost a leg to landmines, and they said the 1999 visit of Princess Diana gave them the inspiration and courage to continue living; BOTTOM: Devastated survivors placed hand-crocheted afghans on the grave of a father and son killed by landmines, hoping to keep them warm during winter.

1999   18 19 20 21 22 23 24 25 26 27 28 29 30 31

1999

Februar	P	U	S	Č	P	S	N	P	U	S	Č	P	S	N	P	U	S
		1	2	3	4	5	6	7	8	9	10	11	12	13	14	15	16	17
1999				18	19	20	21	22	23	24	25	26	27	28			

OPPOSITE: The Bradnaric family's proudest possession hung on the wall over their dining table, a photo of Princess Diana with Malic, right, and his brother. Memorializing her visit to their home in 1999, shortly before her death, the family placed fresh wildflowers above the photo every day; ABOVE: The Bradnaric family sat on their Princess Diana bench with Jerry White, center, Malic's other hero.

ABOVE: Members of Bosnia's "seated volleyball team," sponsored by Landmine Survivors Network, practice with their floor-level net, hoping to compete at the Paralympic Games; OPPOSITE, TOP: Jerry White visits a lab in Tuzla, Bosnia, where prosthetic limbs are crafted and fitted by hand; OPPOSITE, BOTTOM: In towns across Bosnia, disabled people face barriers to accessibility. This shop owner in Tuzla lost both legs to a landmine and now needs to be carried up steps to his own store.

The city of Sarajevo, Bosnia, suffered major destruction during the siege that lasted a thousand days. This apartment building suffered heavy shelling from Serbian forces who occupied the higher ground surrounding this 1984 Winter Olympics host city.

CHAPTER SEVENTEEN

SARAJEVO AFTER THE SIEGE

*Navigating landmines with a Nobel Peace
Laureate and a Jewish hero*

BOSNIA, FEBRUARY 1999

My "Princess Diana reprise trip" with Jerry White actually began in Sarajevo, Bosnia's capital city, which had survived a brutal siege of some one thousand days. After traveling to the former Yugoslavia several times during the war, I felt an obligation to see for myself the extent of the damage to Sarajevo's infrastructure and also to its citizens. Dropping down over the snow-covered mountains that surrounded the city, we landed on a runway defined by war refuse, including a one-winged propeller plane and a dented World War II–vintage tank, both of which interested our travel companion, Howie Buffett. As we taxied between piles of military debris, I reflexively pulled in my elbows to help the pilot navigate the narrow landing strip that reminded me of the scrap metal junkyard behind my friend Barbara's house in Denison.

I had not been to the former Yugoslavia for several years and never had visited this formerly cosmopolitan city, but I felt a special bond with Sarajevo. In 1984, Los Angeles hosted the Summer Olympic Games, and the Winter Games were held in Sarajevo, so the two became sister Olympics cities. Also,

I had always been fascinated by Sarajevo's role as the setting for the event that sparked World War I, the assassination of Austria's Archduke Franz Ferdinand and his wife, Sophia, which took place on June 28, 1914.

Most of all, the recent siege captured my attention and compassion as a brutal war crime that lasted 1,425 days and killed some 11,541 people, including 643 children. The siege and the war of ethnic cleansing ended with a peace agreement known as the Dayton Accords, which had been negotiated in Ohio by U.S. Ambassador Richard Holbrooke and signed on November 21, 1995, by the presidents of Bosnia, Croatia, and Serbia—after three long and bloody years of civil war.

I had flown to Bosnia from Washington, D.C., along with Jerry White and Howie Buffett, a Landmine Survivors Network supporter. On the long flight, I told the men about recent experiences in Bosnia, such as being on the dangerous triangle road near Sarajevo called "sniper alley." Anxious to photograph war scenes, Howie had brought his trademark Canon cameras and several impressive long lenses, and he began taking photos as soon as we exited the plane. I had known Howie for many years and appreciated his boyish enthusiasm.

During the flight, Jerry shared his life story, including details about how he lost his right leg to a landmine in Israel. An Irish Catholic boy from Boston, Jerry majored in Hebrew studies at Brown University and spent his junior year studying in Israel. During that year abroad, 1984, he went camping in northern Israel's Golan Heights with two other American students—and stepped on a landmine. Israel had planted thousands of these inexpensive weapons there in 1967 in an effort to defend that mountainous region during a time of war in the Middle East. Jerry would have bled to death, he said, had his friends not used a belt as a tourniquet and then risked their own lives by carrying him across what they now knew to be a minefield and out to a road, where they waved down a passing vehicle and eventually got him to an emergency hospital. All these years later, Jerry choked up when he talked about the courage of those friends and how they saved him.

"Their quick and selfless actions saved my life," he said, "and luckily they were strong, because I'm a very big guy!" Indeed, he is a big man, a tall man with a big heart who turned his adversity into a full-time career of saving lives and empowering some of the world's most vulnerable people to become advocates for themselves and other so-called "disabled" people.

As Jerry spoke, I listened attentively to every word and then, as a mother would, thought about my own children, Kristin, Steven, and Amy, who were only a few years younger than Jerry. All three of my children had studied abroad during high school or college. What if a terrible accident had happened to any of them? I knew that Jerry's parents had flown to Israel and begged him to return home for medical treatment in Boston, but he insisted on staying in Israel for the following year. He had told his parents that Israeli doctors knew a lot about landmine accidents, and there were other landmine victims in Israel who could support his rehabilitation. That turned out to be true, he said. Amputee survivors in his Israeli hospital ward had allowed no self-pity and had made him get up and move through the incredible pain and depression that nearly crippled his body and his spirit. It was through them, he said, that he learned the healing effect of peer support, from the practical advice and occasional "kicks in the butt" given by other survivors.

"Only survivors fully understand the mental and physical trauma wrought by landmine accidents," he told Howie and me. "They demonstrated the strength to heal, and they gave me no pity, only tough-love." Without that peer support, he confessed, he might not have learned to walk again.

Jerry later reached out to other landmine survivors around the world and invited them to participate in the creation of a United Nations treaty to ban landmines as cruel and inhumane weapons, because they kill more civilians than soldiers. Under the banner *Nothing About Us Without Us,* he even took Third World amputee landmine survivors to global treaty conferences, so they also could share their experiences. For his tireless work on the International Campaign to Ban Landmines, Jerry received the 1997 Nobel Peace Prize, which was also presented to Human Rights Watch and three other tenacious advocates.

All these years later, when I try to describe this brave and generous man, who turned his own adversity into effective work as a champion of vulnerable people with disabilities, I feel gratitude to the Nobel Committee for recognizing Jerry's extraordinary work on behalf of humanity, and I thank Jerry for inviting me to join his bold journey around the world, bringing hope and healing resources to countless innocent people wounded by war.

On this trip, Bosnian LSN staff members, each of whom had lost at least one limb to a landmine, accompanied us to Sarajevo and Tuzla, two cities that Princess Diana had visited, and then south to Mostar, a city in southern Bosnia that I knew well, having gone there during several phases of the war, and having witnessed the most extreme insanity of ethnic tribalism. Mostar's river itself served as a visible metaphor for the separation of people by ethnicities.

After landing in Sarajevo, we were driven straight to our first meeting with a British organization, the Mine Action Center (MAC), where I hoped to find hot coffee to restore my energy. Driving through this once beautiful city, we saw piles of rubble and many destroyed buildings, evidence of the constant shelling endured by this devastated city. Howie and I reached for our cameras, and through the back windows of a moving van, we photographed the rubble of buildings that appeared to have been hit by a category five hurricane.

By the time we reached the offices of MAC, I was feeling the numbing effects of jetlag. Strong coffee and a cold metal folding chair helped me to stay alert while I served as note keeper. We were told that thirty thousand minefields containing more than a million individual landmines remained in Bosnia, a region half the size of the state of Virginia. I recorded these incredibly high numbers and many other facts in my journal, along with details about the tedious hand labor involved in demining efforts. Men worked in teams, each man clearing a small patch at a time, one square meter marked off by strings tied to stakes. Just writing such details made me numb, and I had to shake my head in disbelief at the callous inhumanity that had invented such an evil weapon.

We later got to witness some demining work, with men spread out across a minefield in order to prevent one chance explosion from taking out more than one man, dangerous work that required great patience, but it paid good wages for men desperate to feed their families. We were told that, after months of work, only 1 percent of the minefields in Bosnia had even been marked with warning signs, a despairing problem that presented substantial danger for returning civilians.

We left the MAC office to visit a minefield around Sarajevo's Forest University, where landmines had forced closure of the campus. The Norwegian People's Aid was conducting a demining operation there, with 125 men and five trained dogs working along with soldiers from the Bosnian army. Across a field of tall grass, men on their hands and knees used sharp prods to poke at a 45-degree angle into the ground, probing carefully for metal or any hard surface that might indicate a landmine—the angle reduced the likelihood of hitting the activator on top.

Because mowing could be lethal, the grass had grown tall enough to hide the "trip wires" attached to mines, wires designed to catch a foot and trigger an explosion. Eight men and several dogs had died in the past year, because dogs accidentally tripped such wires. Thinking of our beloved black Labrador retriever named Aspen, my grief extended to the dogs.

After a long day, Jerry, Howie, and I arrived at a dimly lit restaurant in time to meet Jakob Finci, a heroic Jewish leader and a riveting story teller. In fluent English, Jakob shared his fond memories of Princess Diana and expressed the deep sadness he still felt about her death. We drank a toast to "the People's Princess" and emptied the first wine bottle before our food arrived, not a good idea for me. I decided to do a lot of listening.

I had greatly anticipated this visit because, while preparing for this trip, I discovered by surprise that this region had quite a large population of Jews. In fact, when Sarajevo was founded in the late 15th Century, Jews comprised 20 percent of its population. Here's the reason: in 1492, an important date in "New World" history, Queen Isabella expelled all Jews from Spain. (Through that brutal act of expulsion, Spain lost a talented population and also another treasure, an illuminated and beautifully illustrated manuscript of the Passover Haggadah. One of the world's oldest Sephardic Haggadahs, which originated in Barcelona in 1350, ended up in Sarajevo at the National Museum of Bosnia and Herzegovina, and fortunately remained safe there throughout the siege.)

Jakob told us that in September 1992, Sarajevo's Jewish community wanted to organize a cultural event to commemorate the five hundredth anniversary of the Jewish flight from Spain, and they asked for help from leaders of the three other religions. "Surprisingly," he laughed, "we discovered that they all trusted us Jews but not each other. Imagine that!" In this formerly cosmopolitan city, trust had broken down between the various Slavic groups because of the war, but Jews had never taken sides.

"That realization of trust gave us the inspiration to try other initiatives," Jakob said. "We got permission to bring food into the city, because everyone knew we would distribute it fairly."

When Mr. Finci described aspects of the siege, many that I had never heard before, I noticed that he always spoke in the present tense, as if the violence were still happening. In describing the constant barrage of gunfire from the hills, he said, "Many of the snipers are just kids, teenagers high on drugs and alcohol; they are positioned all across the hills surrounding the city." Knowing the siege had ended in 1996, I mentally translated his present tense use of grammar to the past tense. I pictured those teenagers lying on their bellies above the city, peering through scopes at the streets below in search of a victim, any human being who dared to step outside. Reports said that a thousand people had been killed every month by shelling, mortars, and snipers, nearly a fourth of them young children. Kids killing kids. Killing randomly. Aiming at anything that moved.

A bit of history and perspective is needed here. Sarajevo, the capital of Bosnia, had been a cosmopolitan city until trust and communications broke down among its population of Croats, Serbs, and Muslims. In early 1992, the Republic of Bosnia and Herzegovina signed a referendum declaring its secession from Yugoslavia. Bosnian Serbs challenged the initiative and captured Sarajevo, a city encircled by mountains. In May 1992, the Serb army blockaded all roads, cutting off supplies of food and medicine. Then the Serbian military took the high ground and bombarded the city with heavy artillery, tanks, and small arms for more than one thousand days, three times longer than the siege of Stalingrad, Russia. During the entirety of the Serb blockade, the city had no water, no light, no heat, and no hope.

"Anyone who ventures outdoors provides a target for the snipers," Jakob continued. "Dead and wounded citizens lie in the street until someone musters the courage to retrieve their bodies." I reflexively looked out the window, just in case. By now I was calling him Jakob and giving him reassuring pats on his shoulder, trying to imagine what he had endured. I also wondered how Princess Diana had responded to Jakob's story. Jerry noticed that I had barely touched the over-fried and unidentifiable meat on my plate. Always thoughtful, he ordered some excellent brown bread, warm and crusty, while Jakob continued his narration.

"We lived like moles in basements and underground tunnels," Jakob said. After the Serbs cut off all utilities that supplied the mountain city, they had gathered all the generators they could find in order to provide some heat and light. "That allowed us to set up an underground school for children," Jakob said. The weary expression on his face spoke of emotions and memories that required no words.

Thinking about moles had made me wonder about rats, and I asked about health conditions in the underground city. Jakob just nodded, then told us that a pharmacy and small medical clinic were also created by the Jewish community to serve everyone. "Our outpatient clinic has three doctors and five nurses. They are my heroes," he said. I wondered whether the pharmacy and clinic were still operating but didn't ask. Howie, however, asked many questions of Jakob, and I felt proud to hear him evidence the caring and sensitivity of a humanitarian.

While barely touching his own dinner, Jakob had described such courage and achievement that I was overwhelmed with admiration for him and for the Jews of Sarajevo. I knew that he had been talking about a community effort, not a solo achievement, but a significant humanitarian program like that depended on inspired and competent leadership. I set down my glass and took both of Jakob's hands in mine. Looking directly into his eyes, I declared that Queen Isabella's draconian expulsion of the Jews from Spain had provided a gift to Yugoslavia, the gift of talented citizens with exceptional entrepreneurial skills and the heart to serve others. I felt my cheeks flush, embarrassed by my overly emotional response, perhaps enhanced by the wine, but Jakob seemed pleased by the recognition.

We had moved on to coffee before Jakob told us about a major turning point in the city's inter-ethnic relationships. "Encouraged by the successful anniversary commemoration in September 1992," he said, "we suggested other things that would benefit all ethnic groups." The Jews had organized eleven evacuations for some 2,500 people, mostly children. When Jakob described how parents of all ethnicities had pushed their children onto buses, not knowing whether they would ever see them again, I realized that those children had probably arrived in Split as unaccompanied minors, some of the many children recorded and cared for by a woman named Theresa and her organization that I visited in Split back in 1995.

"We even got permission to bring food into the city, because everyone trusted us to distribute it fairly," Jakob told us proudly. The Jewish community had organized the delivery of essential supplies in two trucks every month, one filled with food and the other with medicine, just enough for bare subsistence living.

"And the food products we received, mostly donated by the United Nations, caused some difficulties," Jakob said. "Rice, pasta, and beans are hard to cook when you have limited water and fuel, so we decided to set up a soup kitchen, and it's still working. We put everything into big pots and kept them boiling," he explained.

The subterranean Jewish community, we learned, had cooked and served 350 meals a day in an "open door" kitchen, giving priority to children, the elderly, and other vulnerable people, and taking food to shut-in people. "We also opened a school to teach people how to start and run a small business. More than six hundred people graduated from our business school," Jakob boasted, "only three of them Jews." No doubt having work and a daily routine, whether cooking food or studying economics, kept many people from going mad.

As I listened to Jakob, I was struck by the paradox of the experience he described. Throughout history, Jews had been targets of hate crimes, with Queen Isabella's expulsion and Hitler's genocide being dramatic examples. But in Sarajevo, Jews had served as trusted facilitators of actions that saved many lives, a fact that gave me hope. I would have believed the city to be free of religious prejudice had Jakob had not told us about Sarajevo's four-hundred-year-old Jewish Cemetery, one of the most famous in Europe.

"When the siege finally lifted, courageous deminers cleared 236 landmines that had been planted in our cemetery," Jakob said, "tedious work that took many months. But later," he said, bowing his head in sadness, "we found new mines in the cemetery, mines that had been put there after the clearance. Those mines caused a lot of damage and disheartened our people." Jakob took note of the shock registered on my face and reached over to hold my hand. It was only a moment, but profound truths are revealed in moments like this. I felt glad that he saw how deeply his story had affected me.

After we left Jakob, I told Jerry and Howie about the two different cemeteries in my home town, one for Catholics and the other for Protestants, a common practice in most towns. As a child, I had wondered why Denison created cemeteries on two different hills. I'm sure the dead do not care about the religion of their underground neighbors. Why would the living care?

When I returned home, I told Rabbi Leonard Beerman about the Jews of Sarajevo, and he set up a special program for me at Leo Baeck Temple, inviting rabbis and peace activists from other synagogues to participate. The stories I shared about Jewish leadership in Sarajevo resonated with the audience, and Jakob Finci received many offers of support from California.

A few years earlier, I had joined Rabbi Beerman and George Regas in creating a diverse group of Los Angeles clergy and lay leaders called Interfaith Communities United for Justice and Peace (ICUJP). The organization, which grew out of the Interfaith Center to Reverse the Arms Race, met weekly to discuss problems and opportunities for cooperation.

Immediately after the terrorist attack on New York's World Trade Center on September 11, 2001, members of the ICUJP recognized the threat of retaliation against Muslim Americans and gathered their congregations, hundreds of people representing the broad religious and racial diversity of Los Angeles, to protect the Islamic Center in Los Angeles. I happened to be in New York City the entire week of 9-11, experiencing firsthand the tragedy, the heroism, and the collective trauma. On television I saw the Los Angeles Islamic Center encircled by people holding hands and singing songs of peace, and I fell to my knees.

OPPOSITE, TOP: While Howard G. Buffett looked for a good camera angle in this bombed-out building in Sarajevo, I framed him in my lens; OPPOSITE, BOTTOM: Bottom, The director of MAC, the British organization Mine Action Center, displays a map of the thirty thousand minefields remaining across Bosnia, preventing civilians from returning to their homes; ABOVE: The Jewish community of Sarajevo suffered targeted hate crimes but found the resilience to serve as an underground lifeline and trusted broker between all ethnic groups, saving countless lives.

OPPOSITE: Howard G. Buffett called Jakob Finci the most courageous and resourceful man he had ever met, a true leader and hero; TOP: Cemeteries in Sarajevo say it all. The football field at the Sarajevo Stadium was used to bury massive numbers of people killed by snipers, most of them Bosnian Muslims, marked by stakes; BOTTOM: The landmark old Jewish cemetery, where landmines were placed repeatedly.

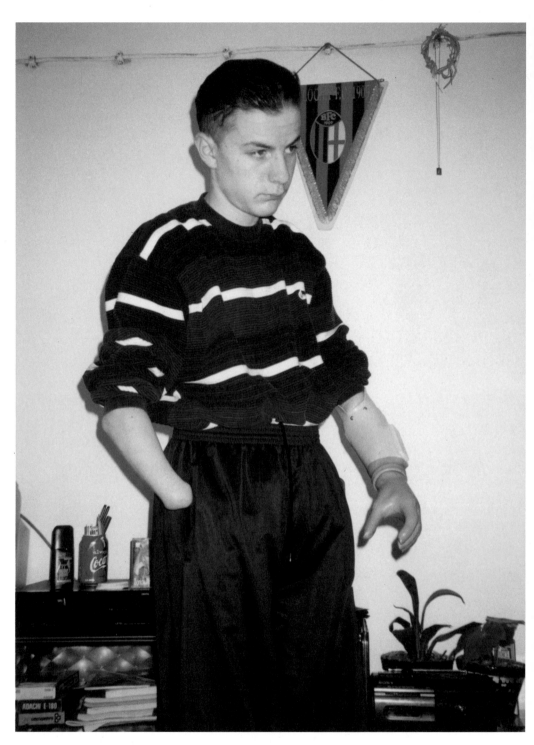

Six months after the war in Bosnia ended, Tihomir Ostojic, sixteen, a Serbian boy in Sarajevo, fell out of an apple tree and set off two different landmines that had been planted in an orchard. He lost both arms and the toes of one foot.

CHAPTER EIGHTEEN

PEER SUPPORT

*A computer whiz with no hands and a mother rejected
by her son personify human resilience*

BOSNIA, FEBRUARY 1999

When Jerry White and I visited amputee survivors of landmine explosions across Bosnia, I noticed a pattern in our conversations. Each survivor began telling his or her story by stating the date the accident happened. Jerry always shared his date, April 12, 1984, as did members of the Landmine Survivors Network staff who were traveling with us. Following that opening ritual, we would examine prosthetic devices to see how comfortably they fit the remainder stumps of arms and legs. I was amazed at how willingly survivors displayed their body parts and exposed the skin of stumps, often red and swollen, where doctors had patched it together after limbs were ripped off violently and without warning. There were no secrets among peers who had shared such shock and trauma. Whenever tempted to feel shame about not having a perfect body, I think about these courageous survivors.

Many amputees complained about pain caused by friction from the rubbing of their prostheses. They also described a sensation of aching or itching in the missing limb, which Jerry called "phantom pain." (Phantom pain is a phenomenon of the nervous system, whereby severed nerves from a missing extremity continue to send discomfort signals to the brain. It was called "phantom," but I knew their pain was real.)

In a Serbian neighborhood of Sarajevo, we visited sixteen-year-old Tihomir Ostojic. His date was June 14, 1996, six months after the war ended and the city siege broke, the day he went swimming in a river with a dozen friends and then climbed trees to pick fruit in an adjacent orchard. In the middle of telling us his story, Tihomir choked up and had to stop. His mother comforted him, and then she continued the tale, rushing to the climax—that her son came down from a tree and stepped on a mine.

"The explosion took off two of his toes and projected his body several feet from the tree," Tihomir's mother said, "and that caused him to fall on the second mine that blew off both his arms." She covered her eyes, and I moved closer to comfort her, losing my composure as we stood holding each other in the center of their small living room, where Princess Diana looked down on us from a framed photograph on a wall, three mothers of sons, in a trinity of kinship. I hoped that I could offer the same quality of care that "the People's Princess" had shared so freely from her heart. My mind drifted to London and a golden coach drawn by four white horses, and I felt caught up in a fairy tale. How I wished I could evoke some magic to give Tihomir back his hands.

I noticed that Tihomir had again taken up the narrative. He was telling us how his friends had applied pressure to stop the bleeding before carefully carrying him out by retracing their steps back to the river. Jerry inhaled sharply, no doubt reliving his own traumatic rescue. "There were no warning signs around the orchard, and we didn't know it was mined," Tihomir said.

Still holding me, his mother added, "A woman recently fell on a mine in the same area." Really! I reminded myself that we were in Sarajevo, which had been a rather sophisticated city, and that this boy was Serbian, the same age and ethnicity of the teenaged sharpshooters who had been positioned in the hills above the city during the siege, following orders to kill anyone they saw in the streets. I wondered who had planted landmines in that orchard and whether they had considered the ethnicity of potential victims. It seemed like random madness.

In an earlier briefing, Jerry had told me that when LSN peer counselors visited Tihomir a year ago to ask whether he had any needs, the boy had requested a computer. After missing a full year of school during his recovery, he told them, he needed a computer to catch up. The LSN staff gave him a brand-new laptop as a Serbian Orthodox Christmas gift.

When I asked Tihomir to show us the computer, his mood brightened instantly. Ah, I smiled, boys and electronics. He turned on the laptop with the stump of his right arm, which seemed a feat in itself, and then actually began playing a video game by using the stumps of both his arms on the keyboard— with amazing dexterity. I had seen many landmine survivors who lost both legs, but this was the first who had lost both hands, which somehow felt like a greater tragedy in the hierarchy of handicaps, at least from my perspective as a writer and photographer. But this boy seemed determined to push the limits of his capacity. His first important step was imagining that he could use a computer, a wish that our staff had facilitated rather than prejudged as impossible. That made me feel so proud of LSN! I, too, was learning how to see potential, not limitations, in the body and spirit of a "handicapped" person, a term that I would never use again.

I watched the screen while Tihomir played a video game, which reminded me of a Pac-Man game my daughter Amy had tried to teach me. While I was still trying to locate my yellow character, she had wiped the screen. When I asked Tihomir the name of this game, I laughed out loud at his answer, "Minesweeper." Honestly, the irony stopped me cold. Tihomir grinned broadly as he wiped all the mines off the screen. If only it were that easy in real life!

Tihomir's mother told me how proud she was of her son's courage and commitment. "He does school work all the time," she said. "He's a smart boy, and he wants to go to college and become an engineer or a teacher." It was remarkable, as was the interaction between Jerry and Tihomir. I could see how deeply they understood and admired each other. I knew that survivors often experience guilt and depression, the *why me* question that cannot be answered, but these two were striving to make their rescue count by living lives worth saving. I shared this revelation with Jerry after we left and said that I was so proud of him. While I could relate with Tihomir's mother, only a fellow amputee could stand as a role model for the son. Peer support. This boy would fulfill his dreams, of that I had no doubt, and LSN's support would be one major reason for his accomplishments.

In Tuzla, the second largest city in Bosnia, we visited a physical therapy center and a prosthesis clinic. We were shocked to learn that the therapy center was located on the third floor of a building that had no elevator. Seriously? And then we bumped into an empty wheelchair blocking the stairway and had to move it aside before climbing the steps. On the way up, we encountered two men carrying a woman down the steps, an awkward and dangerous procedure in that narrow passage. That explained the abandoned wheelchair on the ground floor. In order for them to pass, we went all the way back down.

That evening, Tuzla's mayor, Selim Bešlagić, and his wife, Amira, joined us for dinner at a noisy restaurant. Having learned that this was his birthday, we planned a special surprise for him, but first we had a menu of specific suggestions about how to make Tuzla safer and more navigable for disabled people. We described the third-floor rehabilitation center and several other accessibility problems encountered that day.

Mayor Bešlagić responded, "Disabled people used to stay home or just beg in the streets, but now they want to work. There are a lot of them, and they deserve a chance." In the same empathetic tone, he added some horrendous statistics. Within Tuzla's population of 650,000, more than ten thousand people had suffered significant disabilities because of the war, including seven hundred who had lost their eyesight, mostly from landmine accidents. Elected to his first term in 1990, Mayor Bešlagić had managed the city's security during the entire war of ethnic cleansing. "As the cheapest, fastest, and most effective defense," he said, "we laid landmines in the hills and fields around the city." We told him about our visit with a boy named Malic, who had been injured by a landmine that his own father had buried in a hillside. That caused both the mayor and his wife to bow their heads, unable to respond. Just then, a waiter arrived with the special cake we had ordered, and everyone in the restaurant stood up to sing "Happy Birthday." While the candles were being blown out, I made a wish that the mayor would act on our suggestions by reducing sidewalk curbs, installing ramps, and widening doorways for wheelchair access. Yes, I am goal driven, and I do believe in miracles.

After our visit to Tuzla, we drove south toward Mostar. I felt very anxious for the return to my favorite Bosnian city, but Howie, an avid and serious photographer, kept asking our driver, Slago, to stop at every bombed-out village and destroyed farm so he could take pictures. Slago, who had served in the Bosnian militia, told Howie that we were now driving through a very dangerous part of Croatia, that policemen and volunteer militias guarded these destroyed and abandoned homes, and he did not want to take chances or put us at risk.

But Howie insisted on stopping, one last time, to photograph some collapsed buildings. He jumped out of the car with two cameras around his neck and a variety of lenses in his pockets, while Slago drove a mile or so down the narrow road with Jerry and me to a place he could make a U-turn. Suddenly, Slago yelled and sped up the car. In the distance, he had seen a car approach Howie and two policemen throw him into their back seat. Swearing in Serbo-Croatian, Slago followed that unmarked car at a distance until it reached a town and stopped at what he said it was the city jail, where the "policemen" had already taken Howie inside.

I felt terrified, certain that Howie was in deep trouble and not knowing what to do. Never, in all my years of traveling with various guests and companions, never had anything like this happened, policemen in a dangerous country taking my traveling companion to jail for taking photographs in a "forbidden area"! Slago told Jerry and me to wait in the car while he went in to deal with the authorities, but Jerry and I couldn't stand it. Feeling responsible for Howie's safety, we jumped out of the car and followed him inside, where Howie was apparently being "booked."

As soon as Howie saw me, he grinned and whispered a request that I give him a new film cartridge from the supply in my jacket pocket, which I foolishly did, trading it for the exposed film he had rolled up while in the police car. His desire to save the pictures he had just taken mattered more to him than his safety—or ours! Clearly Slago was very concerned, knowing this was a serious matter. I showed him the card of a distinguished Croatian attorney that I carried in my purse, a friend in Zagreb who would respond to a telephone call. Slago gave that information to the police and added that the U.S. Embassy knew our whereabouts. Finally, they released Howie, thanks no doubt to Slago's military experience.

When we got back in the car and drove away, the first thing Howie did was to pull out his cellphone and call his mother in San Francisco, waking her up at 3 a.m. with the news of his arrest in Croatia. He was laughing, but I was still shaking. When he handed me the phone, all I could say is, "Howie is safe. Please don't worry." I wanted to tell his mom that I would turn him over my knee and give him a good spanking. But then I realized how sweet that phone call had been. Even grown men call their mothers when they are frightened or have big news to share. This experience would give Howie—and his mother—a story to tell for years.

After all that drama, we finally reached Mostar, the southern city divided by a river with destroyed bridges, where I had left my heart during earlier visits. Slago stopped near the river, and I saw that the rope bridge Angela and I crossed in 1995 had been replaced by a more elevated and substantial structure. I was sorry I couldn't show them the swinging bridge I had crossed and brag about my courage.

Many of the people we visited in Mostar remained in "borrowed" housing, having not yet returned to their homes. An LSN outreach worker, Polata Iset, took us to meet three generations of a family named Kara, Muslims who lived in a third-floor apartment owned by a Serbian family. Polata had told us that a young mother, Safeta Kara, had been only twenty-three years old when her landmine accident happened six years earlier, adding that Safeta's long recovery still required all of her energy, making daily life difficult to manage.

Safeta's story: in September 1993, Safeta's family received orders to evacuate across the river to the old city. During the violent and chaotic displacement of Mostar's various ethnic groups, Safeta had been running through the streets when she stepped on a landmine in a separation zone next to the main street. At the same time, many people nearby were killed in a vicious crossfire. Ironically, Safeta's landmine accident helped her survive the crossfire because she had already fallen, a fortunate but cruel fact. A Bosnian soldier risked his life to pull Safeta to safety against the barrier of a building, where she stayed for several hours during the battle and lost a great deal of blood. When finally someone took her to a medical clinic, one of her legs had to be amputated above the knee. She told us that she could not remember anything from the time the soldier dragged her to the building until she woke up missing a leg. After that initial amputation, Polata added, she had to endure four more painful surgeries.

At the time of Safeta's accident, her son Benjamin was only two years old, but when Jerry and I visited the apartment, where her husband and his parents also lived, the boy was eight. I noticed something odd about the boy, and I wondered whether he had experienced trauma himself. As a mother, I knew that a child would naturally respond to the intrusion of strangers by going to his mother for comfort and assurance. But this boy seemed reticent, as if estranged from her. This was not normal shyness. Safeta answered my unspoken question.

"I had to be away from Benjamin for so many months," she said, fighting back tears. "After each of the surgeries, I had to go to Sarajevo to be measured for a temporary prosthesis, and then it took three months to get each of the legs. I had to go back for fittings five times during the next three months," she added. "Now I am a stranger to my son, and he seems to be afraid of me. Benjamin is angry that I can't go to his school events or do things other mothers do, like shopping for school supplies." Safeta continued, "I simply cannot. There are seventy-three steps down and seventy-three steps up every time I go out. My new leg hurts, and my crutches slip on the stairs."

Feeling overwhelmed from imagining Safeta's long journey, I sat down on the arm of her faded red velvet chair and reached across her shoulders. Surprised, she looked up at me and said sadly, "My son will not sit with me. He won't even look at my missing leg." I noticed her husband and his parents still standing in the kitchen doorway, where we had greeted them, watching silently. We occupied the only chairs in that small sitting room.

While comforting Safeta, I noticed Jerry engaging Benjamin. As a father of four, teaching and nurturing came naturally to Jerry. He had gone through a similar journey during his own healing and throughout his life, one that no doubt affected each of his children, their cousins and friends, in different ways. I felt so proud of Jerry's capacity to empathize. He often wore short pants, in sun or snow, so that other survivors would know at once that he was one with them.

Now, Safeta and I both smiled, watching as Jerry showed the child his own prosthetic right leg, a state-of-the-art graphite and titanium limb. He took it off and handed it to Benjamin. Not anticipating the heavy weight, the boy would have dropped it had Jerry not held on. Together, they carefully set the leg on the floor so that Benjamin could examine it in detail. He looked inside the sturdy shoe, comparing it with the shoe Jerry wore on his normal foot. He rotated the ankle joint and pressed his thumb on the plastic button that releases the leg from the remainder stump. When the boy's curiosity seemed to be satisfied, Jerry drew attention to the stump of his right leg, which he crossed over his left knee. The stump extended below his knee, a great advantage over Safeta, who had lost her knee.

I knew what was coming when Jerry asked me for the red lipstick that I kept in an outside pocket of my backpack, just for this purpose. Using the lipstick, Jerry drew a red happy face on the bottom of his stump and then, with both hands, he squeezed it into funny expressions while speaking gibberish, like a Punch and Judy puppet show. Benjamin laughed and interacted with the stump puppet. Eventually, bravely, he touched it, and Jerry allowed the boy to wiggle and move the stump up and down. Then he pulled Benjamin onto his lap and embraced him. Looking small next to the six-foot-three-inch gentle giant, Benjamin leaned into Jerry's chest contentedly. I held my breath but not my tears, too captured by this moment of pure human connection to reach for my camera. Instinctively, I knew that Safeta needed the warmth of my arms holding her, as our tears, mine and hers, merged on her right cheek.

Suddenly, as if making a connection between Jerry and his mother, Benjamin sat up and looked at his mother. Then, while I moved aside, he jumped off Jerry's lap and climbed onto hers. Jerry and I locked eyes, acknowledging this powerful moment. It was time to leave. Jerry bent over to busy himself with the replacement of his prosthetic leg, and to hide his tears.

After the trip, I helped Jerry compose a detailed report of Bosnia's post-war problems that circulated widely to international agencies and organizations. A

German organization called Step by Step built ramps for rehabilitation and prosthesis centers. The governments of Norway, Canada, Austria, and England contributed a combined sum of nine million dollars to assist with demining, so that refugees and displaced people could return to their homes more safely. Mayor Bešlagić carried out a curb reduction program for the streets of Tuzla, greatly improving accessibility. The International Rescue Committee sent an orthopedist, who was head of the American Prosthetic Association, to train doctors at University Hospital in Tuzla. Through that program, Safeta received an excellent new prosthetic leg.

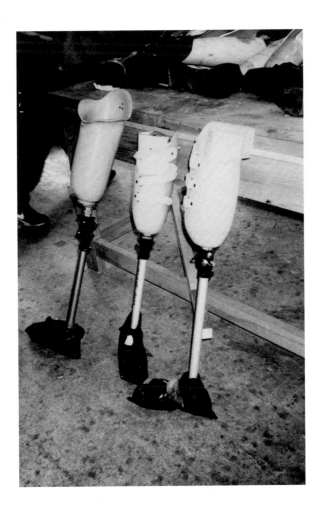

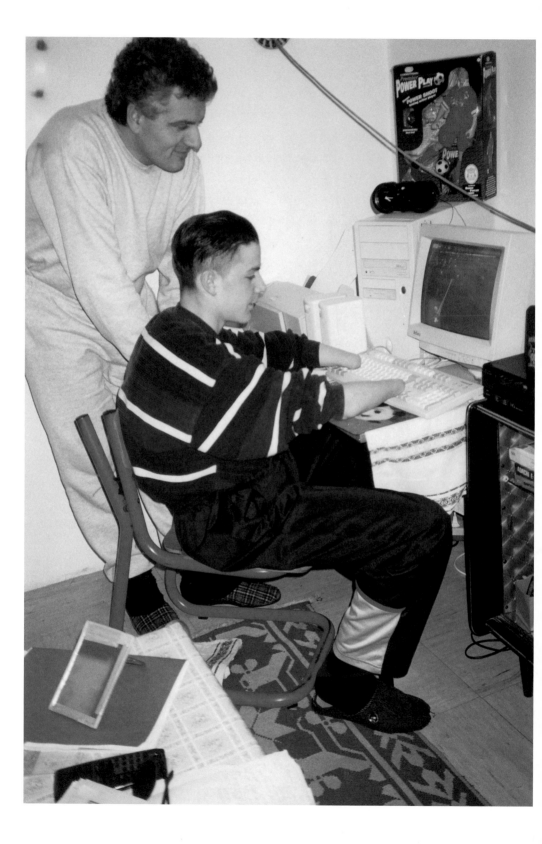

PREVIOUS SPREAD: Craftsmen created a thriving business in prosthetic limbs to serve survivors of landmine accidents; OPPOSITE: Using the stumps of his arms, Tihomir Ostojic plays a video game ironically called "Minesweeper." A photo of Tihomir with Princess Diana hangs on the wall, just out of view; TOP: Safeta Kara sits beside Jerry White, as he displays his prosthetic leg for her son Benjamin. Safeta lost her left leg above the knee during heavy shelling in Mostar, Bosnia; BOTTOM: During our visit, we experienced a family reconciliation and saw Benjamin smile for the first time.

THE CAUCASUS

Map of Armenia and Azerbaijan

Drive to Sisian
Yerevan Dorm
housing — N part of Yerevan
since Dec. '88
Red Cross helped
6 ppl here
husbands in Russia
selling glasses
Health Care
only bright moment
1000
1000
8
Visas
Entries/Entrées
SALIDA COLONIA
U.S. IMMIGRATION
FEB 27 1999

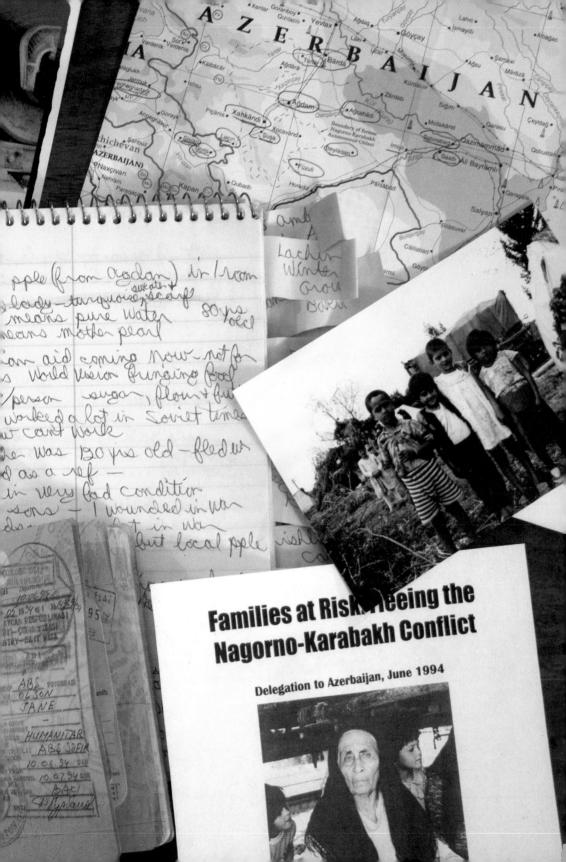

My great-grandmother Dillie Wubbels in Holland, Nebraska, holding our first child, Kristin, who represents the fifth generation of her family.

CHAPTER NINETEEN

WATER FOR LIFE

As war deepens the well of human suffering,
water and tea are precious gifts

AZERBAIJAN, JUNE 1994

My family's relationship to water was on my mind during a journey across the barren landscape of Azerbaijan, a mission with colleagues from the Women's Refugee Commission. We drove through the Caucasus region of the former Soviet Union in June 1994, the first of several trips to investigate conditions for refugees and internally displaced persons, people who had been forced to leave their homes because of violence but remained within their country. A bitter war had been raging between Azerbaijan and Armenia for three years. Like many of the conflicts that erupted following the Soviet Union's dissolution, it involved a border dispute.

We had timed our trip to follow a recently declared ceasefire, and we expected to be doing "post-conflict" research. Even though there had been no formal settlement of the very contentious land dispute, we thought the armed conflict had ended. When we discovered that belief to be false, we worried about encountering violence—but the primary and critical problem we found involved Azerbaijan's lack of potable water, which had become a humanitarian crisis across the country.

The issue of water runs deep in my midwestern roots, going back several generations. Great-Grandmother Dillie Wubbels, my father's paternal grandmother, lived most of her 102 years in the Dutch communities of Holland and Firth, Nebraska. Born in 1869, she survived two husbands and raised seven children in that challenging climate, where rain ruled. The vegetable garden and the chicken coop behind Dillie's house sustained her and several neighbors throughout long winters, thanks to the surplus vegetables she stored in a "root cellar."

When she reached her eighties, Grandma Wubbels finally got indoor plumbing. In 1966, when Ron and I took our first baby, Kristin, to meet her great-great-grandmother, Dillie proudly showed off her new kitchen sink, which had a pump handle instead of faucets. She vigorously pumped water into a kettle and made tea for us.

As a child, I took water for granted, but not so for our parents. They served as role models for the vital importance of water. They had lived through the Dust Bowl and the Great Depression, desolate years that left an indelible mark. When we finished a meal, Mother often poured the water remaining in our glasses into a pitcher and used it to water her roses!

For the June 1994 journey, I flew from Los Angeles to New York to meet WRC staff member Beth Verhey and fellow board member Jane Kronenberger. Jane, an attorney, boarded the flight to Baku wearing an Ann Taylor red skirt and jacket with matching red pumps, having come straight from her office. By contrast, I wore safari clothes for the long plane trip, which seemed appropriate, because we would be undertaking a kind of safari in our search for displaced and refugee families who were sheltering all across Azerbaijan in a variety of barren and desolate places. Our goal was to evaluate the various living conditions and determine the special needs of the women and children we met.

During our flight from New York, I met a woman from Kansas who said she worked for a relief organization in Baku. I asked her about the Azerbaijan Hotel, where we would be staying in Baku, and she replied, "It used to be an intourist hotel, during Soviet days, but I think it now serves mostly prostitutes and the Mujahideen militia." I gasped! My first instinct was to wake up my travel companions and suggest a change of plans, but I decided not to alarm them. Since we would be at the hotel only two nights, perhaps they would not notice the other clientele. As it turned out, we did encounter a militia, but I am getting ahead of my story.

When we arrived in Baku the next morning, the dense, smoggy air smelled like the tar used to resurface asphalt roads. Later, we got a closer look and smell when we drove out of Baku past acres of sludge bordering the Caspian Sea, oil-drilling projects that had been abandoned when the Soviet Union collapsed.

In the lobby of the Azerbaijan Hotel, we entered the black iron cage of an ancient elevator. Three bearded young men wearing camouflage fatigues followed us and pushed their way in among our luggage. We held keys to rooms on the fifth floor, but I pressed the third-floor button and directed the younger women to get out when we stopped. Then we waited for the elevator to return, and I told Jane and Beth that I didn't want the soldiers to know our floor, just in case they thought we were "ladies of the night." That frightened them, but after seeing my room, I developed a greater fear of bedbugs. Hoping to take a quick shower before our first meeting, I stepped into the tin-lined stall in my bathroom. Rusty orange water with the stink of sulphur trickled from the small shower head attached to an exposed lead pipe. It took a long time to rinse off soap and shampoo, but luckily I had short hair.

The dispute between the former USSR republics of Armenia and Azerbaijan began in 1988, during the Gorbachev years. It had escalated over the past three years, with the combined death toll now topping twenty thousand. The conflict primarily involved control of Nagorno-Karabakh (N-K), a mountainous region historically important to Armenia's Orthodox Christian religion and culture. In 1923, Soviet premier Joseph Stalin redrew borders between the Caucasus Republics in an effort to weaken ethnic groups and maximize his authority. He cut N-K out of Armenia, despite its 80 percent Armenian population, and gave it to Azerbaijan, a mostly Muslim republic. Now Armenia wanted to reclaim N-K and force ethnic Azeris to leave. Nearly one million Armenians had been living in Azerbaijan, a country the size of Maine, and they now faced the choice of either fleeing to Armenia or remaining in Azerbaijan as internally displaced people. Either option, they knew, was likely to result in terrible living conditions.

Before leaving the city of Baku, our WRC group spent two days visiting refugee shelters throughout the city, along with a young woman interpreter named Yereda, who gained our confidence by demonstrating the language skills and sensitivity needed for our intimate conversations with refugee women. She seemed equally comfortable in our meetings with both Armenian and Azeri women, displaying a warmth of understanding about their difficult living conditions, because she had faced the same problems here in Baku. I liked her immediately and knew that the refugee women we met would feel comfortable confiding in her. Yereda proved her resourcefulness by securing three cases of bottled drinking water, which proved to be critical for our journey across this hot, dry region.

The first refugee settlement we reached, east of Sabirabad, had pre-fab wood houses with tin roofs that a European organization had provided. It looked like a model village, with latrines set up on an elevated bank above a ditch that ran beside the road. However, the refugees who clamored around us told a much different story. Anxious to capture our attention, several women shouted complaints: "These unshaded houses are unbearably hot, even at night!" "We have no fuel for our cooking pots!" and so on. Then several women said in unison, "There is no safe drinking water!" Yereda told me the Azeri word for water and I pantomimed the question, "Where do you get your water?" They all pointed to a ditch running below the latrines. We walked down to examine it, discovering to our surprise that it also served as a refuse dump.

When we returned to the housing area, a woman carrying twin babies, one on each hip, stepped forward. She pointed with her head to an irrigation canal across the road, and we could see that it held water. Ah, I thought, that looks like an ample supply, but then Yereda said the canal water was polluted by fertilizers and pesticides from the fields. The women had told her that the canal water contained "green and white stuff," and sometimes dead animals floated by. On a sudden breeze, I caught the scent emanating from the canal, a toxic smell that reminded me of fertilizer plants in Iowa.

The women told us they understood that they should boil the water, but they did not even have enough fuel to cook food. I had noticed lots of tree stumps around these pre-fab houses and on the land surrounding it, stumps of the trees that should be standing here providing shade (and oxygen), and I realized the trees must have been cut down to provide fire for cooking pots, a short-term solution with serious long-term consequences.

Scores of children crowded around us, many with their heads shaved to prevent lice. Their bare scalps could not hide scabies, a very infectious skin disease caused by mites, which I had often seen on children in Africa. It shocked me to see so much scabies here, a condition that I considered to be a Third World disease.

"Do your children suffer diarrhea?" we asked. The few men in the group shook their heads, but all the women nodded yes. I wanted to sit down. Sometimes, when being confronted with one dismal condition after another, I am overwhelmed by a sense of sorrow and inadequacy. I was about to suggest that we leave a case of water, when I remembered how a similar act of generosity had once caused a riot. So instead, we promised to send out water tanks as soon as possible, a request later fulfilled by the International Rescue Committee.

In the Saatly region, we came across a settlement with hundreds of families living in abandoned railroad cars. The scorching heat and scarcity of water had made conditions intolerable there. Women and children of all ages sat on rusty train tracks under boxcars, taking advantage of the shade they provided. What must have seemed like a playground to children clearly stressed their mothers, due to countless visible hazards. I watched kids running and ducking under train cars that had sharp and rusty mechanical parts, kicking up dirt and gravel as they jumped over and around the babies and old women who were trying to sleep on the ground.

Kubra, forty-three, lived in a cramped boxcar with two other families and four of her five children. She said that her soldier son was still fighting the Armenians on the front line near Nagorno-Karabakh. "I have only these clothes," she said, indicating the dirty green skirt and orange blouse that hung on her slim body and bowing her head as if feeling defeated.

"We are always hungry and thirsty. Sometimes we get buckets of water from villagers, but that water often makes the children sick." As I watched her body slump in a combination of mental and physical exhaustion, I wanted to embrace her in a physical demonstration of compassion, but frankly, the filth of this entire situation repelled my natural impulse. I had embraced women in all sorts of terrible conditions with no fear, even in refugee camps known to have cases of tuberculosis, but this place seemed to pose an even greater health risk, the risk of no way out, of being dragged down into hopelessness. My own health, I knew, depended on maintaining a positive attitude, which meant finding ways that we could improve this gruesome living system and make a difference in the lives of these women and children. But we looked in vain for problems with easy solutions in this barren settlement.

Circles of cooking fires smoldered between boxcars in the paths of children's games. Branches with green leaves still attached had been stockpiled under the cars to feed the fires, green wood that burned poorly and created a lot of smoke. Clotheslines strung between boxcars held recently washed clothing, from which precious water dripped, making mud puddles below. Several women, when asked why they were wearing wool sweaters in this stifling heat, explained they had fled their homes in the middle of winter.

"I am wearing all that I have," Kubra said. I looked beyond the train encampment and across miles of flat, dry desert land, trying to imagine what this place had looked and felt like in winter, wondering how much the temperature dropped. No doubt parts of America's vast prairie land and deserts, regions that experienced bitter cold winters, had looked like this to pioneers who crossed them in search of fertile land. Here, there were no wagons or trucks or even train engines in sight. The parallel lines of railroad cars ended abruptly on both sides, as did the tracks; I wondered how the railroad cars, and the people, had even come to be here.

Further down the road, we encountered hundreds of people displaced from the most recent spring offensive. Families had set up camp sites along the road, some using tents and others simply sheltering under trucks and wagons. I walked past a rather large canvas tent, its floor covered by a worn and faded oriental rug, but lacking any furniture. At the entrance, a woman knelt over a large metal bowl in which she was kneading bread dough. I longed to kneel beside her and help with the kneading, but she gave me a pleading look that seemed to beg me not to see her this way. I had already taken a photograph of what I considered to be a beautiful domestic scene, but I put my camera down, smiled with what I hoped she saw as the kindness of sisterhood, and turned away.

I next came across a young couple in their early twenties, newlyweds I learned, whose simple shelter next to a tree consisted of clear plastic sheets tented over the metal frame of a double bed bearing a thin, sagging mattress. The husband's dirty white shirt hung open, exposing his sunken chest. His eyes betrayed some sort of mental illness. His pregnant wife, Aigun, twenty-two, sat beside him on the mattress, patting his back. She brushed curly black hair away from his glazed eyes, as if assuring him that I posed no threat.

"He lost himself in the war," Aigun said, "but I know he will come back to me. I built this shelter. Now I am doing everything for both of us." After taking a quick photo, I knelt beside Aigun (whose name means "the day") and asked when her baby would be born. "In four months. Then I will have two babies," she answered, keeping one hand on her husband's shoulder and using the other to comfort her rounded belly. "He just sits and stares. But when we go back home, he will be better."

Aigun startled me by asking, "Do you think we can go home soon? I need to find my mother." My mother. Of course, I thought to myself, we all need mothers for comfort and nurture, no matter our age. Around the world, I have stood in for missing mothers, giving from a full well of love that I had received from my own mother and grandmothers. I could not resist embracing this rail of a girl and touching her stomach in a silent prayer for assurance that she would survive, and so would her baby. I felt the fetus kick, as if answering my question about this young family's resilience.

When I stood to take another photo, wanting to remember this young couple and hold them in my heart, I could hardly focus my camera through a blur of tears. My poor vision continued as I recorded Aigun's words in my journal. I just wanted to carry that fragile pregnant girl to our car and drive in search of her mother, but all I could give her was a final reassuring pat on her belly and a large bottle of water.

Closer to the front line, in a field near Sheki, we found refugee farm families living in tents next to their livestock. Cattle grazed near a pond, the only obvious source of water for both animals and humans. To me, the water didn't look clean enough even for the animals. Scum and algae had formed near its banks. Nearby, I met three older women who were working in a small garden, a plot fenced off with sticks and twine. Two of the women bent over hoes, loosening the soil, and the third gently attached stems of green plants to long stakes. She reminded me of my great-grandmother, thin and spry, full of energy, familiar with and respectful of the soil, so like Dillie Wubbles. I asked Yereda to inquire whether the plants were beans, and she smiled while translating the answer. "Yes, from her garden. They had to leave in a hurry, but they dug up tomato and bean plants and brought them here." I admired the sturdy vegetable plants, and all three women responded in unison, "They need water!"

Tending sheep nearby was Nurlana, twenty-three, also in an advanced pregnancy. She said, "We live here like pigs. What kind of life can I give to my baby?" Nurlana pointed toward her village, which she said was less than three miles away. "The Armenians took all of our farms. Look over there," she said, pointing again. I saw smoke rising in the distance, a sight that startled me. If the ceasefire had in fact halted the violent conflict, it apparently had not stopped the destruction of property. I wondered whether tanks were still being used.

While Jane and Beth went off to examine sanitation facilities, I walked across a field toward a big wagon piled high with household goods. It had intrigued me from a distance because its profile resembled that of covered wagons during pioneer days in the American Midwest—except that here a tractor replaced the 19th Century oxen. A tent had been erected next to the wagon, and people sat near it on rocks and logs. On the other side of the wagon stood an old woman leaning on a cane. A gray canvas tarp covered a mound of possessions that the wagon carried. As I watched, a young man came from behind the wagon, opened his arms wide, and embraced the old woman, nearly picking her up.

Intrigued, Yereda and I approached them. The soldier proudly answered our question, "This is my grandmother. Today is her one hundredth birthday, and I wanted to surprise her." The old woman's deeply creased face broke into a broad grin, exposing her missing front teeth. The soldier told me he was thirty-six years old and had just come from the front line. Tall and thin, he wore a gray shirt and dirty black jeans, not an army uniform. His grandmother wore many layers of clothing, with a plaid blanket wrapped around her shoulders. I thought she must be suffocating, because I felt hot wearing a thin cotton shirt. When I took out my camera, the happy twosome posed for photographs beside their over-loaded wagon.

The matriarch took my hand and led me around the wagon, then pointed to a tree stump, where I should sit. Then, like a sheep dog, she herded all her family members to sit down on logs nearby. We all watched her place a silver samovar (can you imagine? A silver samovar in the middle of this turmoil? I wondered what else she had brought in that big covered wagon!) over a small fire and then dip water from a pail to fill it for tea. While the water heated, the centenarian said she had survived three previous wars, and she hoped this fourth war would be the last time she ever had to watch young men go off to fight.

I wanted to produce a birthday cake with one hundred candles, so that she could repeat that wish and make it come true, but instead, I found some granola bars in my backpack. I broke all the bars apart and gave pieces to four generations of family members. After tasting my humble offering, the amazing matriarch walked over to the wagon and returned with a small wooden box, which she set on the ground beside the samovar. Then, with lines of concentration across her face, the birthday girl lifted a delicate pink china cup from the box and brushed off straw that had cushioned its journey. She filled that precious cup with tea, and offered it to me. I understood the honor, because whenever we visited my great-grandmother Wubbels, she served tea in special blue cups that her family had brought when they emigrated from the Netherlands.

Taking the fragile cup with both hands, I returned her smile. Then she reached into the pocket of her apron and handed me a sugar cube, demonstrating how I should place it under my top lip in front of my teeth and sip the hot tea through the sugar. I suspected this was her last sugar cube, because no one else received one, not even her grandson. She may have been saving it for her own special birthday treat.

Now imagine this—I felt certain that the samovar had not yet boiled the water and suspected I was holding a cup full of bacteria—but I drank every drop of that tea. And I did not get sick. Sometimes our guardian angels do take over.

OPPOSITE, TOP: Near Sabirabad, Azerbaijan, children of internally displaced families were tasked with carrying water from a contaminated creek that gave them diarrhea; OPPOSITE, BOTTOM: In a railroad car settlement, internally displaced mothers coped with heat, filth, and the lack of water, their greatest concern; ABOVE: I could not resist taking this photo of an Azeri woman kneading bread on the floor of her tent shelter. Her eyes begged me to see her dignity, which I certainly did.

ABOVE: At a tent camp in the Saatly region of Azerbaijan, which housed families displaced from the Nagorno-Karabakh region, curious children came forward. Their mothers, who were less trusting of strangers, apologized that they had no water to waste on laundry; OPPOSITE: The face of this grandmother sitting under a train spoke volumes about the perils of sheltering families in railroad cars on hot, barren land in southwest Azerbaijan. I called her the "queen mother," and we used her photograph on the cover of our report for the Women's Refugee Commission.

OPPOSITE, TOP: Refugee mothers and children wandered around tent camps as if lost in a maze; OPPOSITE, BOTTOM LEFT: A strong Azeri farm woman, who brought crops from her garden when she fled, reminded me of my great-grandmother. "We need rain," she said; OPPOSITE, BOTTOM RIGHT: This sad but beautiful boy could have been a poster child for UNICEF; ABOVE: This refugee woman carried her baby on her back like African mothers, reminding me that we are one global family, bonded by the love of our children and a shared desire to shelter, protect, and nurture them in safety.

ABOVE: A young woman named Aigun built this flimsy shelter from plastic sheeting because her husband lost his mind in the war and could do nothing. She said she was pregnant and asked me to help her find her mother. I wanted to take over that role and help her through this challenging situation and the ordeal to come; OPPOSITE, TOP: An impressive reed house sheltered two large Azeri refugee families. They had set up a sink for washing, but the tank held no water; OPPOSITE, BOTTOM LEFT AND RIGHT: An Azeri grandmother celebrating her one-hundredth birthday welcomed me into her multi-generational family and introduced a grandson who had just come from the front line for her birthday. Surrounded by love, she served me tea in her finest china cup.

Having fled from her farm in Armenia, this young Azeri woman felt challenged to keep her children safe and healthy while living in a hot, stuffy train car in rural Azerbaijan. When she expressed anger at the helplessness of her unbearable situation, I thought, "Right on! We all should be outraged by these inhumane conditions!"

CHAPTER TWENTY

LOOKING FOR HOPE AMID HORROR

Toxic chemicals, snakes, and rapists plague refugees

AZERBAIJAN, JUNE 1994

After a long, hot, and dry drive west from Baku through the center of Azerbaijan, our delegation from the Women's Refugee Commission (WRC) reached its destination, a small town in western Azerbaijan that marked the front line of this war with Armenia. On the outskirts of the town, we came upon a gathering of two dozen or more people who had their backs to the road, facing an open field. We tried to guess what had gotten their attention, because we could only see some tractors in the distance.

Jane Kronenberger, Beth Verhey, and our interpreter, Yereda, and I got out of the car to ask what was going on, assuming that the tractors carried farm families who were coming to celebrate the recent ceasefire agreement. I raised my camera and focused it on the nearest tractor. Through the long lens, I could see two adults and two children on the tractor and a wagon filled with what looked like furniture, which seemed strange. Just after I took a photo, a loud explosion caused the tractor to bounce up and roll over.

"Damn," I exclaimed, "I missed that shot!" Beth responded more appropriately. "Landmine!" she yelled. We all jumped back in the car, and we did not have to tell the driver to gun it. A frightened Yereda reported that she had learned from the crowd that the approaching tractors held Azeris fleeing from Nagorno-Karabakh, because their farms were being shelled. I suddenly realized that we had actually been standing on the "front line" and looking into N-K, the region that both Armenia and Azerbaijan claimed, the land that was being fought over. After hearing so much about N-K, I thought I would recognize the land, as if a sign would identify it, like a national park, but it looked similar to the surrounding land we had driven through.

"But what about the ceasefire declaration?" I asked. We all concluded that either the Armenian militia had not heard about the temporary treaty, or it had chosen to ignore it and continue its goal of reclaiming the N-K.

Let me back up and explain how we got here, the trip we had taken across Azerbaijan to the N-K border. I have held these stories in my heart and mind all these many years and never told some of them, even to my family, because putting words to such surreal experiences is painful. I have to look at my photos to conjure details I have suppressed. But it feels important at this time to share these experiences about depth of depravity that can overtake humanity, and about what it means to be humane. If anyone learns anything about being humane, it is worth the pain of remembering and sharing.

Right after the trip, I helped to write our official reports and recommendations for the WRC, listing specific humanitarian relief that needed to happen, but in reports, I could never really give flesh to the stories I am about to share. For me personally, this journey was a revelation of so much brutality against women and girls that it took many years for me to process the reality captured in my journals and photos and to find some rays of hope. I have always needed to find hope, even in the most dismal places. *HOPE* is oxygen to the human spirit.

As we drove across southern and western Azerbaijan, we discovered terrible situations in every town. All of the schools, hostels, and public facilities were filled beyond capacity with refugees and internally displaced Azeri Muslim people, many of whom had been removed from their homes, some for up to five years. Although this conflict began in 1988, most international relief organizations did not come to Azerbaijan until early 1993 (yes, seriously—almost six years later!), a response delayed in large part because of corrupt Azeri government officials. More than twenty international organizations were working here now, all of them struggling to support basic survival of the masses, with very little help from the country's own government, despite the fact that it had been accruing substantial revenues from oil drilling operations in the Caspian Sea. Such greed and callous disregard.

From Baku we had driven west and south, where we knew that tens of thousands of displaced Azeris had congregated in the Saatly region of southern Azerbaijan, near its border with Iran. Along the way we visited an IRC office and met with other international aid workers, the real heroes who remain on the front line and serve desperate people every day, for as long as it takes. From them we learned that Iran had created eight different settlements to house and feed some fifty thousand displaced people in this region. That sounded like a very generous humanitarian gesture, but we were told that Iran's motivation was not entirely altruistic. They wanted to prevent the Azeris from crossing into Iran, and because of that, Iranian guards tightly controlled access to these camps.

When we heard that very few outsiders ever gained admittance, Jane K. and I, of course, decided we that we simply had to find a way to get into an Iranian camp. We assured Beth, the young WRC staffer traveling with us, that we two Janes would take personal responsibility for whatever happened. However, Beth did not look very assured when we directed our driver to take a detour and go to the Iranian Saatly Camp, a very large tent camp.

At the camp's entrance, we encountered a serious fence and a large gate across the road, secured by a heavy padlocked chain. Just inside stood a small house occupied by Iranian guards wearing khaki uniforms. Jane K., taking personal offense at that padlock, got out of the car and shook the chain to summon attention. With the help of Yereda, she called out to the guards and told them that we had come all the way from America to see their medical clinic (which we were not even sure they had). She added that we'd heard their clinic was exemplary, and we wanted to offer medical supplies to the Iranian health care staff.

Whether or not the guards understood the translation, I knew that Jane would get her way. Maybe the word "America" did the trick, but for whatever reason, the guards opened the gate and allowed us to enter. Then, as soon as we passed them, we headed toward the clinic, which they had pointed to in the distance.

There, we stopped to take in the full scene. A mix of shelters, included railroad cars and tents, surrounded the clinic, all looking hot and dusty. Some simple tarps raised on stakes shaded piles of belongings—and people. We had not walked far before scores of refugees crowded around us, shouting and pointing toward a rectangular wooden building across a stretch of dirt about the width of a football field, beckoning us to go there.

After checking to make sure that no guards had followed us, we stepped over a rope fence that separated the field from rows of tents. As we walked across the field, an acrid chemical smell made me feel sick. I recognized the scent of DDT, because that pesticide had been sprayed in my home town every summer to kill mosquitos. That toxic smell made me recall how on hot summer days in Denison, boys loved to ride their bikes behind trucks that sprayed DDT all over town and get soaked in that stinky liquid. The vapors alone hurt my nose and eyes. In the 1950s, we didn't understand the real danger, but I never saw girls doing anything that stupid.

The refugees guiding us told Yereda that this field had been used as a runway for crop-dusting planes carrying fertilizers and pesticides. When we reached an open doorway at the end of the rectangular wooden building, I saw a lot of empty white vinyl bags scattered on the floor inside. Walking diagonally across the building's interior, we made footprints in the thick white dust covering the floor, a powder that emitted the same intense odor. My eyes teared up, my nose started running, and my throat tightened.

In the dim light, I could see several children playing among full bags that were stacked in piles along a corner wall, bags no doubt filled with that chemical powder. Let me be clear—the children were running and playing among stacks of bags that contained fertilizers and pesticides. The improvised playground reminded me of my father's feed mill and its piles of cotton sacks filled with chicken feed where my sisters and I used to play. We used to climb stacks of feed sacks and play hide and seek in the feed mill's storage room. But the bags in my childhood had been safe; these bags were toxic, and they posed a grave danger.

Noting my alarm, Zembira, one of the young women who had led me across the field, grabbed my arm and turned me around so that she could look directly into my eyes, which had begun tearing from the chemicals. She began talking rather hysterically, so I took her other hand to calm her down until I could find Yereda to decipher what she was trying to tell me, which was that her four-year-old daughter used to play here. Zembira blurted out in Azeri, "One day she dropped chewing gum into the powder and then put it back in her mouth. She died shortly after."

Even before I heard the translation, I knew that something terrible had happened, something so awful that, all this time later, this frail woman crumpled and nearly fell, leaning against me for support. I embraced and held Zembira, absorbing the impact of her statement. In shock myself, I could do little more than hold us both upright, as our sweat and tears comingled.

Still holding on, Zembira led me away from the warehouse and back across the field toward a small gray tent where, just inside, I could see the profile of a young woman sitting on the ground and holding the limp body of a child across her lap, in the pose of Michelangelo's *Pieta*. Just when I thought my own heart could not take in more grief, Zembira dropped my hand and entered the tent. Neither woman acknowledged the other, as Zembira sat down next to this Madonna-like figure, whom I guessed to be her sister. Together, the two women rocked the child side to side as one, both crying softly, a primal scene that held me transfixed. Two mothers and two daughters, one already lost and the other on a journey to join her. As the women stared into the dark space around them, I could only witness this absolutely searing moment and hold them both in a silent prayer.

I could not erase the *Pieta* scene from my mind when we drove north from Saatly to the hills above Sheki. In sacred silence, we processed what we'd experienced in this faraway place. I felt numb. I could not take in the scenery unfolding outside the car, until we came to a rural encampment with scenes familiar to me, families tending livestock in an idyllic valley beside a small lake.

In contrast to the desert land of the south, the hillsides here, dotted with sheep and a few tents, looked like paradise. I couldn't wait to get out of the car and breathe fresh air.

Our driver, happy that the melancholic mood had shifted, led us on a short walk up a hill for a closer look at shelters that he called "dug-ins." When Yereda translated that term, I thought about early American pioneers and homesteaders, including my own ancestors, who settled prairies in the Midwest during the 19th Century. Pioneers crossing the U.S., unable to construct cabins before winter arrived, had built shelters they called "dug-outs" or "sod houses" and survived by burrowing underground until the spring thaw.

As we walked up the hillside, we saw small caves with straw roofs concealing them from the road below. In front of one of the caves, we met a friendly man named Niftaly, who was sitting on a rock while milking a goat he had tied to a stake. He picked up a gourd full of milk and invited us to enter his home and meet his wife and his older sister. The two women, who looked like mother and daughter with their matching henna-dyed hair, sat on cots, knitting with purple yarn. I looked at their knitting admiringly, their even rows of knit and purl, no fancy Irish fisherman patterns. Then I examined the dug-in's construction and complimented Niftaly on his carpentry. Wooden posts supported rafters that he had cut from smaller branches, and woven reeds formed an adequate ceiling. Niftaly said he had lined the interior walls with plastic sheeting, then reeds, and finally with carpets brought from home. He pointed to colorful oriental rugs on the walls and told me that his family had escaped in such a hurry that they had to leave behind some fifty other carpets that they owned. (For Azeris, carpets are a measure of wealth.) I asked whether they had any problems with the shelter.

"Rain!" his wife answered. "We could not keep the water out this spring. Mud seeped through the walls and floor."

"Snakes!" Niftaly added. "On hot days, snakes come through the walls. We live in fear of the poisonous ones whose bite kills your flesh."

Niftaly took us to visit a woman named Sona in a nearby dug-in. "Sona means 'the swan,'" he told us. "She is ninety-four years old and lives all alone. In our village, she was very wealthy, but she came here with nothing. Now we take care of her. My wife has been treating her arm, where a rat bit her," he said. White gauze covered both of Sona's arms, and she looked old and fragile sitting on her cot next to a chipped enamel teapot on a rusted wood-burning stove.

Before we departed this hillside encampment, I pulled Niftaly aside and told him, with the help of our sensitive interpreter, that I truly admired his courage. He had lost all of his property and wealth, but had managed to create two homes and sustain himself and three women. When I called Niftaly a hero, he must have thought I was strange, a foreign woman who openly showed so much emotion, but he stood a bit straighter and seemed to gain strength from my acknowledgement. To me, he embodied real strength, not the kind demonstrated through fists and guns.

On our way to Barda, we passed a tent camp in a valley, home to a few hundred displaced families, near a creek that flowed down from the foothills of Nagorno-Karabakh. We had not planned to stop here, but we met a group of teenaged girls and young women walking along the road, and asked whether they would speak with us. They agreed, but just as we were getting out of the car, several older women and men came up from the camp to ask what we were doing. While our interpreter calmly explained that we wanted to talk alone with the girls, the elders eyed us suspiciously, but they allowed us to pass. Two teen-aged girls who looked like twin sisters led us to their tent, and a dozen other girls followed, as we all crowded into the stuffy space and sat on mats wherever we could squeeze in.

We asked the girls if they wanted to share anything with us about their recent experiences. Silence. I looked around the circle at bowed heads. No one made eye contact. Recalling WRC guidelines for speaking with young women in refugee settings, I asked the most important question for such a setting,

"Do you feel safe here?"

When my question had been translated, all heads lifted immediately, but still no one said a word. We waited quietly until one woman, who gave her name as Irada (a name that means "courage"), age twenty, filled the silence by telling us that her husband was away fighting in the war. After a long pause, she continued. "Two older men came into my tent and raped me, right next to my baby," she said, wincing as if the act of sharing this terrible secret caused her physical pain. "I need help to clean out the new baby they put here," she said, touching her lower abdomen.

The other girls looked even more startled than I felt, but again we sat in silence. Then suddenly, as if Irada's courage had given the others permission to open up, they started pouring out their feelings.

"There is no protection for us here," one said. "I need a pill."

Gunai (whose name means "the night") said she had been raped several times by older men who left their family tents in the night. "If I don't clean myself out, I will have no life," she said. "I climbed the hills and found some weeds to make a tea, but it made me so sick that I wanted to die. And now my stomach is growing." Again, a shocked silence fell over all of us.

As I recorded words of trauma, pain, and fear coming from these victimized girls, I struggled with questions, internal thoughts that nearly paralyzed me, about what we could do to help in this dangerous situation. As a mother and humanitarian, I simply could not leave here without somehow securing real protection for these girls, protection that they needed immediately. None of us had anticipated being asked for help with birth control and abortion in this Muslim population, but the topic of sexual violence is part of every WRC mission briefing. Because women, teenaged girls, and children are always vulnerable to sexual abuse in refugee settings, we had been trained for just such a situation. Nevertheless, I felt an awesome sense of responsibility—with no clear idea about what to do. I wrote "CONTRACEPTION" in capital letters in my journal, then underlined and starred the word.

I knew that Jane and Beth shared all my feelings and my gratitude for the courage of these girls to tell their painful experiences, stories they obviously had not even told each other before our arrival. They must have seen us as their last hope.

Just then, three older women barged into the tent. Startled, the girls immediately stopped talking. I wondered what the older women had heard and whether they had come to quiet the girls, to enforce female religious and cultural traditions. Perhaps, I speculated, some of them knew about their husbands' predatory behaviors and wanted to protect their men. Even that cynical thought enraged me. Sensing how upset I was, Jane calmly asked the intruders to leave, saying there was no room for them inside the tent and promising we would meet with them later.

After the older women left, reluctantly, Beth moved over and sat at the entrance to the tent, making sure no one else could enter. Her movement seemed to give all of us permission to stretch out our legs and release some of the tension in our bodies, then settle into more comfortable positions with a renewed and palpable feeling of trust and intimacy. The conversation resumed when Aida, a pretty brunette with stunning green eyes, who looked about sixteen years old, blurted out, as if she had been holding back a confession, "I have been inserting aspirins here." She pointed between her legs, then asked, "Will that stop me from getting pregnant?" Jane K. shook her head. From her sad expression, I thought she was going to cry, and if she did, I would surely join her.

Two other girls, sisters, told us they had made a paste from aspirins and inserted it into their vaginas. "I cannot stop the men," one said, tears rolling down her cheeks. We sat quietly together for several minutes, feeling the impact of the life and death secrets that had been shared within this safe space. These girls had confessed such trauma and terror that I could not imagine how they had contained it in their slim bodies. Even though we all knew that sexual exploitation happens in refugee settings, we never could have anticipated the enormity of the abuse here, nor its horrific impact on these girls, who had been separated from their families.

Because security seemed the highest priority, Jane and I began to suggest protective measures that the girls could begin right away and accomplish by themselves, such as sharing tents, performing tasks in teams, and pairing up at all times, so they were never alone. Most of these girls had been orphaned, many had been raped, and they had endured unspeakable pain. I drew a circle on a page in my journal, with triangles representing tents just outside the circle. I showed how they could protect themselves by placing their tents in a tight circle, openings facing inward toward the center, so they could see and hear each other if any intruders came near. I then drew a fire circle in the center, with a pot over the fire, suggesting that they could cook together.

Beth suggested, "Perhaps if you told them, the older women would stand up for you," but they scoffed at that idea, which really worried me. How could mothers fail to protect children? These girls were still children. In Bosnia, I had formed intimate relationships with girls and young women who had been viciously raped by the enemy, mainly by the Serbian militia, but these girls were being abused by "their own kind," Azeri men who could have been their neighbors before this war had caused such unforgivable lapses in their humanity.

In the dim light, I looked around the tent at each girl, wanting to memorize all of the faces. In order to protect their privacy, I had taken no photographs, but I wanted to remember them and all that had transpired within this tent, which had served as a girl cave, a sanctuary of trust. Clearly, no one wanted to leave the palpable energy of love and unity that had been created here, the safety of oneness. In this brief time, we had helped to create a community of oneness. That realization, and the hope that these vulnerable girls would now protect and support each other, gave me strength for the journey.

Then Beth opened the tent flap just slightly, a signal that we needed to depart. A bright shaft of light suddenly pierced the darkness within, reminding me of a song I had learned as a child in Sunday school, "This Little Light of Mine," a song I had taught to a courageous woman doctor in Serbia, a simple message that always reminds me of a great truth: *It takes only a little light to put out darkness.*

At the end of our trip, we told IRC and UNHCR officers in Baku about the girls near Barda and their immediate need for both protection against sexual assault and counseling on reproductive health care. The Women's Refugee Commission decided to launch a major global initiative focused on reproductive health care.

Our report on chemical pollution at the Iranian camp also prompted action. International Red Cross and Red Crescent relief workers in Azerbaijan confronted the Iranians and demanded that they move the camp further away from the contaminated field. We later learned that truckloads of fresh dirt had been brought in to bury the white pesticide powder, but because the ground had not first been dampened to absorb the powder, two of the men who did the work died within a few days from inhaling the toxins.

The railway camp held thousands of refugees but little hope or joy. When I returned four years later, its population had doubled, but hope had only dimmed.

ABOVE: In the hills above Sheki, I met a hero named Niftaly, who dug two caves into the hillside to create "dug-in" shelters that reminded me of sod houses built by early pioneers in the American Midwest. Niftaly lived in one with his wife (center) and older sister; OPPOSITE: The other cave was for Sona, "the swan," who at age ninety-four left her wealth behind and now depended on the kindness of neighbors. I found them again when I returned four years later in 1998.

Duru, "mother of pearl," took me into the reed shack where she lived with her daughter and three grandchildren to show me the rare and greatly prized gift she recently received, an electric cord from which a bare light bulb dangled. She feared the flimsy ceiling made from cardboard (stamped "USA") would collapse on the children.

CHAPTER TWENTY-ONE

THE CHICKEN CAME FIRST

A background in poultry is useful in refugee camps

AZERBAIJAN, JUNE 1994

My dad's hatchery was a kid magnet. Farmers came to town on Saturday mornings, carrying kids and dogs in the beds of pickup trucks that would return home weighed down by bags of chicken feed and groceries. When they arrived at the Triple T Hatchery, men headed to the feed mill, but the moms and kids went straight to the hatchery building, where magic happened. Although a child myself, I often led them into the nursery room, where we would watch with awe as chickens pecked their way out of egg shells inside glass-enclosed incubators. The hot air of the hatching room carried a unique odor that I called the "fuzzy smell," a scent that I forever associated with birth. We children would stare in wonder at trays of fertilized eggs on racks that were being gently rocked. I told the children to look for signs of life, tiny holes on top of egg shells. After struggling to peck out larger openings, wet baby chicks would gradually wriggle up and out, emerging as floppy-headed little beings that collapsed onto the tray, exhausted from the effort of birthing themselves. Even as a teenager, I never tired of watching that miraculous theater of new life.

By the time chicks transformed from alien beings into fluffy yellow balls, my father hired two Japanese men who specialized as chicken "sexers." They would pick up a chick in each hand, hold them under bright lights, and look between their tiny legs, quickly separating them into crates marked "hens" and "roosters." I could never see any difference in the private parts of chickens, but these men knew their gender at a glance. I never learned whether chicken sexing was a special talent of the Japanese or only of these two men who came to Iowa, but I knew that my father respected them, even though he had fought against the Japanese in the South Pacific rather recently. And that added to my respect for him.

My knowledge of chickens proved to be helpful when I traveled to the Caucasus region of the former Soviet Union in April 1998, four years after my first mission there with the Women's Refugee Commission, to check on the welfare of long-term refugees and internally displaced people in both Azerbaijan and Armenia. In the four years since the active war over Nakorno- Karabakh had ended, it seemed that fear, hatred, and resentment between the two countries had only intensified, and we found that conditions for these homeless people had deteriorated. Seeing the extent of suffering truly discouraged me. In Azerbaijan, about a million people still lived in squalid and unbearable conditions, despite the discovery of oil deposits in the Caspian Sea. The deep-sea extraction of oil had brought billions of dollars into the country, but Azerbaijan's corrupt government continued to ignore the desperate needs of its people and rely on international humanitarian organizations to provide their basic survival needs, while the greedy authoritarian president and his cronies lined their own pockets.

Our WRC delegation for this return trip included Elizabeth Jackson, a staff member, and Xuan Sutter, a Vietnamese American who had recently joined the board. I briefed them on the settlements I had visited in 1994 and shared personal stories of refugees whom I remembered. When we reached encampments in the west, I looked for familiar faces but recognized very few people; however, conditions at nearly every camp looked familiar. We found women and girls doing household duties and sweeping bare dirt yards under the feet of scampering children and chickens, while most of the men and older boys sat around talking, smoking, and playing games, and only a few were doing "manly work," such as tending livestock or repairing shelters.

At one tent camp, Xuan approached three men she saw drinking coffee under a tree. She pointed to the poultry pecking at cigarette butts on the ground near their feet and asked how often they fed the chickens. In a loud chorus, the three replied emphatically, "That's women's work!" Their response made me, the daughter of a man who fed thousands of chickens, grit my teeth. I could see disgust on Xuan's face. In so many countries around the world, both she and I had seen thousands of women performing the bulk of daily chores and most of the work needed for families to survive.

In the village of Shahvalilar near Barda, located just six miles from Armenian-held land, we found eighty families living in shelters made of mud bricks and straw, with tin or cardboard roofs. Mhabuba, thirty-four, cared for her three children with the help of her mother. On the ceiling of their primitive home, a sheet of cardboard had been used to patch a thatched roof, and polka dots of blue sky appeared through a piece of cardboard that had "USA" printed in large red and blue letters. That flimsy ceiling served as a metaphor for the lack of substantial support from the USA and other Western nations for these homeless families. Since the fighting stopped, this region had gone radio silent. I never came across news of Azerbaijan in the media. Only human rights and humanitarian organizations seemed to know and care about these vulnerable people, and they were finding it difficult to raise the funds needed to help them. Donor fatigue. Donors thought this problem had ended, just as many believed the nuclear arms race had ended when the Soviet Union collapsed.

While we were talking to Mhabuba in her fragile home, her mother entered. She told me her name was Duru, meaning "mother of pearl." Duru said both her husband and her son-in-law had helped to build the house, but then both men left to find work in Baku. "They have never returned," she said in a low voice, bowing her head in resignation. "When I sing my grandchildren to sleep, I worry that the roof will fall in." She proudly showed us what she planned to cook for dinner—a small blue egg and two brown eggs received from a generous neighbor. "If we were not so hungry," she told me, "I would try to hatch these eggs and raise hens."

I thought again about the magical mystery room at my father's hatchery, and how my mother used to crack nearly two dozen eggs into a frying pan to make a single breakfast for our family, but I could not share those memories with Duru or Mhabuba. I would have liked to tell them that my mother never used "normal" eggs, because Dad always brought home the eggs he couldn't sell, the peewees, double-yolks, and also those that had blood inside the shells (which could be seen by holding eggs up to a candle.) Dad said he could not sell these odd eggs, because people expected all eggs to look the same. Thinking of those years, when Mother put such bountiful meals on the table three times a day, I felt guilty standing in this cardboard shack, which did not even have a kitchen—no refrigerator, no pantry, no shelves holding food supplies, and not even a table. They survived on eggs from a few hens. I would never again take abundance for granted.

We stopped at one of the railroad camps that I had visited four years earlier and discovered it had expanded to nine hundred families—shocking! Many of the women we met said they had been there for five years, but I didn't recognize any of them, probably because they had aged so much. I almost didn't recognize the place either, because it had doubled in size. Many new lines of railroad cars had been brought in, mostly boxcars with double doors and sliders.

Trains had always fascinated me. During the war years, my mom used to take us down to the train depot to watch the Union Pacific trains that crossed through Iowa and stopped in Denison en route from Chicago to Omaha, and we loved watching both freight and passenger trains roll through, free entertainment during times of scarcity. In this refugee settlement, I shared my knowledge of railroad cars with our WRC delegation. I pointed out the cattle cars, which now stored household goods, the boxcars with slider doors, and a water tanker that was leaking its precious contents onto the ground. Beneath the tanker, children in ragged clothing were playing in a mud puddle, while hens and roosters pecked at the wet ground in search of insects.

We learned that more than six hundred babies had been born here in the four years since my previous visit. I didn't want to imagine the terrifying experience of giving birth in these conditions, especially for a first-time mother. We met a young mother named Zahara (whose name means "only") who showed us her newborn son. She said, "Last year my teenaged son Shamil made me sad by asking why I was going to have another baby, because I had nothing to give a baby." That broke my heart, but then she smiled and looked directly into my eyes. "Today," she said, "I watched Shamil talking happily to his brother while they lay on a mat together. I told Shamil that I had given my new baby a great gift, a big brother to protect him." Her eloquence and the sensitive nature of her story made my throat tighten, and I noticed that both Xuan and our interpreter, Yeganda, had tears on their cheeks. As a mother, I could think of no greater gift, no greater truth. I had come here once again with the intention of helping to make the lives of these women better, but, as often happens on these trips, I became the beneficiary. I had just been taught another critical life lesson, one that I would keep and savor.

We drove away from the camp in silence, but later during the drive, we talked about the breakdown of families here and how few men or older boys we had seen in the camps. Xuan pointed out that men showed up to make babies, but the women bore the burden of keeping them alive. I agreed on both points, and added that their burdens looked immense, especially because we had seen no income-generating programs.

We discussed the feasibility of various empowerment projects for women, such as breeding and selling rabbits or chickens, and Xuan expressed her opinion that most of these refugee women seemed to have adapted to their situations and settled well into survival routines. Not wanting to dampen her optimism, I responded that I was glad to see more life around the camps. Instead of the feral dogs and cats that had scared me before, we now found scrawny goats providing milk. But I hid my true feelings of devastation at seeing that thousands of families remained in these camps, still coping with primitive conditions. Imagining the cold winters that they had endured since my last visit, I shivered reflexively.

My father and his parents occasionally shared stories of their lives during the Great Depression, how they had lived on eggs and shriveled root vegetables during frigid winters in Nebraska. Dad said he often had been so hungry that he would crack open an egg in the roosting house and swallow it raw. I think he started a poultry business out of gratitude to hens for keeping him alive during his youth. Seeing the devastation among refugees here, his stories affected me more than ever before.

After we arrived at the town of Imishli, we went to the International Rescue Committee's regional office to register our initial findings and recommendations. An IRC social worker took us to a school building that was being used to house twenty-three families from Agdam, all of whom had been here for nearly six years, with seven or eight people crowded into each of the twenty by twenty square foot classrooms. I recognized a young woman named Raisa, who was now eighteen years old but still radiated the girlish charm that I remembered. Raisa and I embraced, excited by the recognition and grateful for the reunion. She called to her mother, who also seemed to remember my previous visit, and together they proudly showed us Raisa's "dowry." Treasured rugs and linens, including a purple comforter made by her mother, had been brought from their home and protected all these years.

"Thanks to my mother, I have all of this," Raisa said, "but there are no men to marry me. All the boys left to fight in the war and never came back. Now, I guess they are off somewhere trying to find jobs." Her sadness touched me so deeply that I refrained from expressing my first thought, that at least she didn't have a baby needing her care. When Xuan admired the purple comforter, Raisa confessed that she and her mother had been using her dowry to keep warm.

In another of the classrooms, we met Yerada (whose name means "willpower") sitting on the floor near a small propane heater. She was sharing the small room with her husband and two other elderly couples. I suddenly heard a familiar sound and jumped back in surprise. Seeing two hens nesting in a box under a small table, I laughed at my reaction and then, on impulse, began to cluck and cackle, a precise rendition of sounds that hens make. Then, I just could not resist flapping my elbows and crowing like a rooster, which made the hens perk up. Yerada joined my laughter.

"These hens are better than my husband," she said. "They lay eggs for us to eat. If my husband gets any money, he just buys gasoline for his car and drives around." I leaned over the box and sniffed, searching for the fuzzy smell, but my nose told me there were no baby chicks in the nest. I wondered whether Yerada knew that a rooster had to visit the hens in order to produce fertilized eggs that could hatch into chicks.

Yerada said the day was a Muslim holiday, a holy day of sacrifice. "At home, we would slaughter a cow or sheep and cook a feast," she said, "but here we have no animals, water, nor electricity. I am guarding my hens, because I think the neighbors want to make a feast with them," she said, looking suspiciously around the square room and nodding her head to underscore her certainty. When we asked about her health, Yerada reported that a doctor occasionally visited them. "The doctor gives the same pill to everyone for every complaint, a drug called 'Regedral' that comes from Iran," she said. "He gives Regedral for coughs and also for aches and pains," she continued, "but if I give the doctor an egg, he will give me the blue pills that really help me." I wondered whether those Iranian pills were actual drugs, or perhaps placebos, which made her feel better, thinking she was getting something special.

When I smiled and pointed to a beautiful brown hen, Yerada reached into the box and put her hands across its back. "Caca," she said. Pinning the wings down, she gently lifted Caca onto her lap and began stroking the hen's autumn-colored body from head to tail. I could see that she received as much comfort from the bird as I did from petting our dogs. Her face relaxed, and she began rocking from side to side, humming softly to comfort Caca. I felt certain this hen would die from old age. More importantly, I hoped Yerada would live a long life.

OPPOSITE, TOP: Hens and one rooster pecked at the dirt yard around a primitive shelter created by Azeri refugees, who shared the few eggs that they provided; OPPOSITE, BOTTOM: A lone sheep provided precious wool to be spun by Jeyran, sixty-two, into yarn for knitting and weaving. She slept with the sheep to protect it from being slaughtered for meat; TOP: In the town of Imishli, I recognized Raisa and her mother, who had been living in a schoolhouse for four years. Raisa, now eighteen, said they were using the quilts of her dowry to keep warm, "because there are no young men here to marry me"; BOTTOM: I met many trios of mothers and daughters who sustained each other and kept babies alive.

ABOVE: This railroad car refugee camp, which I had visited in 1994, grew to nearly a thousand families. Women and girls worked all day, while men and boys sat and watched; OPPOSITE: Refugee women often held up photos of their missing husbands and sons, asking whether we could find them. Their desperation outweighed any hope of having such wishes fulfilled.

Armenian refugees who had lived in Azerbaijan survived a violent conflict, but the destruction and poverty they found in Armenia gave them little hope for the future.

CHAPTER TWENTY-TWO

A JOB WORTH DOING

*A refugee from Vietnam teaches others
the importance of work*

ARMENIA, APRIL 1998

After returning to Baku, our Women's Refugee Commission delegation split up
in order to visit two other countries in the Caucasus region, Georgia and Armenia. I would be going with Xuan Sutter to Armenia, to see that side of the war
I had been witnessing in Azerbaijan. During our flight from Baku to Yerevan,
the capital of Armenia, Xuan asked a lot of questions about my previous WRC
trips. As a new board member of the WRC, Xuan wanted to learn everything
she could about how we conducted our research and advocacy work.

In an effort to diversify its board, the WRC recently had elected three new
members, all of whom had come to the United States as refugees from different
war-torn countries, immigrants who became U.S. citizens. Xuan had fled from
Vietnam with her family. I felt certain she had experienced the deprivation of
war, but when I tried to probe gently, she seemed unwilling to discuss her
childhood. All I knew was that her family escaped Vietnam in a crowded boat
near the end of that fateful war, which the Vietnamese call their "American
War." Now that she would be traveling alone with me, I hoped Xuan would

talk about her life and how she became a refugee. Life stories can be the best way to understand world history and culture. I also hoped we could become friends. I planned to tell Xuan about the peer support methodology of Landmine Survivors Network. As a refugee herself, she could empathize with refugee women and intuit their feelings.

This flight from Azerbaijan to Armenia reminded me of my solo trip to Belgrade, Serbia, to see the other side of war in the former Yugoslavia. During that war of ethnic cleansing, I had begun to sympathize with Bosnians and condemn the Serbs, but I learned that war is an equal destroyer of lives. And now, after spending so much time with destitute Azeris during this war in the Caucasus, I had begun to see Armenia as "the aggressor," even though I have many Armenian friends in California, and I share their grief over the Armenian Genocide early in the 20th Century, a tragedy never properly acknowledged by Turkey.

I reminded myself that there are two sides to every war situation, and that Armenian refugees deserve equal support and compassion. During our brief flight, I asked Xuan about her impressions so far, and she replied that this trip, being her first return to a war zone, had ignited traumatic memories from her childhood. I gently probed for more information, but she did not seem ready to talk about traumatic memories.

In Armenia, we planned to examine the needs of refugee women and children in both urban and rural areas. After first visiting refugee settlements in the city of Yerevan, we would travel by car, with a driver and an interpreter, into remote rural areas, including the disputed region of Nagorno-Karabakh (N-K), which I had seen from the other side four years earlier. We dove right into the morass in Yerevan, where thousands of ethnic Armenians who had grown up in Azerbaijan now lived as refugees, the majority in crowded Soviet-era apartments. The concrete block buildings we visited looked drab and decrepit. Their stairways, reeking of tobacco and urine, reminded me of apartment buildings I had visited in Kiev and Moscow ten years earlier. But at least the towers here offered fabulous views of Mount Ararat, the mystical mountain where Noah's ark is widely believed to have first met land. I loved pondering that myth, but views of Ararat did not make up for the horrid conditions we were about to see.

In one densely packed and filthy apartment, we met Julia Oseypian, forty-three, living with her grandmother, sisters, and many children. "Our husbands left and went to Moscow to find work," Julia said. "My husband complained that carrying buckets of water up the stairs was the only sport he found here, and he wanted to play football in Russia."

When I asked about sanitation, we learned that each floor had only one bathroom, which explained the overpowering stench that made me feel nauseous. We routinely examined "water closets" for our assessment reports, but in this case, I chose to imagine their conditions from a distance. After years of experience with disgusting toilet facilities, I had learned to restrict my water consumption and thus the urgency to visit them. As soon as we entered Julia's apartment, several other women materialized and crowded into Julia's room, as if they had anticipated our arrival. Even before introductions had been completed, the women fired facts of their lives at us. Clearly, we were not their first experience with international humanitarians.

"We cannot earn any money here," Anjuta said. "Education is free, but our children have to be seven years old before we can apply. They started younger in Baku." When I asked about her job in Baku, she said she had worked as an engineer and earned a big salary. Another woman shouted, "We need dental care," pointing to her brass-covered front teeth. A younger woman named Kristina chimed in, "I have epilepsy, and I cannot buy seizure medicine. I haven't seen a doctor for many months." I wondered whether Xuan shared my sense of exasperation about hearing only complaints, one after another. As always, I looked for signs of hope and optimism, but so far, none appeared.

I inquired whether they got any support from the Armenian Diaspora, because I knew that Armenians (especially Armenian Americans) had donated a lot of money, and also sent over workers to rebuild shelters and roads, including a new highway to the N-K region. (This knowledge came from Armenian taxi drivers at the Bob Hope Airport in Burbank, California, a frequent stop for me. I had learned over the years that cab drivers in the U.S. commonly are immigrants, and I always asked about their countries of origin, many of which I have visited.) My question to these women about the diaspora brought out smiles and a softening of the negativity that had built up. I noticed Xuan's initial defensive reaction had relaxed a bit, too.

Our hostess, Julia, said, "Our people who moved to the West have helped us a lot. My brother is in California, but I haven't been able to write to him." I told them that I live in Southern California, home of the largest Armenian Diaspora. Out came the teapots, which caused Xuan to smile broadly and embrace several of the young women. She understood the symbolism and importance of serving tea, a ritual throughout Asia, and this generous gesture made her feel welcome. I was glad to receive black tea with no sugar!

Amazing as it sounds, nearly every family seemed to have relatives who lived near Pasadena in Glendale. Julia showed me the most recent letter she had received from her brother, Vardanian, and I jotted down his name and North Hollywood address in my journal. Julia said she had not heard from her brother for two years, but I assured her that I would find him and deliver her letters and copies of my photos. Starting that afternoon, I made many such promises, and I hoped that I could remember and keep all of them. In fact, I received so many letters and photographs, that I gave away all my snacks in order to make space for them in my backpack. It gave me joy to anticipate meeting their relatives when I got home, and that felt nourishing enough.

Before we left the city of Yerevan, Xuan and I told aid workers at several international relief organizations about the complaints we had heard from refugees in Yerevan. Their explanation surprised us. Many refugees, they said, wanted to keep their jobless refugee status in order to receive foreign aid and to avoid disappearing into the general population's sea of poverty. That made sense, but it also made me feel very sad. We had seen widespread deprivation in Azerbaijan. Displaced people there had been living in much more horrendous conditions than the Armenian refugees we had met so far, but in my experience, the Azeris had not complained as much. They seemed better able to cope with their situation, perhaps because they held fewer expectations.

Staff members of the United Nations High Commissioner for Refugees (UNHCR) office in Yerevan expressed a great interest in our itinerary. They confessed that they knew very little about rural refugee families, because government officials denied access to rural areas. We had decided on a "don't ask, don't tell" strategy and planned not to seek formal permission. If we got caught, we reasoned, we could plead ignorance and beg forgiveness. We would have to travel incognito, which might be more difficult with my Asian colleague, but I did not share that concern with Xuan. The alternative was to be stuck here in the city, but we'd already seen enough to write our reports on Yerevan, and I was anxious to explore more of the country.

From the UNHCR briefing, we learned that about three hundred thousand ethnic Armenians still lived in Armenia as refugees. Most had fled homes in Baku and other Azeri cities between 1988 and 1991. They had primarily been educated urban dwellers and skilled factory workers whose families had lived in Azerbaijan for generations. They experienced discrimination here for speaking Azeri instead of Armenian. As a result, UNHCR officials explained, they could not find jobs or even hope to secure citizenship. I took that as a marching order, to find out about jobs while I was looking for hope.

The following morning, Xuan and I, along with a driver and translator, reached the outskirts of Yerevan, with Mount Ararat barely visible through low fog. Sheep and goats dotted foothills above groves of apricot and almond trees in full bloom. Vineyards climbed rocky hillsides, yellow mustard plants spread out between the rows. No wonder so many Armenians come to California; the terrain is remarkably similar.

Finding refugee families in the rural areas of Armenia proved to be difficult. Instead of large settlements, they lived on scattered farms and in small villages, where they blended in with the locals. After recapturing Nagorno-Karabakh, Armenia had resettled many of these city people on farms, into rural homes that Azeris had abandoned. We learned that the Armenian government wanted these refugees to repopulate the region in order to bolster its claim on N-K, but most of the new population resisted, having had no experience with rural living nor any desire to learn about farming.

But after visiting so many refugees living packed together, either horizontally or vertically, these rural settings seemed much more inviting to me, a girl from Iowa. We drove into one rather large farmyard that had a wood-framed house and several barns and sheds. As if we had banged a drum, women suddenly rushed toward us from every direction. Xuan and I barely got out of the car before they closed in on us, holding passports in outstretched hands and demanding to know what we had brought for them. Having had similar experiences in the USSR, I understood the expectations of people who had been raised in a communist culture with welfare traditions.

Our interpreter told the women that we were not aid workers, and we had brought no goods. We had come to learn what they and their children needed, so that we could inform international relief organizations that did provide aid, such as food, shelter, and medicine. At that, many of the women turned away, expressing disappointment and even disgust that shocked me, as I had never experienced rejection from refugees. I felt like apologizing to Xuan for their behavior, but it didn't seem to bother her. As usual, she kept her personal feelings to herself, but I could see that she was observing and taking in everything.

Along the route, as Xuan and I spoke with refugee women and documented their primary needs, we noticed that local people were also suffering from poverty and unemployment. I knew that the recent war was not the only reason for this sad state of being. In December 1988, a massive earthquake had struck Armenia and destroyed a lot of infrastructure, devastating the country's economy. Shortly after the quake, the war with Azerbaijan broke out, greatly accelerating poverty and causing a decline in living standards.

At a rural village about two hours east of Yerevan, we gathered a group of about forty women, sixty children, and a few elderly men for a discussion in the village center. These refugee families, we learned, had come from various parts of Azerbaijan about eight or ten years earlier. When our interpreter asked about the history and the current conditions here, a chorus of requests began at once.

"We want a medical clinic."

"We have no heat or electricity."

"We need food."

I calmly stood up, raised one hand, and waited for the room to quiet down, a trick I learned from a second grade teacher, who also taught me to whisper if I wanted to get attention in a noisy classroom. Thinking of that teacher, Paula, I suddenly smiled, feeling tempted to use another of Paula's tricks by saying,

"One, two, three; eyes on me," but I doubted that would translate well into Armenian. When the room quieted, as I knew it would, I calmly asked:

"Are these children in school? Who is teaching the children?"

Iliayva, thirty-one, replied, "The schoolhouse fell down ten years ago during the earthquake." She added that her three daughters, ages two, four, and six, had no books or even writing material.

Then Xuan, as if suddenly taking charge, came over and stood beside me. Side by side, we looked into pleading faces around the room. Xuan asked, "What are you mothers doing to help your children?" Raia, forty-two, told us that this was the first time they had ever met together. "In ten years?" Xuan questioned, incredulously. She asked Raia what her previous job had been.

"I was a financial specialist in Baku," Raia answered proudly. "Can you teach math?" Xuan asked. Then, looking around the room, she asked, "Were any of you teachers?" Five hands went up. "Are there any doctors or nurses?" she continued. Three women raised their hands, including Iliayva.

Xuan exploded. "When I was a child, my family had to leave Vietnam suddenly in a boat full of strangers," she said, shaking with emotion. "The boat started sinking, and we barely made it to a small island in the sea. We all had to work together to survive, even the children."

Our translator, clearly taken aback, asked Xuan to speak more slowly. Xuan lowered her voice and began, finally, to share the story of her refugee experience. The Vietnamese refugees, she said, took everything they could salvage from that boat and laid it onto a canvas sail they had retrieved from the sinking boat. The resulting pile included food, water, seeds, small tools, and extra clothing.

"We had to ration and share everything. Everyone had to work to benefit all," she explained. "I was young, but I took care of babies and toddlers while their parents worked to build shelters," she said, "and I worked in the garden. We did not know if we would ever be rescued."

A long silence followed Xuan's words. Even I was speechless and in awe of my colleague, stunned to hear the riveting story of her refugee experience. It felt powerful and appropriate, and I wondered how these women would respond. Would they turn their backs and walk away, as we had experienced at some of our first stops, or would they stay to learn how they could change their ways and improve their lives?

After some time had passed and no one left, I asked some of the women who had not raised their hands whether any of them had work experience. Most said they had been specialists in factories, where they used tools and machines. "But there are no machines or tools here," one of the women said. That sounded to me like an excuse to do nothing. I thought about all the skills I had always used as a mother and homemaker, the most important of which did not require machines or tools.

"What else can you do?" Xuan pressed. Silence again filled the room, but I felt no need to speak, enjoying the role of observer. What a transformation had just taken place in my travel companion! I watched Xuan's body language as she stamped her foot and raised her voice, barely concealing her outrage.

"Why are you not helping each other?" After a round of excuses came back, Xuan clapped her hands loudly. I nudged her with my elbow, fearing that we had pushed too hard, and I whispered that maybe we should leave, but she ignored me.

"Get organized right now!" she insisted. "Who will be the leader?" Raia looked around, shyly, and then cautiously stepped forward.

Xuan nodded at her. "Will you all support this leader?" she asked the room. A few women held up their hands, tentatively, and then a few more responded the same way. I exhaled with relief, realizing that I had been holding my breath.

"Very good," I said. "This is the perfect time to plant a garden. I'll show you where the garden used to be and where some tools might be. You can start by clearing the weeds and turning the soil. There must be tools in these sheds. Has anyone looked?"

Blank faces stared back at me. I had noticed a shed beside a weedy plot of land, where we parked our car, and hoped we could find tools. Then I could demonstrate how to turn the soil with a spade, break up clots of dirt with a hoe, and create rows of raised beds for planting. I told the men in the room they had to help to prepare the soil, and if they did a good job, we would send out seeds and fertilizer from Yerevan.

"By summer, you can start selling vegetables," Xuan said. "Raia, your leader, knows how to manage money, and she will be fair. But now, each of you must take a job." Xuan divided the teachers and nurses into cluster groups and got them talking about what they could offer the community, if they worked together, while I took the others out to the shed in search of garden tools. I thought about my sisters and how we always divided the housework as children and earned a weekly allowance. Mother would check our work and remind us, "A job worth doing is a job worth doing well." For this small community, if they all learned how to do a good job, they would improve their spirits, their health, and their quality of life.

When I returned to California, I wrote letters to all of the Armenian relatives for whom I had contact information. Several families drove to my home in Pasadena, bringing gifts of bread, flowers, and desserts made with honey, expressing tearful relief to learn that their relatives and loved ones had survived the war, since there had been little or no communication. I served tea, displayed my photos, and shared all the details I could remember. I told them they would be proud of their relatives, because they were learning new job skills and adjusting to life in their beautiful native land.

At the next WRC board meeting in New York, I shared the story of Xuan, the "labor organizer." I told board members how she had motivated refugees in Armenia by sharing her own story of survival. Xuan had taught the Armenians how Vietnamese emigrants had survived and coped with an impossible situation by working together and combining their skills. By sharing her own inspirational story, I reported, Xuan had empowered victims to become survivors.

It was a job well done, I thought to myself, one that would have made my mother proud—proud does not begin to describe my feelings about Xuan.

ABOVE: As the mother of a son, I could feel the crippling pain of this Armenian woman named Nora Sarkisova, whom I met in the city of Shusha, Nagorno-Karabakh. Her son had died in the war with Azerbaijan, and she wanted "to lie across his grave and follow him to heaven"; OPPOSITE, TOP: Many refugee Armenian women came from factory jobs in Baku, Azerbaijan, and they needed to learn survival skills in rural Armenia; OPPOSITE, BOTTOM: My WRC colleague Xuan Sutter (lower left in purple), a refugee herself from Vietnam, offered tough love and practical advice from her own experience.

OPPOSITE: Living in a battered and abandoned building with only one small bed, this mother and son depended solely on each other to survive. The poignancy of the scene touched me deeply; TOP: This tiny Armenian woman lived in sparse conditions, but her buoyant spirit, warmth, and positive attitude left no doubt she would survive and help others; BOTTOM: This neighborhood in Shusha, Nagorno-Karabakh, had been shelled heavily. Bottom floors of the building on the left had been burned out, but we saw signs of resilience on the upper floors.

AFRICA

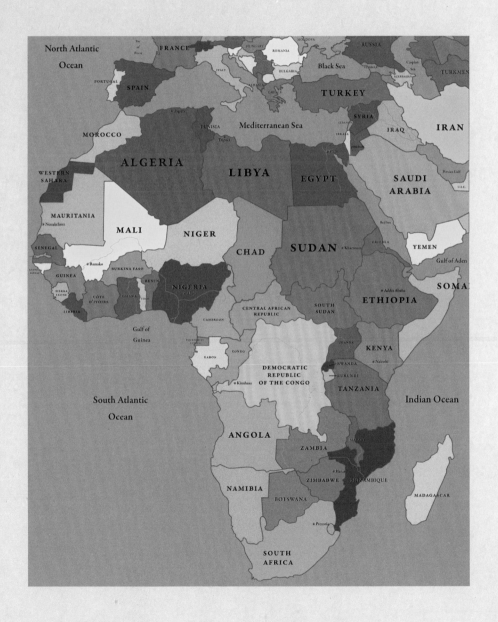

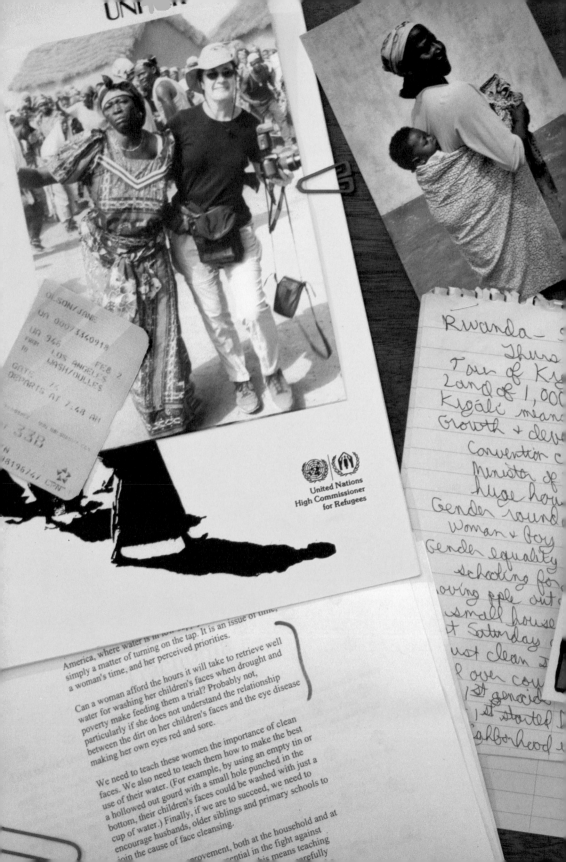

United Nations
High Commissioner
for Refugees

America, where water is in low supply, it is an issue of time,
simply a matter of turning on the tap. It is an issue of time,
a woman's time, and her perceived priorities.

Can a woman afford the hours it will take to retrieve well
water for washing her children's faces when drought and
poverty make feeding them a trial? Probably not,
particularly if she does not understand the relationship
between the dirt on her children's faces and the eye disease
making her own eyes red and sore.

We need to teach these women the importance of clean
faces. We also need to teach them how to make the best
use of their water. (For example, by using an empty tin or
a hollowed out gourd with a small hole punched in the
bottom, their children's faces could be washed with just a
cup of water.) Finally, if we are to succeed, we need to
encourage husbands, older siblings and primary schools to
join the cause of face cleansing.

... improvement, both at the household and at
... essential in the fight against
... his means teaching

Rwanda —
          Thurs
     Tour of K?
 2and of 1,00
 Kigali mean
 Growth + deve
      Convention c
      Minister of
        huge hou?
  Gender round
  Woman + Boy
  Gender equality
     schooling for
  ?oving ?ple out
  ? small house
  ? Saturday
  ?ust clean ?
  ? over cou?
  1st genocid
  1st started ?
  ?ghborhood

I met Happy at the United Nations when she testified about surviving near death during the horrific genocide in Rwanda. Ron and I adopted her informally and later gained two additional grandchildren. Here, she cooks traditional Rwandan food in our California kitchen.

CHAPTER TWENTY-THREE

HAPPY FROM RWANDA

*One girl's story encapsulates
gruesome details of an unfathomable genocide*

NEW YORK CITY, DECEMBER 1997

She stood tall and regal in front of a green marble wall at the United Nations in New York. "My name is Happy," she said. "I was the youngest of five children in my family, living in Kigali. When the genocide started in Rwanda, during the month of my nineteenth birthday, the Hutus killed all my family except for me and one brother, who was out of the country. My father was hacked to death with a machete. My mother was shot. My two sisters were buried alive. The Hutus shot me and beat me and left me for dead."

Happy paused for a long moment and stared straight ahead, seeming not to see the audience, then lowered her head and her voice. "I would have died also, except for the mercy of a Hutu captain," she whispered. I held my breath, wishing I could hold Happy, and waiting for what would come next. Then, as if gaining composure, she began, from the beginning, to tell her personal experience of Rwanda's historic blood bath, which began in April 1994.

I had not met Happy before I introduced her to the audience at this conference, which was being held at the United Nations on International Human Rights Day in December 1997. I simply read from my program Happy's name, age, and this brief description: "survivor of the genocide in Rwanda." Then I reached out to take her hand and help her step up to the podium. Now I sat in the front row, and Happy stood before the large crowd, slowly reading unfamiliar English words that someone had translated from the personal story she had recorded earlier in French.

The Women's Refugee Commission, Human Rights Watch (at the time I served on the boards of both), and other international organizations were co-sponsoring this conference, which focused on war crimes against women, part of an effort to promote the establishment of an International Criminal Court under UN auspices. Women survivors from all over the world had come to New York to share their stories of violent abuse and to express how much they wanted perpetrators of war crimes and crimes against humanity to be punished in a forum of justice. As they described crimes against their own bodies, their families, and their communities, they articulated the importance of making the perpetrators face their victims and receive punishment.

Happy, one of the first speakers, said that in Rwanda, tensions between Hutus and Tutsis had been worsening for several years before the massive genocide began. As a dancer in a professional girls' troupe, she had been performing at many public events. Because some of the events were considered to be political, she and her family had been receiving death threats months before the massacre began.

"When the killing started, my family sent me to a Catholic mission three miles away from our home in Kigali, assuming that I would be safe there," Happy continued. "One of my sisters and her baby son went with me. We were among the scores of Tutsis seeking refuge there."

Happy described how some thirty soldiers of the Hutu militia attacked the Catholic mission. While working in the kitchen, she saw them crash the gate and begin beating and killing Tutsis, so she ran to hide in the priests' latrine with a dozen other people, crushed together and scarcely able to breathe. I imagined Happy in that latrine—the stench of fear, the deafening screams, the cramp of arms and legs unable to stretch or move, the pain of lungs desperate for oxygen. Happy paused for a moment, reliving the terror, before continuing, "The militia finally left, and I ran to search for my sister, Gustine." I could not allow my imagination to follow Happy into the next scene, when she described finding Gustine and her infant on the floor among some 150 bodies. The bodies of nuns and priests who had tried to shield the Tutsis lay dead among them.

When I thought I could bear no more, Happy added that a few of the victims remained alive, including her sister, who apparently had leaned over to protect her son and then fallen on top of him when men slashed her head and body from behind with machetes. Discovering that Gustine was alive, she lifted up her sister's body and found the seven-month-old baby drinking blood from his mother's wounds. A loud collective gasp filled the room. I willed myself to sit still and give this courageous girl the respect of my full attention.

Happy continued, sharing even more traumatic events. While priests transported Gustine to a Red Cross clinic, she had stayed at the mission with her infant nephew, with very little food. She managed to keep the baby alive for two more weeks by giving him water mixed with some sugar and salt that she found in the kitchen. He pooped blood for several days and gradually grew weaker, she said, closing her eyes as if to unsee the baby's decline and death.

She remained at the mission for several more weeks, with very little to eat, while other Tutsis arrived daily, desperate for refuge. Then, looking around the grand UN hall, Happy took a deep breath before telling us that the Hutu militia had attacked again in early June, this time with guns, more efficient weapons. During an earlier scare, Happy had hidden in a doghouse, but this time she had no warning. Hutus rounded up some seventy-five Tutsis, including herself, and ordered them to stand in a circle, crowded together. Then they fired guns at everyone and, horror upon horrors, threw grenades into the circle. Vivid pictures of bodies falling across each other and of blood, so much blood, filled my mind. How, I wondered, had this child survived? I knew myself to be an empathetic person, and every cell of my body vibrated with a desire to hold Happy.

Somehow, Happy carried on. She told us that she remained conscious, which was not a good thing, because she felt such intense pain. She could see and hear the Hutu killers as they pulled bodies out of the pile, stripped them of valuables, and shot those still breathing. When a killer turned Happy over to search her pockets, she moaned from pain, and he cursed her for being alive, complaining that he had no more bullets. Then he kicked her in the head and lower back, picked her up and threw her into a truck loaded with dead bodies. I bowed my head, unable to watch or listen, and just then her voice choked. It seemed torturous to allow Happy to continue, but surely she had gotten through the worst. Then she spoke these words:

"When the truck arrived at a Hutu military station, other men pulled me out, saw that I was alive, and they kicked me again. Then they left me beside the road to die, saying that someone would come along later to pick up my body. I could hardly move, but I managed to crawl away from that station." I turned and looked around at the audience to see how people reacted to that last part. Many had hands over their mouths, perhaps holding back sobs. I imagined they were as much shocked by Happy's strength and resilience, past and present, as by her story, which continued.

"A Hutu army officer found me beside the road. When he realized I was still alive, he said that, because he was a Christian, he would save me. He took me to a hospital run by the International Red Cross.

"Fortunately," Happy went on, "a nurse at that hospital lived in our neighborhood and recognized me. He dressed my wounds and gave me medicine, then he wrapped my head and body in bandages and put me in a cold room with piles of dead bodies."

Happy said the nurse checked on her several times a day but told no one of her presence. "The smell was so bad in there that I couldn't eat anything," Happy added. "I had to stay in that morgue for a week, because the Hutu militia kept coming to find and kill Tutsis. Eventually, I got a bed in a room where doctors treated critical care patients, and I stayed there for a month."

And then came another heartbreak. Happy told us that when she finally got to return home weeks later, hoping to see her family, a neighbor told her that the sister wounded at the mission, mother of the baby boy, and an older sister both had been buried alive in a pit beside their house. She found her parents' decapitated bodies in shallow graves in the backyard. It is hard enough to write about that scene, knowing the cost to Happy's psyche, her physical and mental health.

After ending her gruesome story, Happy announced that the Seventh Day Adventist Church had sponsored her for refugee resettlement in Southern California. The audience clapped and rose to their feet as one. The applause continued and continued. I clapped louder than anyone else, having just learned that this bright and heroic young woman would be coming to California.

As I took her hand to help her down from the podium, I whispered in her ear, "I live in California. Would you like to have a mother?" Happy smiled and nodded. She understood the English word "mother." Our eyes met for the first time, and I felt the exchange of heart energy, the giving and the receiving.

Happy settled in a town two hours from where I live. She learned English as her sixth language, studied at a nursing school, and worked in a teaching hospital. Eventually, she became an American citizen. She calls my husband and me "Dad and Mom." Although we did not adopt her formally, we have supported her financially, while encouraging her independence. Eventually, she fell in love with another survivor, a Rwandan man who had been resettled in Europe after losing most of his family in the genocide.

When Happy learned that I would be going to Rwanda with Survivor Corps in February 2009, she and her fiancé set the date for a traditional tribal wedding, and I helped her select a beautiful bridal gown in Los Angeles. On Valentine's Day, I flew to Kigali and met Francois, who would become her husband the following day. As "mother-of-the-bride," I attended the wedding, along with eight American members of Survivor Corps. When we arrived, we saw the cow we had sent as a dowry gift for the bridegroom's family. It was tied to a stake in the back yard of the house where the traditional Tutsi wedding would take place. The poor cow looked skinny by Iowa standards, but she seemed to please Francois's uncles.

As I watched costumed young girls, who had been hired to perform traditional dances during the wedding ceremony, I remembered that Happy had danced in a similar troupe before the genocide began. I will always remember this joyful dance and the beauty of the bride, my resilient daughter, Happy. She now has a daughter and a son, our beautiful Rwandan grandchildren, a constant source of light and love, and lives nearby in California.

Shortly before the twenty-fifth anniversary of the genocide, Rwandan president Paul Kagame ordered all Rwandans living abroad to return home, find the bones of all their family members, and take them to the genocide museum in Kigali. Happy complied. She went back to her family home, uncovered the skeletal remains of her parents and sisters, washed all the bones and bagged them individually with identifications, then took them to the museum.

Unimaginable.

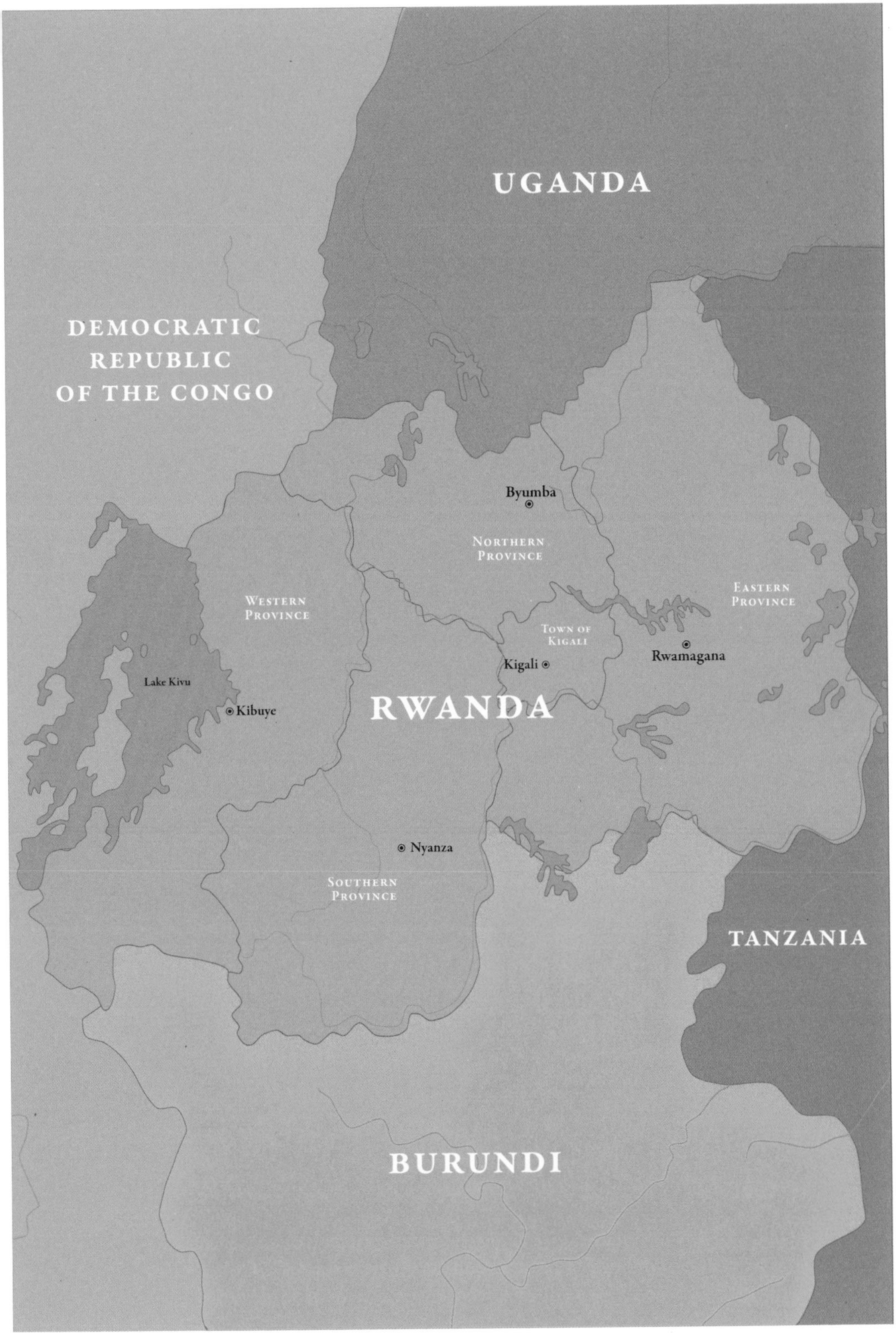
UGANDA
DEMOCRATIC REPUBLIC OF THE CONGO
Byumba
Northern Province
Western Province
Eastern Province
Town of Kigali
Kigali
Rwamagana
Lake Kivu
Kibuye
RWANDA
Nyanza
Southern Province
TANZANIA
BURUNDI

Alison Des Forges, highly esteemed expert on the Great Lakes region of Africa who headed Human Rights Watch's work there, famously wrote a comprehensive report dubbed "the encyclopedia" on Rwanda's genocide. Here she greets a tall man, who seems to symbolize her beloved Africa. Was she saying "hello" or "goodbye"?

CHAPTER TWENTY-FOUR

JUSTICE ON THE GRASS

A self-confessed killer and a Catholic priest face justice,
and a tiny woman is a mighty warrior

RWANDA, SEPTEMBER 2005

During my first trip to Rwanda, in September 2005, I stayed at the Hôtel des Mille Collines, setting of a true story depicted in the film *Hotel Rwanda*. I regretted my choice of hotels after the first night. Even though they had cleaned and remodeled the hotel, bullet holes remained in many of the walls, and new carpeting did not eliminate the stench of carnage. While swimming laps in the pool early the next morning, I recalled film images of the hotel's pool slowly being drained of water to quench the thirst and wash the clothes of many frightened Tutsi families who were hiding in the hotel from mobs of hate-crazed Hutus, who were hellbent upon killing them.

Other board members and several supporters of Human Rights Watch (HRW) who came with me on this journey were staying at less haunted hotels. After breakfast, we all met at the HRW office for a briefing with Alison Des Forges, our expert on Africa's Great Lakes region, who famously documented the Rwandan genocide in an eight-hundred-page report called *Leave None to*

Tell the Story. Human rights experts across the world still refer to her report as both "The Encyclopedia" and "The Bible" on the genocide.

Over strong Rwandan coffee, Alison briefed us on the gacaca (pronounced "gachacha") trials that we would soon visit. While describing the history and rules of this unique grassroots justice system, she interspersed stories of victims and survivors, speaking of them with so much knowledge and compassion that I knew they had been her friends. After all, Rwanda was her second home. Through her stories, she let us know how the trials had been helping people process the long, dark nightmare of genocide, and move on.

I could not stop watching my friend Alison's expressive black eyebrows, which moved up and down over her soulful gray eyes, seeming to punctuate every other word. She smiled with her eyes, and she smiled often, with a tenderness that expressed her humanity and humility. I felt so happy to see her, to meet all the HRW staff, and to know that our office in Kigali had survived unscathed, in part because of its obscure location on the second floor of a small professional office building. We always need extra security in authoritarian countries because of the work HRW does to expose violations of international norms and laws, such as the Universal Declaration of Human Rights. No government appreciates having its dark and nefarious deeds exposed to the light.

In the early 1990s, HRW issued many reports about growing tensions between the two major ethnic groups in Rwanda, the Hutus (majority population) and Tutsis (who represented less than 20 percent of the population but held influential positions). The reports documented an increasing level of hate speech, including incitement to genocide, and frequent acts of violence, primarily perpetrated by Hutus against Tutsis. Hutu radio talk shows had constantly been calling Tutsis "cockroaches" and other vile names. Hutu military leaders had distributed machetes by the tens of thousands to Hutu civilians. The signs were clear, but no one, not even Alison Des Forges, could have predicted the absolute madness that exploded into one of the most horrendous genocides of the 20th Century.

As well as I know these facts, I still can hardly believe the numbers, figures that represent human lives lost forever. Starting in April 1994, in the first one hundred days, some eight hundred thousand people were massacred. The victims primarily were Tutsis, but they included Hutus who had been married to Tutsis. The vast majority of killers were Hutus wielding machetes. By the end of 1994, the death count reached a million and a quarter.

Unconscionable.

Those stunning facts are well known, but Alison told us a lot more details, facts that she included in her massive report, but which had received less attention from the international media. She talked about the Rwandan Patriotic Front (RPF), a Tutsi-led militia, which had finally moved in to stop the genocide. During its sweep across the country, the RPF had killed tens of thousands of Hutus.

After the massacre, a Tutsi-led government arrested some 130,000 Hutus, accusing them of perpetrating and committing genocide. Those charged with major war crimes, such as incitement to genocide, were also to be tried at the UN Tribunal in Tanzania, but the vast majority of prisoners received no definitive charges, nor did they receive any due process. Over the next ten years, these accused "genocidaires" overwhelmed Rwanda's prisons and led to the deaths of more than ten thousand prisoners in those crowded cells.

Of the 120,000 prisoners remaining in jail at the time of our visit in the fall of 2005, only a small fraction had been tried in conventional courts. At that pace, Alison explained, it would have taken a century to complete the judicial process. It may have dragged on indefinitely, except that the International Committee of the Red Cross (ICRC) announced in 2005 that it would no longer feed the prisoners, as it had been doing for a decade. The ICRC announcement led to the release of some fifty thousand men, those accused of lesser crimes. Because many of the fifty thousand men released had actually committed murder, perhaps several murders, it was important to resolve their cases before releasing them back into their neighborhoods. To resolve this dilemma. the government initiated a gacaca process (a Kinyarwandan word meaning "justice on the grass"). Normally this traditional practice had been used only for minor offenses.

After the long briefing, everyone in our delegation needed time to process, but there would be no rest for the overwhelmed. We got into cars and drove with Alison to a remote district of Kigali, where a gacaca hearing would take place. Actually, this was the part I had looked forward to—the opportunity to witness firsthand how peace and reconciliation was working in the places where people lived and worked.

It seemed incredible that this procedure, as Alison had explained, was taking place across the nation, on the same day each week in 9,500 different gacaca cells, with mandatory attendance for all adult citizens. Community members in each cell had elected nine to twelve judges, who were trained with the help of an international organization called Advocates Without Borders.

When we arrived and parked our car on a bare dirt yard, Alison instructed us to leave our cameras in the car and to sit quietly throughout the procedure. She would translate and pass notes to us. The setting here in a Kigali suburb looked like a Little League baseball field, but with no diamond or bases. As we walked across that dirt, I couldn't help but wonder how much blood had spilled into the soil. Knowing the horror that transpired twenty years before, the land itself seemed to be a sacred memorial.

As we approached, our group attracted considerable attention from about one hundred neighbors who had gathered there under a blue plastic tarp. Instead of elevated bleachers, there were rows of flat benches facing a long table with folding chairs behind it. We took seats on two benches. Some of the spectators recognized Alison, and she spoke with them softly, listening intently and nodding. She tried to share bits of their conversations with us, but we had to suspend our conversation when the crowd grew quiet. We noticed that six men and three women, the local judges, had emerged from a small shed near the parking area and were walking solemnly across the field to take their seats behind the long table. Each wore a sash of blue, yellow, and green stripes—the Rwandan flag.

Then, as if following theatrical cues, three additional men emerged from the shed, and we identified two armed guards escorting a short Hutu man wearing pink shorts and a shirt, the uniform of all prisoners, a bright color that made escape nearly impossible. He stood before the judges, near to us, and stated his name, Jean-Baptiste Navatorre, a defendant charged with killing three or four people in this district. (Before the trial began, Alison had spoken with a young woman who called Navatorre "the evil person who killed my husband." She recounted fleeing into the brush and giving birth alone to the now ten-year-old girl seated next to her.) In his brief testimony, Jean-Baptiste confessed that while guarding a roadblock in this neighborhood, he had ordered a man to exit his car and kneel beside the road. When asked what came next, he insisted that another guard, not he, had beheaded the man with a machete.

Suddenly, a different woman, one who had been seated behind us, stood up and walked forward. She pointed to the prisoner and shouted with great emotion, "I saw that man kill my father and my husband on the porch of our house. I know it was Jean-Baptiste! After that, I ran with my son, who was four, and we hid in the swamp for many days." The woman, who had seemed very brave to me, suddenly lost her balance and asked if she could sit down. On impulse, I reached out to steady her, but Alison raised her imposing eyebrows, and I retracted immediately.

Facing the judges, the woman continued, speaking more calmly.

"My son and I joined a big crowd of people walking on the road toward the Congo border. Injured and bleeding people walked beside men holding bloody machetes," she said, "and not just men with machetes. There were women killers also, all trying to run and hide. My boy got lost, and I went crazy for three days, but then this man found my son and brought him to me. I can no longer hate him so much." This was not quite a statement of forgiveness, but the woman clearly had considered the humanity of the accused man and his potential for redemption. Perhaps it is true that time can help to heal wounds.

In many respects, I realized, especially after witnessing another hearing, Rwanda's gacaca justice system resembled South Africa's Truth and Reconciliation process, which had been designed by three men: South Africa's president Nelson Mandela, Archbishop Desmond Tutu, and Justice Richard Goldstone, two of whom I knew very well. Justice Goldstone served on the board of Human Rights Watch, so I worked with him directly and counted on his knowledge and judgment.

Desmond Tutu, during the long dark days of apartheid, came often to All Saints Church, Pasadena, which he called "my church in America." Tutu was a bishop then, and he considered All Saints' rector, George Regas, to be his soul brother. He preached a sermon every time he came, and the large Gothic church would have to set up overflow seats on the lawn. In one sermon, Tutu answered a question that George had asked him about how he could keep his faith while surrounded by such violent racial hatred.

"As a Christian," Tutu had answered, "I am just a prisoner of hope." I wrote down those words at the time and have tried to live by them.

In the grassroots systems of both Rwanda and South Africa, victims and perpetrators could speak about their experiences and create a public record. In both countries, public hearings allowed people to vent deep emotions they had held for decades, hoping that such purging would help to maintain peace, restore communities, and allow people of different races and tribes to live and work together; perhaps even to respect each other.

On the drive back to Kigali, we saw men wearing pink prison uniforms working to clear brush and plant trees along the roadside. Alison told us that for the past decade, tens of thousands of prisoners had been doing this kind of labor to rebuild Rwanda. "The government may not be eager to release them and lose this free labor pool," she suggested.

As I watched the men in pink swinging machetes, I remembered a frightful encounter with men swinging machetes that I experienced on a country road in Nicaragua in 1984, during my first journey to a war zone. Those machetes caused momentary fear, but the Nicaraguan men turned out to be friendly farm workers. Here in Rwanda, that common agricultural tool that had become the primary instrument of death.

Back at the office, Alison shared her concerns about this improvised justice system. "There are 350,000 direct victims of genocide living in Rwandan neighborhoods, right next door to perpetrators," she explained. "They fear reprisals if they testify." She said that many of the gacaca judges were illiterate and poorly trained, and she worried that they would be biased if any of their friends or relatives were implicated in genocide.

We also discussed the problem of collective guilt and of people making false accusations. Alison talked about gacaca's negative impact on Rwanda's economy from having work shut down across the nation one day every week while people attended trials. (As I write this during the global shutdown caused by the COVID-19 pandemic, I realize full well the negative impact of work stoppage.)

Then Alison stated her greatest concern: "One-sided justice." She said that since the Rwandan Patriotic Front (RPF) stopped the Hutu killing binge and took power in July 1994, no one had been allowed to speak about the tens of thousands of Hutus slaughtered by the RPF army in its march across the country.

"Murder is murder. Hate crimes are hate crimes. International law is impartial. It does not make exceptions for tribe or nationality," she concluded.

It always comes down to politics, greed, and control, and so was the case here. As the Tutsi general who led the RPF, Paul Kagame became an international hero. He fought on the side of justice to avenge the primary victims. But when he became president, Kagame refused to admit to crimes that RPF soldiers (Tutsis) committed, the massive killing of innocent Hutu civilians, and he declared that charges and trials against Tutsis must be excluded from the criminal justice process. Most observers, including Western countries trying to assuage their guilt for not intervening to stop the genocide, accepted Kagame's version of "victors' justice." But for her comprehensive Human Rights Watch report, Alison courageously investigated and reported all the slaughter, including that perpetrated by the RPF.

Early the following morning, Alison roused us unexpectedly. As usual, she had spent most of the night on the phone. She learned that a close friend of hers, a Belgian Catholic priest, had been arrested at the airport and charged with a category one crime, the highest offense. An open public trial would begin soon in central Kigali, and she wanted to be there to testify on his behalf. What an amazing opportunity to witness an important event! My reporter instincts went into overdrive, as I grabbed my camera and spiral notebook.

Before 9 o'clock, we arrived at an open field beside a large Catholic church, where some six hundred people already sat under large blue canopies stamped *United Nations*. We found seats on two benches near the front. Because Alison had to pay close attention and could not serve as our translator, we busily planned how a local HRW staffer, who spoke no English, would translate the Kinyarwandan court proceedings into French, then pass her notes to Kevin Ryan, an HRW board member from New York who spoke fluent French. Kevin then would quickly translate to English and share his notes with the other five members of our delegation. Complicated.

As church bells rang the hour, nine judges entered and took their seats. Armed guards followed, escorting the gray-haired white priest, who wore a pink shirt and shorts like all Rwandan prisoners. The priest had not been allowed the dignity of wearing his white clerical collar. Father Guy Theunis, age sixty, maintained a posture of composure while the presiding judge read the charge, "incitement to genocide," a level one crime. Then the judge surprised everyone by announcing that the use of cameras and recordings, including television cameras, would be allowed. Television camera crews suddenly materialized and scrambled for good positions.

Alison turned, her eyebrows raised up to her hairline. "Show trial," she declared in a voice loud enough to be heard by the TV crew that now stood in front of her. I entered the date, September 11, in my journal and under it wrote "show trial." Then, remembering the traumatic events of 2001, I wrote and underlined, "today is 9-11."

The priest calmly looked around at the large crowd, his face expressionless, and I noticed the instant that he recognized Alison in the front row, made eye contact with her, and relaxed his shoulders. At the same time, my shoulders tightened. My entire body tensed, and I felt sweat dripping down my spine. I realized that our small group of white people really stood out, especially seated as we were in the first two rows. By now the crowd, nearly all black, had doubled to about 1,500 people, many of whom stood outside the canopies in the hot sun.

When the presiding judge asked Father Theunis to state his credentials and explain what he had done in Rwanda before and during the genocide, he replied that he was a member of the Catholic Order of White Fathers, and that he had served as a missionary in Rwanda from 1970 to 1994. He said he had served at various parishes in Rwanda, between occasional trips back to Belgium and France. He added the important fact that the church had evacuated him and all other Belgians right after the infamous airplane incident—the tragic event that killed the presidents of both Rwanda and Burundi. (This plane crash, which sparked the massive genocide in April 1994, is widely believed not to have been an accident.) In conclusion, Father Theunis said he had been in Europe during most of the massacre. Then, turning the table on the court, Father Theunis asked the presiding judge to explain the basis for accusations made against him.

"You wrote anti-Tutsi articles for a church paper called *Dialogue*," the judge declared. He went on to quote an article, reportedly written by Theunis in 1995 and published in Europe, in which the priest had labeled President Paul Kagame as "a dictator replacing a dictator." Alison quickly wrote a note: "*Gacaca* jurisdiction covers only 1990–1994" and held it up for us to see. At that moment, I heard soft organ music coming from the church, an incongruous intrusion of the divine into this dramatic setting, which I, ever the optimist, took as a good sign. Suddenly, a woman wearing an orange dress rushed forward and yelled in a deep voice, "Theunis sent faxes to Europe saying that RPF soldiers killed many Hutus, even children. He hates Tutsis!"

Another woman shouted, "Make him admit his crimes." Alison wrote, "Witch hunt! This is all 'BS'!'" as if she wanted me to see those words and take heart. Many more people yelled criticisms, but they lacked spontaneity and appeared to be orchestrated, starting with the woman who yelled about faxes.

Then, Alison rose to her full height of four feet ten inches and stepped forward, the moment I had been anticipating. I noticed that many people in the crowd seemed to recognize Alison as she approached the judges' bench. She reminded me of Desmond Tutu, another small and mighty warrior for truth and justice. When Alison started speaking, slowly and in the Kinyarwandan language, our passing of notes sped up, pieces of paper written in English and French that I later collected and kept in my file. I have always been an obsessive keeper of paper files, slow to trust digital record keeping.

"Thank you for letting me speak," Alison began. "It is my obligation as a citizen of the world to testify. I completed a doctorate degree in the history of Rwanda, and I have lived here for fourteen years, working to establish human rights for everyone."

After turning around slowly to look at the crowd on all sides, Alison continued, "I have testified nine times at the United Nations International Tribunal in Arusha, Tanzania. Father Theunis and I did research together on human rights violations against both Tutsis and Hutus. He and I believe that laws protecting human rights must apply to all people.

"By creating gacacas and showing respect for justice," Alison continued, "Rwanda has attracted the attention of the world." She pointed toward our delegation and announced, "Today, members of the Human Rights Watch International Board came to witness this important trial. They understand the rules."

Alison paused dramatically and looked at each judge in turn, taking her time, letting them wonder about her next words. She then spoke more loudly, in a voice of authority. "The jurisdiction of this court is for 1990–94, not for anything written or spoken before or after those years." She let that sink in, then added, "The term 'incitement' means pushing people to commit genocide, nothing short of that. Father Theunis is not guilty of the charges made against him."

Alison returned to her seat, and I automatically leaned forward as if to shield her. I heard the crowd again grow agitated, but no one else spoke against the priest, although a few people did condemn the Catholic Church and the Belgian government. One man yelled, "I like seeing a white priest in a pink suit." Finally, the shouting ended, the crowd broke up, and the judges departed.

As Father Theunis was being led out, presumably back to jail, he looked over his shoulder and smiled at Alison. She returned his smile and signed, "two thumbs up." It seemed to me that on this auspicious day, Alison had been the one who gave the blessing and the benediction.

I remained seated, writing in my journal and trying to control my emotions. Alison surprised me by bringing a BBC camera crew over. She asked whether I, as chair of the International Board of Human Rights Watch, would allow them to interview me about the trial. I never said no to Alison. I tried to gather my thoughts and calm my nerves as I followed the TV crew to a place under the shade of an acacia tree that provided a neutral background.

After Alison's powerful performance, I knew that my words had to be chosen carefully. A tall BBC reporter had told me in his Oxford English accent that this interview would be played all across Europe that evening. The camera rolled, and I had no time to think before being asked the first question: "Do you think this trial was fair?"

"This trial was a travesty of justice," I replied, trying to steady my voice. "The judges allowed wild accusations that had no relation to the indictment." Then I paused, looked directly into the camera, and calmly stated my very strong opinion that Father Theunis had become a scapegoat for long-held grievances over European colonization and the power of the Catholic

Church. Alison, standing beside the camera, nodded. When I saw her smile, I finally could relax my shoulders.

After giving the BBC interview, I told Alison that I could do one more thing to help Father Theunis. I happened to know the new U.S. ambassador to Belgium, the Hon. Tom Korologos. In fact, my five-year-old grandson Will recently had served as ringbearer at his Greek Orthodox wedding to a dear friend of mine. I called Tom in Brussels that evening and briefed him on the Theunis trial, and he promised to speak with Belgian's prime minister Guy Verhofstadt. As it turned out, the prime minister then worked tirelessly with Alison to secure the priest's eventual release and his return to Belgium, which they accomplished within two months.

Father Theunis later told Alison that he had ministered to many men within the prison walls and taken confessions from genocidaires who were seeking forgiveness. He felt that his incarceration turned out to be time well spent, because he had been needed in that prison. Everything happens for a reason.

Rwanda's gacaca trials lasted a decade. Most prisoners got off for time already served, but people convicted of multiple murders, rape, and other major crimes had to remain in prison. Because category one perpetrators faced trials at the International Criminal Tribunal for Rwanda in Arusha, Tanzania, our delegation flew from Kigali to Tanzania with Alison to witness her powerful testimony against four indicted Hutu generals. When we arrived at the tribunal, I felt so proud to see how everyone there, attorneys, prosecutors, and defenders, greeted Alison like a rock star and sought her advice.

After I returned home, I sent the following message to HRW staff and board members: "*On our recent trip to Rwanda, we had hoped to educate board members and supporters by showing them the impact of HRW's work. Coincidentally, a trial in Kigali of the first European to be charged with incitement to genocide allowed us to support Alison Des Forges and our staff in Rwanda at a critical time.*"

ALISON THE WARRIOR

Five years later, I went to Uganda, Burundi, and Rwanda with Jerry White and a delegation representing Landmine Survivors Network, which had changed its name to Survivor Corps. Burundi, Rwanda's neighbor to the south, had been experiencing a long civil war, another conflict between Hutus and Tutsis. Because it lacked the explosive impact of Rwanda's genocide, some called it a "genocide in slow motion."

In the capital city of Bujumbura, we met with young women who had been kidnapped and forced to serve as child soldiers and sex slaves. The recovered girls confessed to us that they now had good-paying jobs as city police officers, but their uniforms did not protect them. Male officers raped them if they refused to perform sexual favors. While I listened to their traumatic testimonies, I kept wondering how Alison would respond to these heartbreaking stories. I took detailed notes so I could report to her when I returned home.

On our last full day in Burundi, I got up early and turned on CNN International, just as a breaking news story reported that a small commuter plane had crashed while landing in Buffalo, N.Y., killing all passengers and crew. Suddenly, the face of Alison Des Forges appeared on the screen. Alison, who lived in Buffalo, was the first of some fifty passengers to be identified. I looked at her image on the screen and saw "Human Rights Watch" in large letters below, but I simply could not take it in. Alison, who embodied the "human" part of human rights; it just could not be true! The shock made me dizzy and disoriented.

Alison had stayed several times at our home in California to help me build support for Human Rights Watch in Los Angeles, often coming straight from Africa to share fresh reports of her work. The information and inspiration Alison provided had helped to build HRW's Los Angeles Committee, which became a model for the nearly thirty global committees that followed. During one of her visits, Alison and I discovered that we had been born the same week of August 1942. Although I was four days older and nine inches taller than Alison, I thought of her as my twin sister. I looked up to her achievement and courage, but I always felt a strong need to protect her.

I had been in constant communication with Alison for that past month. She needed me to intercede with the government of Rwanda, because President Kagame had revoked her visa since she did not go along with "one-sided justice," and she had continued to criticize the actions of what was becoming a police state. The very next day, in fact, I was flying to Kigali to meet with the Human Rights Watch staff and help them secure Alison's visa renewal. After that, I would attend my Rwandan daughter Happy's wedding.

All that day, I felt stunned and hollow, unable to eat or take notes at the meetings in Bujumbura. Because of long practice, I was able to push down my grief and move mechanically, but I could not accept compassion from my colleagues for fear I would break down. That evening, when our Survivor Corps group went to a restaurant high above the city, grief suddenly overcame me. Feeling an intense need to be alone, I excused myself, left the patio table, and walked down a dirt path to an open patch of grass on the hillside. Finding myself in total darkness, I looked up and searched among the billions of stars for any sign of comfort from the vast beyond.

Exactly above my head, I spotted the warrior constellation, Orion. Since learning the seasonal positions of major constellations during my childhood, Orion has always been my favorite. And there he was, just when I needed him, right beside the Southern Cross.

On this tragic night in February 2009, the appearance of Orion offered assurance that Alison Des Forges, who had lived her life as a peaceful warrior and a champion of hope, would continue to watch over the Great Lakes region of Africa. I thanked the Universe for comforting me with this powerful spiritual symbol of Alison's strength, resilience, and incredible legacy.

OPPOSITE, TOP: Crowds gathered in Kigali, Rwanda, to observe the "show trial" of a European Catholic priest, seen dressed in the pink uniform of a genocidaire prisoner; OPPOSITE, BOTTOM: Alison Des Forges with her back turned, a small but mighty warrior who presented a convincing defense of the priest, her friend and a fellow human rights defender; ABOVE: Alison reads the names of many friends among the million-plus dead listed at the genocide museum in Kigali. For Alison, the 1994 Rwandan genocide was personal.

In Gulu, northern Uganda, we met former child soldiers of Joseph Kony's Lord's Resistance Army (LRA), children who could not erase horrific memories of acts they both witnessed and committed, nor could they hide their trauma and shame.

CHAPTER TWENTY-FIVE

CHILD SOLDIERS

A generation of children forced to commit
murder and mayhem struggle to return home to their
communities and to themselves

UGANDA, APRIL 2009

What began with a snag in flight plans led to encounters with tragedy, cruelty, and evil that tore my heart apart; it ended with hope for the ability of victims, even young ones, to persevere by holding on to each other. I had never been to Uganda before, and I felt some trepidation on the day that I left home to join members of Landmine Survivors Network, unsure about what I would find there, given the recent history of turning innocent children into brutal killers.

Landmine Survivors Network, whose board I had been chairing for a decade, had broadened its mission statement and morphed into an organization called Survivor Corps. Because LSN's peer support programs had proven to be measurably helpful with the healing of amputees, we began to receive requests from countries that had suffered violent conflict, but did not have landmines, including several in Africa. We changed the name to better reflect our expanded work. In the Great Lakes region of Africa, Survivor Corps had recruited and trained local staff members, all of them survivors of war, to help other survivors heal from physical, emotional, and psychological injuries. Along with Jerry White, founder and director of LSN and Survivor Corps, I wanted to bring board members and supporters to visit these new programs.

I flew alone from Los Angeles and narrowly missed a late night connection in Nairobi, Kenya, which meant that I had to wait at the airport a few hours and sleep on the floor near the departure in order to catch an early morning flight to Uganda, but at least I was not alone. Two Kenyan guards, who looked like teenaged boys, kept me company by marching up and down the corridors all night. Every time they reached me, the boys stomped their boots on the concrete floor and shifted their automatic rifles from one shoulder to the other, making sure that I noticed how well they were protecting me. That sleepless experience prepared me for what I would encounter in Uganda—boys carrying guns.

At sunrise, I boarded a small plane and flew over beautiful Lake Victoria, crossing the Equator just before landing at Kampala, Uganda's capital city, where I caught up with Jerry White and the rest of our delegation. I had not been able to tell them about my delay, but Jerry had traveled with me often enough to trust that I would make it. We spent the first day meeting with government officials, including the foreign minister, to learn more about the long civil war between the Ugandan National Army and a horrendous guerilla force called the Lord's Resistance Army (LRA) that broke out in 1987.

LRA, whose radical leader Joseph Kony claimed to be a god incarnate, had killed more than one hundred thousand people, mostly in the north, and mutilated tens of thousands by chopping off victims' lips, noses, hands, and limbs— or by dousing them with paraffin wax and setting them on fire. I shudder as I write these words with difficulty. They evoke unbearable images. I heard the paraffin story firsthand from an older woman whose head and upper torso had been burned so badly that her face reminded me of photos taken in Hiroshima after the atomic bomb hit that city.

After two decades of brutal fighting, the LRA still rampaged through the countryside, and officials in Kampala confessed they had no idea of Kony's whereabouts. International forces failed to find the LRA in the dense jungles, despite numerous sightings. If there were any government-sponsored humanitarian efforts currently helping the half million survivors, especially those suffering severe mental and physical disabilities (our focus), none of the officials who met with us seemed to know about them.

The next day, we took a small plane to Gulu in northern Uganda, where I learned that more than the Equator divided Uganda. The northern and southern regions of this former British Protectorate (which became independent in 1962) looked like different countries. Kampala and the southern region boasted a snow-covered mountain, lush tropical forests, and the seat of government. In the north, we flew over barren desert and bushland.

Members of a local organization, the Gulu Disabled Persons Union, met us at the Boma Hotel, a small resort that would have resembled a desert oasis had its grounds not been filled with wounded survivors. I noticed a small patch of grass, a far cry from my father's Kentucky blue grass, but a welcome relief from the amber dirt. I wanted to remove my hiking boots and walk barefoot in that grass. On our last day, after walking so much barren land, I actually did that— and I couldn't believe how great it felt.

We ate a lunch of bread and cheese while going over our agenda and learning how our peer support methodology was being used here. I felt so gratified to learn we would be meeting with individual survivors within the enormous camps for internally displaced people, which we had passed on the road. Having been with this organization since its beginning, I wanted to see how our peer support methods worked in the Great Lakes region of Central Africa. In the other LSN programs I had visited, such as Bosnia, Jordan, Vietnam, Colombia, El Salvador, Mozambique, and Ethiopia, "the enemy" had left unexploded bombs and landmines, often invisible, which could tear apart human bodies years after combatants left. Here, "the enemy" used close and very personal encounters to mutilate human bodies.

Our delegation included two teenaged girls, Jerry.White's nieces Kylie and Kaziah White. I had been somewhat concerned that touring the camps would expose these sensitive girls to too much trauma, especially since this war had brutalized Ugandan children and teens. On the other hand, the girls were very mature. I told them I had taken a college course in African history, but many of the names and borders of countries had changed since 1964. Despite such transformation, however, it's the people who matter to me, and cultures are slow to change. If I had anticipated my life path, I said, I would have included anthropology, sociology, and foreign languages in my college courses.

Most kids in northern Uganda had no chance to receive any education. Thousands of teens and young children had been kidnapped by Joseph Kony's soldiers over the course of this war. Boys were forced to serve as soldiers and girls as porters, wives, and sex slaves for LRA guerillas. Many bands of captured child soldiers still roamed the countryside, killing and pillaging. I hoped to meet some of the children who had come out of the bush recently and to assess whether, in addition to their childhoods, they had lost all sense of humanity.

After a short drive on very dusty roads, we came to the Dungaetira camp, home to about fifty thousand war survivors, one of some two hundred camps that had been built for internally displaced people in northern Uganda. The long war had forced two million or more people to flee villages that were later destroyed, so there could be no going home. The round mud huts at Dungaetira, built close together across an acre of dry land, looked like inverted beehives with thatched roofs. Narrow dirt paths meandered between them in such random patterns that I wondered how people could identify their own huts. They all looked alike except for articles of clothing laid across many thatched-grass roofs to dry in the sun— that and the canes, crutches, and wheelchairs beside many entrances.

We split into small groups to tour the camp, and the girls came with me. I was so surprised to see that the young Ugandan woman named Carolyn who guided our group wore an over-sized USC Trojan T-shirt. That made me smile, wondering how that shirt had made its journey from California. Even though the world is huge, this T-shirt and I had both come thousands of miles from the same city, Los Angeles, to reach Carolyn. The ease she showed with her baby, and the love she gave while breastfeeding her, held my admiration.

When I noticed that Carolyn had one shorter leg and walked with a considerable limp, I asked whether she had been injured during the war. She moved the child to her other breast before explaining that she had suffered from polio in childhood. Then, she sat down on a tree stump, and we formed a circle on the ground around her, Kylie and Kaziah sitting comfortably in lotus positions. Carolyn started talking about what she had experienced during the war. She spoke fast, as if needing to blurt it all out quickly, and I listened carefully, hoping to remember every detail. Carolyn explained that when the LRA advanced on her village, her family fled. "They left me behind, because I could not keep up." I took in this horrific news, imagining the despair she must have felt when her family abandoned her.

"I was just a teenager. I tried to hide, but the rebels found me," she said, hanging her head for a moment, then continuing more slowly. "They took turns pointing guns at me and raping me. Some were just boys." Both of the Colorado girls stared at her, transfixed, their eyes wide and filling with tears, as were mine.

"A very young boy tried to rape me, but could not. The men and older boys taunted him and ordered him to be a man," Carolyn continued. "He tried again, and then started yelling at me, calling me ugly, as if it was my fault. He grabbed a gun and jammed it inside of me," she said, pausing for a long moment to look at our faces, needing to know that we understood the horror she described. I held Carolyn's eyes. I had heard stories like this in Bosnia, and knew she needed to see a reflection of understanding and compassion. And my tears.

As if comforted by the depth of empathy that encircled her, Carolyn went on. "I can still feel the pain. When I started to bleed badly, they all left, but first they broke my leg brace and threw it into the brush." She lifted her child, pulled her closer, and began rocking back and forth.

"It was a very terrible time, but she came to me," she concluded, with dignity and calm. We sat in stunned silence until heat and sweat forced us to stand and widen our circle. I asked her daughter's name. "Hope," she answered.

I took in the symbolism of the name "Hope," chosen by a very young mother at a time when she had no reason to hope, and my own heart filled with optimism, as the certainty of her baby's name gave Carolyn the resilience to go on. And this reminded me that even in the depth of true tragedy, and seemingly unbearable despair, Hope survives.

Later I was approached by another unforgettable survivor, Simon Santos, head of the Gulu Disabled Persons Union. A visually impaired young man, he shared his story, quietly and with great pain. Simon first explained that he had been working as a social worker with physically disabled people for the last twenty years. He seemed eager to tell me that his motivation to serve others came from the years of violence he experienced as an enslaved LRA child soldier. Most survivors needed to be prodded, but Simon told me his whole story right away.

"The soldiers came to my village and kidnapped all of us boys," Simon began. "They made us kill our own parents and burn our homes. We also had to destroy many other villages and walk so much; it was so hard to keep up," he told us. "One spring day in 1988, I dropped my gun in the mud, because it was too heavy and my arms ached. The soldiers beat me and tortured me for two days," he said, choking on the words before adding that the brutal beating had caused his blindness.

"After the beating, it was scarier than ever, because I could only hear the violence, not see it," Simon told us. "My imagination created the horrors of hell!" We later learned that when Simon escaped and returned home, he discovered that some twenty-one members of his family had been killed by the LRA.

As I looked at this truly awesome man, whose unimaginable pain had resulted in his devotion to helping others, I realized that even though his large black eyes seemed unfocused, they sparkled, and his cheeks crinkled when he grinned. I wondered how any human being could recover from so much tragedy and loss, and still smile. As if guessing my unspoken question, Simon said that through helping other people, some of whom had suffered even more than he had, he could set aside his own problems.

I asked Simon whether any child soldiers had returned to Gulu recently. I had been hoping to meet a boy or girl fresh from the jungle. I had interviewed so many victims of war around the world, but this was different. It tore children from their homes and made them commit murder and mayhem. I wanted to look in their eyes and see for myself that humanity remained, or that it could be revived. He nodded and offered to take me to meet some teenaged boys living in a small encampment at the outskirts of the settlement.

While the other members of our delegation went with Carolyn to visit a medical clinic, Simon led me down a narrow road, tapping and swiping his cane confidently across the fine reddish dirt. I asked about the boys we would meet, and he warned me that they might not be willing to see me. "They have barely spoken in the past two months since coming out of the bush," he said. "Social workers call them *silent but reactive.*"

As we approached a small grouping of huts, I saw a boy about sixteen years old outside, sitting on an elevated horizontal log. The muscles of his bare arms looked strong, and for a second, I feared violence. "No one knows his name or village," Simon told me. I sat down on the log a bit tentatively, a short distance away from the boy, and Simon stood beside him. I waited quietly for a few minutes, feeling inadequate. "I am Jane from America," I said. When Simon translated, the boy's posture eased a bit.

In my backpack, I found a photo of my eight grandsons, who ranged in age from four to ten, and set it on the log between us. He stole a glance at the blue-eyed, mostly blond boys, and turned away. I realized that my grandsons, who lived far away in a world he could not have imagined, must have looked to him like they came from a different planet. But that photograph was a passport that had opened many doors. I wished I had asked Kylie and Kaziah to join me, certain that they would have gotten a response from him.

Feeling the heat, I dug in my backpack and found a square paperback book, which I used to fan myself. The boy made a curious grunting sound, and Simon spoke to him calmly in Swahili, pausing to watch for any reaction before continuing, patiently. After some time, the boy began to respond, slowly at first, hanging his head, and Simon translated for me: "The LRA attacked his village when he was six or seven and kidnapped him. They gave him a gun and ordered him to kill his parents and burn his home so he would have no place to return. They shot any child who refused to obey."

I saw the boy's body slump, and I wondered whether this was the first time he had talked about what happened to him. He seemed to shrink from the telling. As the blind man and soul-battered boy continued to converse, I sat as a quiet witness, not needing or wanting to know any more details. In this powerful illustration of peer support, I could only be present and hold the space. Perhaps Simon was sharing his own horrific LRA experiences. Both spoke so softly that I took quiet, shallow breaths in order not to interrupt the flow of their conversation. I wondered whether the guerillas had given the boy drugs or alcohol, a practice I remembered hearing about in Sarajevo, where teenagers had been trained as sharpshooters, drugged, and told to shoot anything that moved.

When they paused, I told Simon to ask why he wanted to live apart from the community. "The kids here laugh at me," the boy answered. "I never got to play with balls or anything. The soldiers hit us if we talked, and they made us fight each other. Now I'm too big for school," he concluded. "All I can do is fight and shoot guns."

All during this conversation, the boy's eyes had remained downcast. I suddenly remembered a child named Mark, the bully boy who terrorized other children in the Head Start pre-school program where I volunteered years ago. I recalled how Mark finally had responded to touch and affection. I reached out to touch this boy's shoulder and noticed a V-shaped scar on his upper arm that looked like it had been carved into his sable brown skin. At my touch, he flinched, as if I had whipped him. So, I took a step back and picked up the red book that I had been using to fan myself, a children's picture book called *The Story of Ferdinand*. I set the book next to him beside the photo of my grandsons, two gifts that I would leave with him.

The book told the story of a gentle young bull named Ferdinand, who was the son of a champion fighting bull. Other young bulls teased and bullied Ferdinand because he loved flowers, but he always refused to fight with them. It had been one of my son Steven's favorite books, and I could picture Steve in his beloved blue pajamas. Thinking of my son, I felt a strong urge to put my arms around this big boy, take him onto my lap, and read to him.

Simon motioned that we should leave. As I got up to go, the boy picked up the red book and glanced at me. I smiled and stood perfectly still, not wanting to frighten him. Slowly, the boy's face softened, and he returned my smile, tentatively at first, and then more broadly.

That smile gave me hope that some resiliency remained in this young man, whose childhood had been stolen by monstrous human beings. I realized in that moment that, if for no other reason, I had come to Uganda to deliver this book to this boy. Not everything can be explained or forgiven, but if, over time, he could forgive himself for the heinous acts he had been forced to commit, perhaps he could help other lost children of Uganda come home to themselves. Then together they could rebuild lost families and lost communities.

TOP: We were greeted by young dancers and drummers, all of them former child soldiers who served in the LRA; BOTTOM: Only two small counseling centers, both in decrepit condition, served fifty thousand people, all of whom fit the description "Conflict Affected Persons."

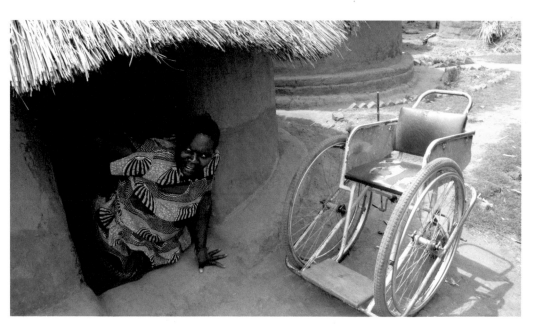

OPPOSITE, TOP: The mud brick huts of Dungaetira camp, home to fifty thousand war survivors, looked like beehives with thatched roofs; OPPOSITE, BOTTOM: The expressions on children's faces made me suspect they had served as child soldiers or been child brides; ABOVE: Wheelchairs and crutches parked outside many huts indicated the presence of disabled people living inside, a very high number. The small therapy center had a long line of patients waiting patiently.

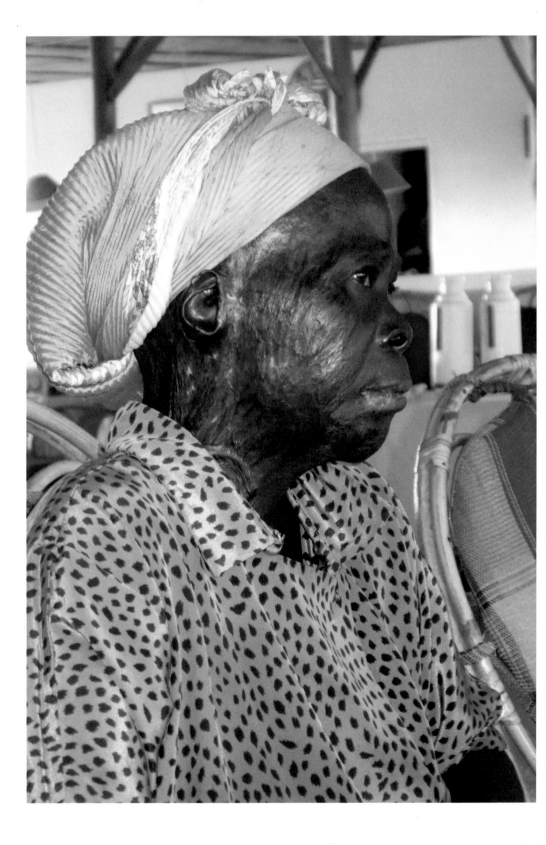

OPPOSITE: Child soldiers from the LRA poured paraffin wax over this brave woman's head and set it on fire. She willingly posed for a photo, wanting the world to see what she had endured; ABOVE: Simon Santos, head of the Gulu Disabled Persons Union, had been enslaved as a child soldier and lost his sight from a severe beating. He served as a social worker for disabled people, especially the blind, and helped other former child soldiers return to heal.

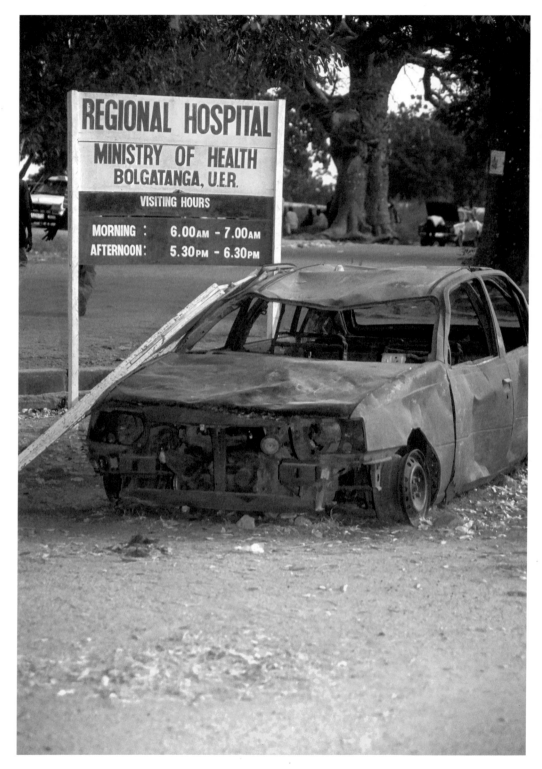

The sign for the regional hospital and ministry of health in northern Ghana did not inspire confidence.

CHAPTER TWENTY-SIX

BUGS, WORMS,
AND YELLOW PENCILS

Stoic people in remote villages
confront diseases from the Dark Ages

GHANA, NOVEMBER 2000

I learned a lot about insects from growing up in Iowa, where the heat and humidity of summer hatched a plethora of bugs that invaded the state on a predictable schedule. Farmers viewed insects as a threat to their crops and fought them with pesticides, but we children used bugs for games, science projects, fishing bait, and personal adornment. We loved them. Well, most of them. June bugs arrived right on schedule, and those fat, bronze-colored beetles congregated on every lighted pathway at night. My sisters and I crunched them on our porch, the way kids today stomp on bubble wrap.

In August, we chased lightening bugs across the lawn in the dark and netted them as they flashed their tiny yellow tail lights to attract mates. We pinched off those iridescent tails and squished them together to create bracelets. Late summer also brought "protein bees" and blackflies, both of which attacked food like dive bombers and made dining outdoors nearly impossible.

These childhood experiences came to mind when I went to Ghana, West Africa, in November 2000 with World Vision (WV), a global aid organization that supported teams of health care professionals working in Ghana to end Third World diseases, such as malaria, elephantiasis, trachoma/river blindness, and Guinea worm. We would be doing a lot of driving to reach the region where these diseases plagued so many people, very remote villages in northern Ghana, some of which were not on the map I brought with me.

On most of my previous journeys, I had met with victims of violence and armed conflict. But for millions of people around the world, the primary cause of suffering is crippling disease, not conflict. Poverty and extreme climatic conditions, such as those found in northern Ghana, can create a perfect storm, intensifying the deadly effects of various diseases. This region exemplified an alarming aspect of global warming. As average temperatures continued to rise in Ghana, the population of bugs, worms, and parasites grew stronger and infected vulnerable human beings in larger numbers.

Our delegation gathered in Accra and had time to tour the city before we left on our drive north. Looking around the town, I realized why a Christian-affiliated organization like World Vision would be warmly welcomed here. Most of the buildings in Accra, shops and houses, had religious phrases painted in bright colors above their doors, such as the *Blessed Grace* hardware store, *Precious Blood* hair salon, and the *God Is Able* iron works. The sign above the blue doors of a photo shop said *Except God*, which really puzzled me until I realized that they meant to say *Accept God*.

I studied the history of Ghana before I left home and decided to go a couple of days early to tour the south-facing west coast and see the fortresses and dungeons from which African slaves had been shipped to the New World. I could not be in Ghana and miss that experience, difficult as it was emotionally. That brutal reminder of Ghana's shared history with slavery in America still haunts me.

One of the most dignified men I knew came from Ghana, Kofi Annan, who was the seventh Secretary General of the United Nations (1997–2006) and a 2001 Nobel Prize recipient. I knew Mr. Annan as a champion of the Universal Declaration of Human Rights and a great friend of Human Rights

Watch. After seeing the slave forts up close and personal, I kept thinking about Kofi and wondering what genius and potential the world had lost because thousands of Ghanaians and other West Africans had died or been worked to death as slaves.

In a journal of inspirational quotes that I keep, I have two quotes from Kofi Annan:

We may have different religions, different languages, different colored skin, but we all belong to one human race.

Education is a human right with immense power to transform. On its foundation rest the cornerstones of freedom, democracy and sustainable human development.

Ghana, a British colony, won its independence in 1957, but a quarter of the population, mostly those living in the south around Accra, continued to practice Christianity. Some 40 percent, especially people in the northern region we would be visiting, followed traditional, animistic beliefs, and the rest were Muslims. I felt eager to experience life in the traditional, indigenous villages.

The guide book said that Ghana has only two seasons: hot, dry, and buggy; and hot, wet, and buggy. Even though we had come at the beginning of dry season, our local guides said the previous months had yielded abundant rainfall, and there would be even more insects than usual in the north. I was glad that all my immunizations were up to date (the infectious diseases doctor at Pasadena Public Health knew me well) and that I carried anti-malaria pills.

In addition to Angela Mason and Howie Buffett, who had been in Bosnia with me, two local World Vision staff members accompanied us in a white Land Rover. Howie kept his camera bag on his lap, as usual, and shot photos out the window of every roadside stand selling colorful produce. The barren landscape of burned fields and clear-cut forests, however, looked unphotogenic to me, and the excessive heat made me reluctant to open a window in our air-conditioned van. My zeal to take pictures had its limits.

When we reached the town of Tamale, we got out for a small stretch and snack, then continued north to a small village for our first visit to a clinic, where we would meet the medical team that would travel with us in a separate van. But first, I am anxious to share my first visit to a traditional, animist village.

Before we went to the clinic, protocol dictated that we had to first greet the chief of this village. It turned out that the chief had retired as a wealthy man from his former government position as director of the interior, or something like that. I failed to write down his name or that of the village because, while shaking our hands, the chief boasted that he had twenty-eight wives! Had I not been wearing sunglasses, he would have seen the shock in my eyes. He proudly took us to see his home, a compound of some fifteen round mud huts attached to each other in a curving line that resembled a caterpillar of condominiums, each with a rounded opening. The undulating sculpture fascinated me, and I could not resist running my hand over the hand-sculpted clay, but Howie and I both felt frustrated, because we had been told to leave our cameras in the van. Darn! The architecture of that compound was beautiful, and it truly looked like a curling caterpillar.

All at once, several women emerged from the huts to greet the chief. He smiled broadly and nodded to the oldest looking woman, his first wife, and then introduced us to his newest bride, a girl whom he said was twelve years old. Looking very pleased with himself, he pointed to her hut at the tail end of the caterpillar. I suddenly felt sick to my stomach about her fate, but truly, I did not know the circumstances. Perhaps the chief had rescued the girl from an abusive family. All the women seemed genuinely glad to see him, evidence of his kindness.

We had an opportunity when the chief departed to sit in with some of the wives, thirteen of them, on a grass mat. Many of the women (and girls!) held infants or toddlers on their laps. When our interpreter asked about their daily routines, one of the older women listed several daily chores and explained that they divided and shared all of the household duties. As I thought about the benefits of "sister wives," especially when it came to doing housework, I started laughing.

"My husband has only one wife," I said. Instead of joining my laughter, the women looked sad, as if they pitied me, apparently assuming I had married a very poor man. The senior wife spoke for all of them by asking, incredulously, how I alone could possibly serve all of his needs. That question startled me into silence, and I decided not to tell my husband about the chief's living situation.

I never did tell him, by the way. He will read it here, but after more than fifty years of marriage, it's too late to change our arrangement.

After that intimate visit, I was still smiling while we walked to the medical clinic, but that expression changed instantly after we entered the children's ward, where we found young mothers sitting helplessly beside the beds of desperately ill children, even infants and toddlers, who were suffering from malaria. The scene inside the clinic took my breath away. As the grandmother of four boys at that time, one toddler and three infants, I could not turn away from this heartbreaking scene. Howie and I both went to our knees, cameras in hand, and captured the pathos on film. Taking photos of such tragic scenes felt disrespectful, but those mothers were so focused on their sick and dying children that they appeared not to notice us. While on my knees, I said a prayer for these mothers and children, hoping my prayer could encompass this entire region, because I knew that more devastating scenes would follow.

It was hard to believe that such a deadly disease as malaria could be caused by a tiny mosquito. I remembered learning that mosquitos are the most dangerous living thing in the world, because they kill through many different diseases, but that had been just a fact. Now I could see the devastating reality of the mosquito's lethal sting.

Overcome by emotions, I went outside and walked around the clinic building with a member of the local WV staff, hoping he could reassure me that the clinic would cure those beautiful children. We were deep in conversation when, behind the building, we met a man named Alalenga, age seventy, sitting on a bench under a tree, who said he was awaiting treatment for elephantiasis (filariasis). Alalenga's physical appearance shocked me, but I greeted him with respect, looking into his beautiful dark eyes, not wanting to lower my eyes. I'll explain why in a minute, but first an explanation about elephantiasis, a rare disease of the lymphatic system found primarily in northern Ghana and caused by the bite of "tiger mosquitos." Parasitic worms resulting from the bite of tiger mosquitos can lodge in the lymphatic system and cause entire limbs and/or genitals to become enlarged, more commonly in men. Now you understand why I fixed my gaze on his face.

Alalenga pointed to his greatly enlarged right leg and told me that he had contracted the disease as a child. He looked stoic and unembarrassed as he spread his legs to display a massive scrotum, which hung in a rigid mass nearly to the ground beside his malformed leg. Realizing that he probably had experienced a lifetime of psychological trauma and social isolation, I carefully contained the shock and pity that I felt. It occurred to me that Alalenga must have assumed I was a doctor or nurse because of my white jacket, so I played along to protect his feelings. When I asked about his pain and range of mobility, he tried to extend the knee of his enlarged leg, using a cane to push from the back of his ankle and wincing at the effort.

Alalenga's wife, Akoroyia, walked toward her husband slowly, supported by a white cane and holding the shoulder of a small boy. Staring at me through unfocused eyes, she introduced their grandson and explained that she had an advanced case of river blindness and could see only shapes outlined by dim light. I decided to tell Alalenga and Akoroyia that I also had a grandson, in fact, four of them, which caused them both to smile broadly. Having established a bond as grandparents, they agreed to pose for me. But before I raised my camera, I asked the boy to stand in front of his grandfather, covering his private parts. I wanted to remember the face of this stoic old man, the expression of kindness that I saw in his eyes, kindness and perhaps surrender. He seemed to accept his terrible fate and to appreciate the support he received. I felt honored to meet him and to photograph him, truly honored. In the future, this memory would help me to put personal health challenges into perspective.

We learned more about river blindness from three non-profit organizations that were working out of Bongo, near the border of Ghana and Burkina Faso—and yes, home of the bongo drum. UNICEF, Catholic Relief Services, and Peace Corps all focused on health and sanitation issues in the region. They told us that oncho, commonly known as "river blindness," flourished here, because blackflies bred in nearby rivers and streams. When these particular flies bite a human, they deposit the larvae of a parasitic worm, which then produces millions of micro-filariae, tiny worms that cause severe itching and eventual blindness if they enter the eyes. Just writing this, years later, makes me shake my head in wonder, and in disgust, that such awful diseases exist in the 21st Century, still causing havoc in human lives, when it seems they could be eradicated through the intervention of First World science.

The Peace Corps directors said that blackflies populate land near waterways, the richest and most productive lands, and make them unsafe for human habitation. "Because of dangerous fly infestations, most people in this region live on one-third of the land, where the soil is less fertile for their crops," he said. "The other third is too rocky." I thought about Iowa's rich soil and its relatively innocent fly species, which seemed to prefer our house and our hamburgers to the banks of Denison's Boyer River.

From Bongo we drove west for nearly five hours on narrow roads toward small remote villages. World Vision health care professionals led the way in a van, and we watched it sink often into soft, silt-like dirt up to its chassis. We had to follow at a considerable distance because of the dust storm it (and we also) created. Even with the windows closed tightly, we all coughed and sneezed reflexively. But despite such conditions, I felt very happy to have such a rare opportunity to see one of the world's most remote regions, and to share the experience with my friends Angela and Howie, both of whom kept me laughing with humorous comments.

When we arrived in Kubori, we found scores of people waiting for us under a beautiful baobab tree, the iconic African "tree of life." After driving through dust for hours, the scene looked like a desert oasis. It looked like all the people from the village had gathered, dressed in bright colors with their faces painted for a celebration. I wondered how long we had kept them waiting, but then I realized there were no clocks or watches here, and they lived in the moment, dressing, waiting, then celebrating. Time had little meaning. We could learn from them the benefits of patience.

As I photographed the expectant faces of Kubori villagers, I could not help but reflect on what I had seen at the slave fortresses on the southwest coast of Ghana. It occurred to me that the ancestors of these villagers were captured, chained, and thrown into the holds of ships to be sold as slaves in Europe and the Americas. That realization brought a deeper understanding of the interconnectedness of all humanity, as the COVID-19 pandemic made clear.

Two women wearing intricate facial makeup and traditional dresses took my hands and escorted me to the center of the circle, then began wrapping blue and gold striped fabric over my shirt and pants and a turban around my head. Boys and men pounded bongo drums in an enticing beat that soon had everyone dancing in the searing heat, three or four generations together, and I joined the swirl of celebration. Soon all my clothes were soaked with sweat, including the extra layer of Ghanaian fabric, but I danced with abandon, moving through the crowd and smiling at each person I passed, having the time of my life. Just give me a drum beat, and I'm transcended to another dimension.

When the drummers finally stopped, we all walked a short distance to the village center. Along the way, I noticed that many blind adults were using a child's hand or shoulder like the leash of a guide dog, and the impact of river blindness really hit me. It gave me joy that we had come with World Vision doctors, who were already working on patients in a makeshift clinic, leaving the rest of us free to mingle with village people returning to their daily chores. I joined a group of women, who were preparing a garden for planting. Using a rudimentary wooden hoe, they broke up the pale brown soil, created elevated rows, and planted seeds, a familiar task that used to leave my hands calloused every spring and summer.

Before we departed, the chief gathered everyone for a ceremonial send off. He bowed formally, and all the villagers followed his motion, as did our group. Then he presented two small pigs, one to the doctors, who had worked for hours and treated fifty-one patients, and one to Howie. Howie looked startled when he received the squealing piglet, but, being a farmer himself, he realized the generosity that this living gift represented. When I bowed to Howie and called him "Bwana," a Swahili word for "master," I could see the boy Howie in his broad grin.

When the chief handed piglets to the doctors, he bowed to them and gave them thanks and praise, saying, "We are so glad that you came. The eye is the human. You have given life and hope to our people." At that, my own eyes became blinded, blinded by tears. Later, when I asked what would become of the pigs, the WV staff said they would donate them to the clinic where they worked; the valuable protein would feed their patients for a long time.

Filled with emotions, we drove away in silence, processing the juxtaposition of the joy and sadness we had just experienced. These villagers experienced sadness every single day, and I hoped we had brought them joy and the comfort of knowing that the world held caring people. As usual, I had a hard time leaving that village. These visits always seemed too brief, but we had much ground to cover while we still had daylight, and so much to learn.

The doctors told us some extraordinary facts about Guinea worm, a global disease that had nearly been eradicated, except for in this remote region in northern Ghana. The simple process of filtering water through a finely woven cloth will eliminate the tiny water fleas that carry Guinea worm larvae. But here, where stagnant rivers provide the only drinking water, most people lack the knowledge and availability of such filters. Once ingested, Guinea worms can grow up to three feet in length. After living in a body for about six months, worms take on the appearance of spaghetti under the skin. Mature worms begin to emerge after a year, slowly pushing out of the skin through a blister, a painful process that could take two or three months. To relieve pain, infected people often immersed their bodies in water, which then causes the female worm to expel tens of thousands of larvae into the water, thus repeating the cycle.

We had been promised an opportunity to witness medical extractions of Guinea worms, but I never could have imagined what that procedure entailed, an experience out of the Dark Ages. The first took place at Gushiegu, where a nurse named Emmanuel Kuma operated on a six-year-old boy who had worms infecting both of his feet. Kuma told us this would be the fifth such surgery he had performed in the past three days.

After inserting a local painkiller, he identified the worm's head and made a small incision beside it. The boy clenched his teeth and both fists but made no sound, a fact that troubled me, because no child needs to be so stoic. Then, using tweezers, Nurse Kuma gently eased the worm's head out about an inch and wrapped it around a yellow pencil. Keeping the pressure tight, he pulled very slowly, waited for a bit more of the worm to emerge, and then twisted the pencil again. He said it required a steady hand and great patience to keep worms intact; if one broke, an infection would likely result. He said it might take several hours to remove the worms from both of the boy's feet.

To take my mind off the boy's pain and fright, I thought about the abundant fat earthworms that we used to dig out of Mother's flower garden in Denison and use for fishing bait. After folding worms into "S" shapes, we would stick fishhooks through each fold. I could perform that operation effortlessly as a child, feeling no empathy or remorse, but now I felt ashamed of how cruel we children had been to living beings.

When I rode with the health care team to the next village, Sampin, I didn't tell Nurse Kuma about Iowa's fat earthworms. Guinea worms were so skinny that he could not have imagined the difference. Instead, I asked how he kept his hands steady and held his focus for so long. Clearly, that required incredible stamina, and great caring for his patients. He just smiled and told me he would be operating on two children who had advanced cases of Guinea worm at Sampin, the next village.

When we arrived at Sampin, an "operating room" had already been set up under a baobab tree in the village center. A board balanced across two sawhorses would serve as an operating table. I was surprised to see people of all ages sitting in circles around the tree, in full view of the surgical theater. It looked like the entire village had come, not to be entertained but to offer support for both doctor and patient. *It takes a village* came to mind.

The nurse dramatically washed his hands in a bowl and put on latex gloves, while two men lifted a boy about eight years old onto the board. When they removed his pants, I immediately spotted the Guinea worm, just under the skin, stretching from the boy's groin past his knee to the inside of his lower leg.

Dozens of children sat on the ground watching the procedure. Their sober expressions suggested that they had seen this before, or perhaps they previously had been patients. The nurse injected a local painkiller into the boy's upper leg and then, before making an incision, he placed tweezers and a yellow pencil on the board. I would never again use a yellow pencil without thinking about Guinea worm and this supportive village.

After all of my global trips, I find it is hard to leave people and places, but this time it seemed especially wrenching. My emotions had run the gauntlet in Ghana. But I needed to go home and find time to think and to write. As usual, I gave away most of my clothes and nearly all of my money before boarding my plane in Accra. I had to make two stops and clear customs in New York before boarding a plane to Los Angeles. I stored all the film in my large leather travel purse and cradled the purse on my lap during the flights, as Howie often did, valuing the exposed film more highly than anything else, except my passport.

When I reached New York, I called Ron's office to apologize for being completely out of touch for nearly two weeks. It was mid-afternoon in New York, noon in Los Angeles, and I had not yet slept. Ron's assistant answered and said, "I'm so glad you called! Ron had a case come up, and he is now in New York. He wants you to go to his hotel and spend a few days with him there."

I had just enough money to buy lunch at the airport, and my duffle bag held nothing but dirty shoes and a few twice-worn safari clothes, and the African fabrics I received as gifts. And this was New York City, before the proliferation of credit cards and cellphones. But I agreed and jotted down the hotel's address, in the Upper East Side, Manhattan. Yikes! Fancy. Well, at least I had only one purse and one duffle, into which I stuffed my camera case and journals.

At the taxi stand, I found a yellow cab with a black driver, wondering whether his ancestors had come from West Africa. After telling the driver where I had been, I confessed that I did not have very much money and assured him that when we got to my hotel, my husband or the hotel's cashier would come out to pay him. Amazingly, all of that worked out, and I shared a romantic reunion with my husband, managed to buy some new clothes, eat fabulous gourmet dinners, and sleep in a beautiful, clean hotel. But those days in New York seemed so strange to me. I could not speak about the powerful experiences in Ghana that impacted me. In fact, I did not allow myself to embody the depth of my feelings, until now.

The streets of Manhattan—the cars, the lights, the noise, the plethora and richness of consumer goods in shop windows, and most of all the fast-moving people on sidewalks, busy people who rarely made eye contact—all of it gave me an extreme case of culture shock. Here I was in my own country, in a very familiar city, but it all felt foreign to me. My mind had not yet caught up. I longed to dance under a baobab tree, sit with people who were blind and deformed, pray on my knees beside malarial babies and toddlers, and witness a dedicated nurse perform surgery on a stoic child with a yellow pencil. I had felt so at one within the multi-generational circle of villagers, children sitting in the dirt, compassion in their eyes. There my heart was wide open, and I could offer hope, love, and the dignity of being seen and respected—gifts of humanity to those who asked for nothing, nothing more than to be seen as valuable human beings.

As I walked the streets of Manhattan, I felt torn between two worlds, in a strange kind of limbo.

OPPOSITE: This home in of Accra displayed respect for the USA, and it called on the Almighty for the gift all mothers require, patience; ABOVE: Ghana's capital city, Accra, boasted colorful buildings that bore inspirational names and mottos. I felt certain God would assume the photo shop meant "accept" instead of "except."

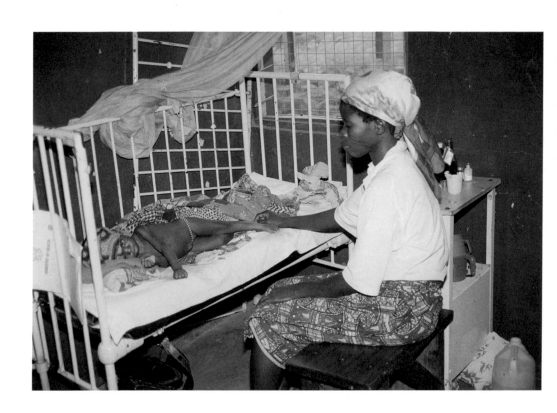

ABOVE: A toddler girl suffering from both malaria and meningitis was treated at a medical clinic in Tamale, northern Ghana, as her mother looked on hopelessly; OPPOSITE: In this beautiful face and erect posture I saw strength and dignity but not acceptance. She knew that she had been destined for something greater, and I hope she found it.

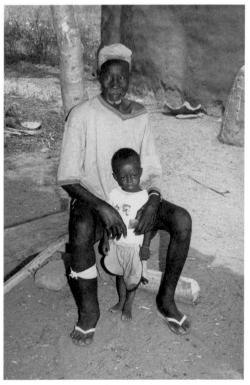

OPPOSITE, TOP AND BOTTOM RIGHT: Blindness is common in northern Ghana, where blackflies cause eye diseases called trachoma and oncho ("river blindness"). Patients awaited treatment by World Vision doctors; OPPOSITE, BOTTOM LEFT, Alalenga, seventy, suffered from elephantiasis, a disease borne by tiger mosquitos, which caused the enlargement of both his right leg and his scrotum, which was covered by his grandson; ABOVE: I could not help wondering whether the baby was her sibling or her child. Either way, this girl already understood that life is not fair.

8a

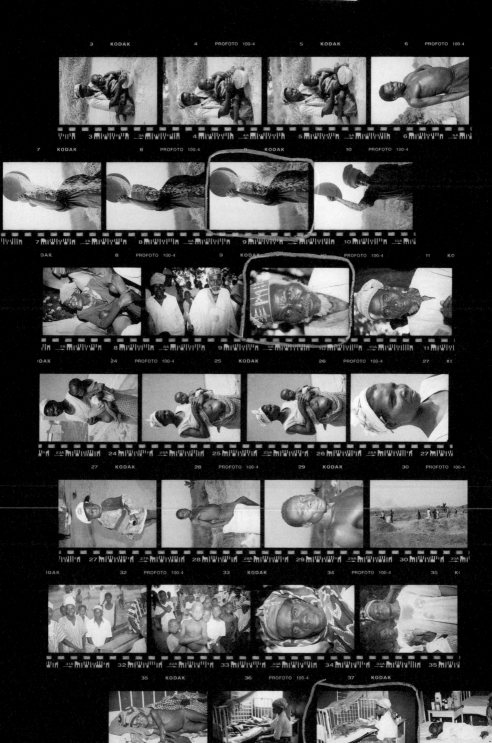

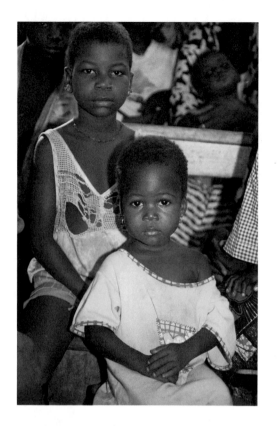

TOP: At Sampin village, everyone formed a surgical theater to watch the World Vision medical team perform delicate surgeries on children who had mature Guinea worms in their bodies. Young spectators expressed so much empathy that I wondered whether they had experienced infections; BOTTOM, LEFT AND RIGHT: World Vision surgeons removed Guinea worms from a boy's groin and a boy's foot; OPPOSITE: Women and children trekked long distances to get water from dirty rivers and carry it home, water that might have contained Guinea worm eggs that could grow in a human body if ingested; FOLLOWING SPREAD: At Kubori in remote northern Ghana, the entire village awaited our arrival under a baobab tree. I expressed gratitude and then danced with joy to bongo drums (photo by Howard G. Buffett).

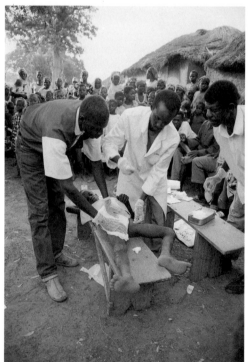

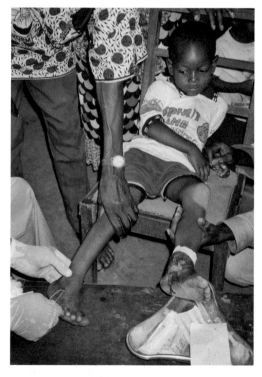

Enterprising boys at an AIDS orphan center in Malawi made their own toys from recycled wire.

CHAPTER TWENTY-SEVEN

THE WARM HEART OF AFRICA AND 17 RESPIRATORS

HIV/AIDS orphans cry "Mama," and teenaged
girls describe ritual rape by their elders

MALAWI, JUNE 2003

During the COVID-19 global pandemic, in March 2020, I became obsessed with tracking numbers of cases and deaths around the world, searching for news about countries where I had traveled and developed lasting friendships. When I discovered a story about Malawi, the "Warm Heart of Africa," my heart sank. Malawi already suffered greatly from the large percent of its 18.5 million people who were infected with HIV/AIDS. The article predicted that Malawi could be absolutely devastated by the dreaded new virus. The entire nation had only seventeen respirators and twenty-five ICU beds.

I felt heartbroken but not surprised. To prevent COVID-19, Americans were being advised to wash our hands constantly, but most people in Malawi do not have running water or electricity. The amazing people I met in Malawi during my trip there in 2003 with the Global AIDS Interfaith Alliance (GAIA) came to mind. I recalled their faces and the strength of their determination to survive

HIV/AIDS—indelible memories that I captured in photographs. Now I prayed for their protection from yet another invisible disease. For me, Malawi was not just a name or a skinny vertical piece of land on the map of Africa between Mozambique and Zambia.

Thinking of Malawi evoked the smell of moist, warm air, a fragrance unique to sub-Saharan Africa, which always made me feel I had come home in some fundamental way. The scent and color palette filled my senses and lifted my spirit. I pictured the rhythm of female bodies swaying under bags of pota-toes, or trays of eggs, that they balanced on their heads while carrying babies strapped to their backs with amazing strength and balance. But those physically strong women and girls did not have the strength or opportunity to negotiate for their human rights, even the right to refuse sex. And then there are the chil-dren—children with runny noses, shaved heads covered in scabies, pleading eyes begging to be seen, and arms reaching out to be embraced. Malawi breaks the heart of any traveler brave enough to venture deep into its soul.

I learned about Malawi from the founder of GAIA, Bill Rankin, an Episcopal priest who in 2003 gave a talk about HIV/AIDS at All Saints Church in Pasadena, California. Bill had served on the church's staff as a young priest at the time when ASC founded the AIDS Service Center, a preeminent non-profit organi-zation that provided extensive services and advocacy for Southern Californians infected with HIV/AIDS.

My notes from Bill's talk that day state that five million new cases of AIDS occurred in the world between 2002 and 2003, raising the total to forty-two million. I found that number astounding! "Seventy-five percent of AIDS victims live in sub-Saharan Africa," Bill had emphasized with gravity, "mostly women aged fifteen to forty-nine." He then reminded us that these were the women needed to birth and teach the children, to nurse the sick, work the fields, and hold families and communities together. "More than one million AIDS orphans are struggling to survive, just in Malawi," he concluded.

Bill Rankin founded GAIA, based in San Francisco, in 2000, in partnership with his wife, Sally, a PhD professor of nursing. GAIA's mission focuses on advocacy and activism in Malawi, a long sliver of a country in southeastern Africa that continues to have one of the highest infection rates. Bill mentioned that because of its friendly people, Malawi is often called "The Warm Heart of Africa." I smiled at that, because I've always thought of Iowa and the Midwest as "The Warm Heart of America."

Malawi, Bill said, is about the same size as the state of Pennsylvania, and it had more HIV/AIDS cases in 2003 than the U.S. and Canada combined. Up to 45 percent of its adult population suffered some stage of the deadly disease, which can live in a body for up to ten years while waging war on the immune system. The life expectancy for women in Malawi had dropped from age sixty-one to thirty-nine in the past seven years, Bill reported, adding that women were six times more likely to contract AIDS than men. Women were especially vulnerable because they could not refuse sexual intercourse even if they knew that their husbands carried the disease. Therefore, they had no way to prevent its transmission from their husbands or to their unborn babies. I wanted to scream.

As I listened to Bill describe the vulnerability of women in Malawi, I thought about the countless rape survivors I had met around the world. What if the traumatic sexual violence they suffered had also infected their blood with a deadly virus? Compelled by that thought, and by a sudden strong desire to hold AIDS orphans in my lap, I joined Bill and Sally on a trip to Malawi in June 2003, along with Dr. Don Thomas, director of emergency room medicine at Pasadena's Huntington Hospital, and his wife, Mary, an attorney.

When we landed in Lilongwe, the capital city, I realized that Malawi represented a different kind of war zone than others I had visited. Here, a life-threatening battle was being waged against a fearsome disease. I had packed carefully for this trip, bringing three cameras and several journals to document AIDS in Malawi, but I had not prepared myself emotionally, and I felt a rush of fear down my spine. Even the welcoming scent of African air could not relieve my sudden anxiety in the beginning. The risk of getting HIV did not worry me. In countless refugee camps, I had hugged people who suffered from skin infections, tuberculosis, and other contagious diseases, and miraculously I had never gotten ill. But fear is not a rational emotion. Even though I knew that HIV/AIDS passes through bodily fluids, and it poses no risk through normal social contact, I could not quite shake my trepidation, but I forged ahead, determined to meet and interact with many people, as I always did. And after the first encounter with people in Lilongwe, I managed to push the fear of diseases out of my mind.

The main program for our trip would be a four-day conference for clergy, which GAIA planned to host in Lilongwe. But before the conference began, we had an opportunity to visit nearby villages. In the first village, a woman named Grace captured my heart. Grace, a single woman, served as grandmother to fifty-six AIDS orphans! Grace took in her own grandchildren after their parents died and then, over the next few years, she assumed responsibility for fifty additional orphans. Her extended family of children lived all together in a one-room hut inside a primitive reed fence encircling Grace's barren property.

When we entered that property, children appeared everywhere, some sleeping outside on straw mats or bare ground. Girls seven or eight years old were carrying babies on their backs, above slim hips that had not yet begun to curve, already demonstrating the protective instincts of a mother. I knelt to pick up a baby boy who was crawling on the ground in over-sized pants that impeded his progress, and immediately a toddler girl, who looked less than a year older, placed a protective hand on the baby's back. He must have been her baby brother, because she gave me a stern look of warning that left no doubt who was in charge of his safety. A faded plaid dress, also too large, hung off the girl's shoulder as she leaned over the baby, facing me down courageously and earning my compliance. I snapped a photo before backing off, sorry that I had nothing to give the girl except my highest respect.

Grandmother Grace. Grandmother Grace. I have to repeat her name, because all these years later, she is still magical to me. Her hair bound in a dirty blue scarf, she sat like a Buddha at the entrance to her primitive home and seemed unbothered by the countless children climbing all over her. I had a sense that her body was used so often as a jungle gym that she didn't even notice.

"Many of these little ones were born HIV positive," Grace said, closing her eyes for a moment. "I want to make their brief lives happy, but love is the only medicine I can give them." Grace appeared to be ageless, her face unlined and her soft smile defying the exhaustion she surely felt. As she sat calmly with us strangers from a foreign land, I dubbed her the African Queen. I had worked hard to parent only three children, and I could not conceive of the responsibilities and burdens she had undertaken. She told us that her neighbors brought clothing and also food from their gardens to help feed the children—but still, just think of the work. At that moment, I saw her as the strongest person I had ever met, and I have not changed my opinion.

We then visited a program in the southern outskirts of Lilongwe, where volunteers brought AIDS orphans from surrounding neighborhoods to a park every Saturday, an opportunity for them to play games and eat a nutritious lunch. Although I'd been warned that there would be hundreds of children, I felt unprepared for the mass surrounding me during a brief walk from our van to a dirt playground. Children with curious eyes and big smiles suddenly materialized and formed concentric circles around me, most likely attracted by the Nikon camera I held; cameras are always a magnet for children.

Most of these kids had some form of illness, skinned knees, or bloody abrasions. In many Third World countries, I had held lots of children with snotty noses and skin ailments quite comfortably, but here the numbers kept growing, and I knew that I would be buried if I sat down. I began to feel overwhelmed as the circumference grew, with children swirling around me like a school of fish, looking into scores of upturned faces of children pleading to be noticed. As I tried to capture them all within the frame of the camera lens, I felt rather dizzy. With no time to change to a wide-angle lens, I turned slowly clockwise, photographing the mob scene a quarter of the circle at a time. As I focused and clicked, bigger boys pushed their way to the front, forcing girls and smaller children out of range. The boys made faces and grinned at me through cracked lips and missing front teeth.

Just when I felt the children become a bit more aggressive, a small voice called out "Mama." That clarion call inspired a chorus of "Mama. Mama. Mama. Mama. Mama," which grew in number and volume, with arms reaching up to me. The dam of my composure broke suddenly, and tears washed my face. Wrapping both arms around my camera, so it would not hurt anyone, I carefully made my way through the crush and rushed to the van. I could always endure a heavy load of emotions, but this experience simply overwhelmed me. I laid down on the back seat of the van and surrendered to grief, sobbing within the protective vehicle. A picture of Grace, the Buddha, came to mind, and I felt like a coward. But I was not alone. The others soon joined me in the van, and we drove in silence all the way back to the city, holding on to feelings that had nearly drowned us all.

The clergy conference opened the next day with a powerful talk by Bill Rankin about the need to reduce the fear and denial attached to HIV. Malawi, as a former British protectorate, had many Anglican churches. GAIA worked through those churches to teach clergy about the prevention of and treatment for HIV/AIDS and the need to overcome the stigma that prevented people from getting tested. Later, during our long drive to southern Malawi, we had time to discuss what we had learned and explore ideas for encouraging churches to serve as a healing force of information and advocacy.

After hearing so much tragedy and grief, I was glad to leave the city and see the beautiful countryside, the lush green tea plantations covering hillsides and the stately palm trees standing as sentries to mark borders of fields that had no fences. Apparently, Malawi had no barbed wire barriers, such as those that enclosed Iowa's cornfields. Lacking borders, the many shades of green blended into each other, like a watercolor painting that bled and fused verdant shades. Those palettes of green helped to heal my emotional turmoil, as they brought me into alignment with the bucolic environment of my childhood.

In every village, vendors lined the streets. The greatest number of roadside shops sold simple wooden coffins, coffins that came in a variety of lengths, the smallest being for babies. I felt a bit disrespectful taking photos of coffin stands, but the irony of merchant signs, such as *The Comfort Coffin Shop*, brought some humorous relief to the deep sadness we all felt.

As we drove across the country, we toured many small hospitals and learned appalling facts about health care in Malawi. They had only one physician for every fifty-sevn thousand people. Three pharmacists served the entire nation of eleven million, as did only one pathologist, very few lab technicians, and no dermatologists. Nurses, it seemed, were expected to cover all health care needs, and because of that burden, many nurses reportedly were leaving the profession for higher-paying jobs, such as secretarial work. Nurses at medical facilities across the country complained about the critical shortage of basic supplies, such as latex gloves, masks, IV tubes, sterilizers, and even sterile water.

Hospitals also lacked supplies of clean blood for emergency infusions. These poor conditions exposed health care workers to infections.

I had looked forward to touring the Nkhoma Mission Hospital, one of the more developed health care facilities. But even before we entered the hospital, we realized that "developed" was a relative term. A dirt yard surrounded the hospital, and patients awaiting appointments sat in clusters on the pale amber dirt, mostly mothers and their children. Here and there small satchels of food lay open, giving the impression of a picnic ground.

Inside the ward, women in earlier stages of labor sat on folding chairs in a hallway, dressed not in hospital gowns but in their own bright fabrics. In the labor and delivery area, twelve narrow beds placed close together held silent women who clearly were enduring the final stages of birth. None of the women, in either labor or delivery, made a sound. (I have to tell you that silence in a maternity ward is not normal. During my own three experiences of labor and childbirth, even with the benefit of sterile conditions, comfortable hospital beds, and a trained medical staff, I had been neither brave nor silent.)

As we entered the post-delivery room, I noticed a new mother who looked pale and feverish. She had captured my attention by moaning when I passed her bed, and I asked a nurse about her. Agnes was her name, age thirty-five. She had just delivered a stillborn infant and was suffering from malaria, but she was not HIV positive. Then the nurse broke my heart by adding that Agnes had four children at home. "She lost a lot of blood and may die soon from anemia," the nurse said, "because the hospital has no clean blood supply." Oh no! But of course, in a country rife with HIV/AIDS, safe blood donors would be rare. But I had clean blood. I had donated blood to the American Red Cross twice a year and had no fear of needles.

I asked Agnes's blood type and discovered that it matched my own, O positive, so I donated a pint directly to Agnes. Dr. Thomas performed the transfusion with sterile needles and IV tubes that he had brought from California in his black leather medical bag. As I watched my blood flow into Agnes, I added another a prayer that it would give her a chance to live. I honestly felt privileged to do one small thing that might help to save a life in this devastated country, where the mere fact of being born female posed a lifelong threat. The next morning, Don asked whether I wanted him to call the clinic and check on

Agnes's condition. Hmm. I considered his question for a minute and answered, "No." I just wanted to imagine my blood sister, Agnes, returning home to her four children, and holding on to that hope felt immensely important to me.

We then drove through several small "traditional" villages to visit a program called the Thunga Cooperative Circle, which operated seven primary schools serving fifteen such villages with a combined population of about forty thousand people. We learned that the death rate from AIDS had spiked here recently because, as a local GAIA social worker told us, many young people had been diagnosed as HIV positive. She blamed the practice of casual sex among young people, explaining that the elders accepted and even encouraged such practice. Sally, Mary, and I discussed that shocking information as we walked around the village.

A teenager named Catherine suddenly approached us and whispered that some of her friends wanted to speak with us. While Bill and Don went to meet with village elders, we three slipped away quietly and followed Catherine to a small wood-framed building, where we found about a dozen girls sitting inside on the floor, in near darkness. When our eyes adjusted to the low light, we saw that a sheet of coarse muslin was taped across the only window in what they described as a school classroom. Catherine cautioned that this meeting had to be kept secret, because they all risked severe punishment if discovered talking to us. Catherine explained that they wanted to tell us about initiation practices performed by village elders, so we agreed and listened in rapt attention, at first only to the shuffling of feet. Then the sad recital began:

"The old men took us to a camp in the forest. They said we had to have sex with them to prove that we were virgins," a girl whispered, "and they said they would teach us how to please a man so we could be married." Two girls translated softly in English, while the others spoke in the local Chichewa dialect. I missed a few words but understood the powerful import. We learned that the elders had raped the girls and then checked to see whether blood came out.

"The old men passed us around and made us have intercourse many times," another girl told us. "I cried for my mother and sister," a small thin girl added. "Why had they not warned me?" Why indeed! I longed to hug her and cry with her, but I focused on breathing softly and listening quietly, barely able to contain my rage. When Sally asked what happened to the boys their age, Catherine told us that the elders took boys into the forest and circumcised them by cutting their penile foreskin, using one dirty razor on all of them.

"We heard that several boys developed infections that took weeks to heal. And some got HIV," she said. I recognized Catherine, as well as these other brave girls, as leaders and potential health care workers.

Catherine continued, "Before we girls were allowed to go home, the elders advised us to have sex with many men and boys in order to prove our maturity. That is so unfair," she said, raising her voice, "because girls have to have their blood tested before marriage, but boys do not. If a girl gets a positive HIV test, no one will marry her."

The old men held that power over these girls, who would have no real future if they did not secure husbands. I looked at Sally's shocked face and noticed tears on her cheeks that matched my own. When we left, the three of us relieved our feelings of outrage by suggesting ways we wanted to punish the elders for their cruel initiation practices, some of them surgical. When we told Bill and Don, who had just met with village elders, they said nothing was mentioned about this barbaric practice. I wondered how common it was in traditional villages like this one, but could guess the answer to that question.

I did not meet any of the old men. Lucky for them!

It was hard for me to leave the Warm Heart of Africa. Countless children had begged me to be their mama. Vulnerable girls had reached out for guardians to protect them from sexual violence. Villages needed grandmothers to adopt AIDS orphans, and new mothers required clean blood, all such critical needs. I felt helpless.

GAIA designed an ambitious program for education and action on all things related to HIV/AIDS in neighborhoods and villages, a "ground up" program that trained and empowered women to be leaders. Starting in the southern part of Malawi, GAIA would build a model that could later be replicated throughout the country.

The southern part of Malawi would be divided into five major districts, with a professionally trained female social worker assigned for each, and they would work under the supervision of a country director. Those five women leaders would then divide each of their districts into five areas, then train and hire a female head for each area. The division and pyramid pattern of five women leaders could continue into every neighborhood and village, with each woman leader receiving extensive training in order to take charge of all things related to HIV/AIDS on the local level, from testing and condom distribution to end-of-life hospice care. The number five, Bill Rankin explained, provided women leaders sufficient power to overcome challenges to their authority. If one died or left for any reason, another woman would replace her immediately.

Once the program received funding and got underway, infection and death rates from the devastating bloodborne disease slowed substantially. Elder male leaders in traditional villages could not help but notice the significant drop in rates of sickness and death. Many village chiefs eventually allowed blood tests and other prevention measures to be conducted. It is hard to know whether teenagers were still subjected to sexual initiation rituals, but we three women made sure that the connection between those rituals and the transmission of HIV/AIDS was part of the leadership training. While I still worry about vulnerable children, they now have women protectors in their villages in whom they can confide.

So how did this impressive GAIA program receive its initial funding? When I returned home from Malawi in the summer of 2003, I felt overwhelmed by the devastation I had witnessed, but also filled with hope that the training and empowerment of women would make a huge difference. I connected with Melinda Gates and told her about my recent trip to Malawi and what I had learned about HIV/AIDS in that country, knowing that she had a great interest in eradicating the disease and that she championed the human rights of women. When I described GAIA's hopeful plans to elevate women leaders at every level of society, Melinda understood both the problems and the promise. The Bill and Melinda Gates Foundation generously donated one million dollars to launch the program, an enormous gift that made all the difference.

In 2019, Melinda wrote and published a book entitled *The Moment of Lift*, in which she told stories about girls and women she met on trips to developing countries around the world on behalf of the Foundation. Her inspiring stories described cultural barriers and biases that held women back and stressed the importance of educating girls and supporting women leaders.

"When you lift up women," Melinda said, "you lift up humanity."

When I read Melinda's book, I thought about Malawi. I suddenly realized that the Gates Foundation's gift of a million dollars had been that *moment of lift* for the girls and women of Malawi, the nation of warm-hearted people that lives in my consciousness.

Coffins are the primary growth industry in Malawi, where 45 percent of adults are HIV positive.

ABOVE: We visited many coffin shops, including at Wodala and Mchesi, but my favorite was the "Comfort Coffin Shop," which the owners would not allow me to photograph; OPPOSITE: There are so many AIDS orphans in Malawi, children who lose both parents and then have to parent their younger siblings. I wept for babies carrying babies but marveled at their mature protective instincts; FOLLOWING SPREAD: This iconic picture of women in colorful clothing carrying cans on their heads looks beautiful, but their faces reveal the weight of their burdens.

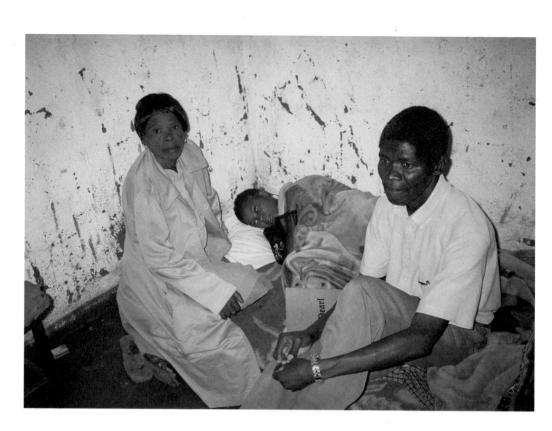

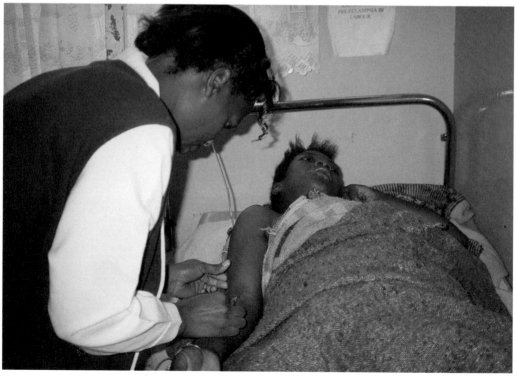

OPPOSITE, TOP: A young woman lay dying of AIDS, surrounded by her grieving mother and her devastated husband, a truck driver, who confessed that he transmitted the deadly disease to his wife; OPPOSITE, BOTTOM: A nurse at Nkhoma Mission Hospital prepared Agnes, who had lost a lot of blood giving birth to a stillborn baby, to receive a direct transfusion of clean blood from me, because the hospital had none. It would give her a chance to go home to her four living children; ABOVE: When I knelt to photograph a crawling baby boy, his toddler sister ran to protect him. Her strong maternal response simply stunned me, and she earned my eternal respect.

PREVIOUS SPREAD: At the Kauma Youth Center, AIDS orphans circled around me in a crush, crying, "Mama, mama, mama, mama," and I became a sobbing puddle of grief; ABOVE: This joyful young girl supported twin infants and two toddlers. There simply are no words; OPPOSITE: The eyes say it all.

WAR AND FORGIVENESS

Children in Crossfire
18 July 2007

I speak here today as a mother, a grandmother of 8 little boys, and as a person who has travelled a great deal to some of the most devastated places in the world. Some of you live in those places. Basically, I am a mommy who raised 3 children and worked the past 40 years as a volunteer first in my community and then in the wo.

For the past 25 years, I have gone to war zones on 5 continents — both during and after conflicts with human rights + humanitarian orgs. It is an honor to participate in this important conference focused on the most vulnerable victims of war — children.

Thanks to Richard Mo... ...ing this program and to ... and teenagers, for ca... these difficult issu... away and hoping ... work for peace ...

You have take... making a differen... to pour your compassi...

UNIVERSAL
DECLARATION
OF
HUMAN RIGHTS

Entries/Entrées Visas

17th & 18th July 2007
City Hotel and Millennium Forum
Derry/Londonderry

International ...

...TH DALAI LAMA OF TIBET

...an of peace. In 1989 he was
...his non-violent struggle for the
...ntly advocated policies of non-
...me aggression. He also became
...recognized for his concern for global

... more than 62 countries spanning 6
...h presidents, prime ministers and crowned
...e has held dialogues with the heads of
...any well-known scientists.

...ss has received over 84 awards, honorary
...es in recognition of his message of peace, non-
...ce, the ...gious understanding, universal responsibility and
...passion. His Holiness has also written more than 70 books.

...is Holiness describes himself as
...a simple Buddhist monk".

JANE OLSON, CHAIR, HUMAN RIGHTS WATCH

Jane Olson has devoted her life to international just... ...man
humanitarian work. She chairs the International Boa...
Rights Watch and serves on the board of the Salzburg...
for International Studies. She also chairs the board of the...
Survivors Network and recently joined the board of the...
Council on International Policy and is a member of the...
Foreign Relations. Jane has received numerous a...
inaugural 2005 Eleanor Roosevelt Award f...
...ievement Award from the ...
...ity Achievement ...

A Promise
for the Future
An International Conference
on Children's Rights

Jane Olson
Human Rights Watch

DONEGAL

NORTHERN
IRELAND

IRISH
SEA

FOR GOD
AND ULSTER

Page

Former Secretary of the U.S. Air Force and Space Force Robert Channing Seamans Jr. and his daughter May Seamans Baldwin on an airport runway on their first visit to Hanoi and North Vietnam, a region he knew well through maps and infrared images.

CHAPTER TWENTY-EIGHT

THE WAKE OF A WAR WITH NO WINNERS

*Former enemies and a father and daughter
inspire hope for humanity*

VIETNAM, MARCH 2004

Of all my experiences witnessing the consequences of war, this trip to Vietnam was the most powerful. Imagine going to North Vietnam with the former U.S. Secretary of the Air Force on his first journey to that "enemy territory" and traveling with him to sites he previously had seen only through infrared images captured by surveillance planes. I had that privilege when I went to Vietnam and Cambodia with Landmine Survivors Network in March 2004. It gives me chills even now to think about that journey from his point of view.

At that time, nearly thirty years after the Vietnam War ended, the country still needed a lot of help with recovery, but very few international humanitarian organizations were working in Vietnam, with the remarkable exception of the Vietnam Veterans of America, U.S. soldiers who had served in Vietnam and knew firsthand the critical wounds left behind, including some 350,000 tons of unexploded ordnance (UXO).

Jerry White and I first went to Hanoi in 1999, seeking governmental approval for the establishment of a new LSN peer support program, and then returned in 2004 to visit that newest program. A large delegation of LSN board members and supporters accompanied us on the second trip. Our itinerary included a tour of Hanoi and an overnight train trip to the Demilitarized Zone (DMZ) in the central part of Vietnam, the Quang Binh Province, where our newest LSN program focused its work. Of all our programs around the world, this one arguably served the most heavily mine-affected area with the greatest percentage of war-injured survivors. We would then fly to Cambodia, which also had a large population of amputees.

Our delegation included a "secret" guest, one whose identity the staff and I had been asked not to reveal to other members of the delegation—Robert Channing Seamans Jr., former U.S. Secretary of the Air Force and Space Force. An aeronautical engineer and MIT professor, Mr. Seamans served as deputy administrator of NASA before being appointed by President Richard Nixon as civilian head of the U. S. Air Force, responsible for overseeing the air campaign of the Vietnam War from early 1969 through May 1973. Secretary Seamans came with his daughter, May Seamans Baldwin, a friend of LSN. When May had accepted an invitation to join our delegation, she asked whether she could invite her father. To her surprise and ours, he said yes.

May Seamans Baldwin, the fourth of five children, told me that she was just becoming a teenager when her father accepted the Pentagon job and moved their family to Washington, D.C.

When her family arrived in Washington, May said, anti-war protestors were marching in the streets. "Members of the SDS, Students for a Democratic Society, came to my school and talked about the war in Vietnam," May told me. "They read a list of bad men. When they read my father's name, calling him a bad man, I felt mortified by his work. But I knew that he had accepted that position, Secretary of the Air Force, because he hoped to end the war. He just got caught up in what everyone else wanted to do," she said.

"I never talked to my father about SDS or the others," May added. "My friends were peeing on the steps of the Pentagon while my dad was working inside. We were a nice 'WASPy' family, and we just never talked about 'the elephant in the middle of the room,'" she confessed. "We children knew not to talk about it," she said, explaining that she had felt somewhat estranged from her father all these years because they'd never reconciled that important issue in their lives.

Thinking about my own father, I asked May whether her father had served in World War II. "He couldn't go to World War II because he was colorblind," May answered, adding that she believed he felt guilty about that and wanted to make it up by doing his patriotic duty in the Pentagon, even though he did not believe in war. That surprised me and greatly elevated my respect for him. "My older brother was at Harvard during the war," May continued, "and he worked for the SDS. We never talked about that either. Dad never said anything about war protestors," she said, "but one night he came into my bedroom and ripped a poster off my wall, a poster of Allen Ginsberg wearing a top hat made from an American flag. Then he walked away without saying a word."

I remembered times when I had felt my own father's unspoken anger, like when I dropped his gun in the river. The silence that day had been more than I could bear. But my father died when he was only fifty-six, too young, and we never talked about things that mattered, that matter still. Perhaps because of that, I closely watched May and her father, whom we called "Bob," during this journey and thought about my own father. I attached my father-daughter issues to Bob and May, hoping they would experience understanding and a reconciliation.

"How did you get Bob to come with you?" I asked May. "Well," she answered, "I just casually mentioned the trip to my dad and was shocked when he said he wanted to come. There had been other opportunities for him to go to North Vietnam, and he knew this was a landmines group, so maybe he just wanted to be with me," she concluded, a question mark in her voice.

"Dad asked if he could go incognito, under an assumed name, and that was no problem, since I used my married name." Then May and I laughed, remembering what had happened at dinner the very first night in Hanoi. While we were introducing ourselves around a long table, Bob stood up and announced he was "Robert Seamans Jr., former secretary of the U.S. Air Force." Jerry and I were shocked; May told me that she had wanted to dive under the table, but everyone else simply took it in stride.

Our tour of Hanoi included a visit to the Ho Chi Minh Mausoleum and Ho Chi Minh home. Having seen Lenin's tomb in Moscow, I felt prepared to view the Viet Cong leader's remains—but an experience at his home really jolted me. We walked through the beautiful Presidential Palace grounds and came to a humble cottage, where the guide stopped and asked us to gather around while he described Ho Chi Minh as a humble leader, a simple man, who had chosen to live in this small cottage instead of the palace, so he would never forget he was one of the people. The guide talked about their "American War," twenty years of fighting that ended in 1975. For them, he explained, it had been a war of independence, beginning with a revolutionary war against France to end its colonialist domination.

Noticing that Bob was shaking his head, I moved closer to eavesdrop on his conversation with May. "We just didn't understand him," I heard Bob say. "We just didn't get it." He shook his head again and added, "We were on the wrong side of this war."

I nodded my head. World War II was easy to classify as a "just war." Hitler had to be stopped. So did Japan. Both enemies and imperatives were clear, and I always felt proud that my father volunteered for the U.S. Navy and served in the South Pacific. But the Vietnam War, planned by the World War II generation and fought by their sons, had no clear justification and no winners. The U.S. simply declared victory and left abruptly, abandoning our South Vietnamese allies, many thousands of whom fled for their lives.

In Hanoi, the friendliness of ordinary North Vietnamese people surprised everyone. They greeted us warmly, eager to ask about education and work opportunities in the United States, and with no apparent resentment for the war that had killed and maimed a million Vietnamese. One reason, perhaps, was that now a large percentage of the population was young and had no personal memory of the war. Their youth gave energy to this recovering society, but historical reminders, elderly people and ancient monuments, kept it anchored in tradition.

When we visited the DMZ region in central Vietnam, I spoke with an old woman sitting on the bank of a rice paddy, wearing a conical hat woven from bamboo reeds. She said she had stepped on an unexploded bomb in that same rice paddy many years before and lost an arm and a leg. When she told me that she comes here often, I realized she wanted to visit the place that holds her body parts, as if it were a cemetery. That old woman broke my heart, as did the miles and miles of graves and family tombs filled beyond capacity. It's always about human loss. Too much loss.

When we watched a demining procedure in central Vietnam, Bob asked many questions about the operation, but he did not give voice to the big questions that no doubt plagued him, whether and why he had ordered the bombing missions that devastated this country and left countless UXOs, deadly debris that had continued to kill and maim civilians three decades later.

We visited a small village where our local LSN had concentrated its outreach. Because there were so many amputee victims of landmines and UXOs here, we divided into groups of two or three to visit them in their small homes. Jerry and Bob were assigned to meet with an old man who had served as a high-ranking officer in the Viet Cong army. I watched them, the tallest two men in our delegation, as they bent nearly in half to enter the door. Once inside, they were offered yellow plastic chairs, the kind used by pre-schools and kindergartens back home. I held my breath when they sat down, hoping that the chairs would not collapse, and then I sat on a square pillow on the floor behind them, leaving space for the occasional breeze coming through the door, which provided momentary relief from the dense heat and humidity. How on earth, I wondered, did American soldiers in full battle gear survive in this stifling climate?

In a back corner of the room, a woven hammock hung above a single bed with a thin mattress and two pillows, an improvised bunk bed. Along the back wall, a decoratively carved wooden plank served as a mantle, holding treasured family possessions, vases, candlesticks, and a teapot—always a teapot. The space created a sanctuary for reflection and healing by two former enemies, each of whom had sent countless young men to their deaths.

A tentative conversation began, with long pauses for interpretation that allowed Bob and Jerry to exchange encouraging looks. When the subject of bombing raids and escape tunnels came up, the two military leaders leaned in, talking softly, their foreheads nearly touching. Only our petite female interpreter could hear them, and her face reflected the solemnity of the moment. I realized that this exchange could take place only because the former U.S. Air Force Secretary was traveling with a humanitarian group, one that had earned the trust and gratitude of the local people.

When I told May about that conversation, she said, "My dad always worked very hard to be on the same level as other people and meet them where they are." Then, after a long pause, she added, her voice choking, "He faced what he did."

Like all tourists, we visited the Hanoi Hilton, an infamous prison where Senator John McCain and other captured American pilots had been held and tortured for many years. It had been converted into a museum of sorts. A big square table in the center of the museum featured a topographical map of Hanoi and the surrounding region, with red arrows pointing to the Hanoi Hilton and to the lake where McCain's plane had crashed.

All twenty members of our delegation gathered around that table and silently watched Bob Seamans, as he studied the landscape and processed his memories, no doubt looking for markers from the infrared scenes that had informed his instructions to bomber squads. He leaned over the table, then straightened and walked to the opposite side, as we backed up in unison to give him space.

"There it is," Bob exclaimed, pointing to a small model of a building, "that's where the pilots were being held before." He became animated, talking with both hands, as he described how military intelligence had identified that site, a few miles outside Hanoi, as the place where downed American pilots were being held.

"Pentagon officials planned a strategic raid to rescue our guys, plotted down to the smallest detail. I gave the orders for a rescue mission," Bob said. "We dropped special forces guys very near here," he added, pointing to a field near the building, disappointment already showing in his face. "But the 'other side' had moved them into Hanoi that very day." He just stated a fact with no excuses and no further explanation, but the question *what if?* hung in the room above that table.

May instinctively moved to her father and put her arm around his back, giving comfort to the reluctant warrior who had carried heavy burdens all these years. Clearly, she had never heard this story, a fact that spoke volumes about her father's integrity. Both stood with their heads bowed for a long moment, and then he turned and embraced May. It seemed that time has collapsed for him, and he was holding his teenaged daughter.

During the second phase of our trip, the journey to Cambodia, May recalled a shocking incident that took place in the midst of the war, an event that helped her to understand the burdens her father carried. "We were on a family vacation in Vail, Colorado," May said. "Every morning, Dad did his exercises on the floor while watching *The Today Show*, and that's what he was doing when he learned that we were bombing Cambodia," she said. "The Joint Chiefs of Staff made that decision in his absence, but my father had to take the hits for it." I could hear compassion and love in her voice.

Before I heard that story, I had wanted to ask Bob how he felt about all the amputees we saw in Cambodia, but I already knew the answer to my question. Although professional to the core, Bob was a compassionate man and a loving father. I had no doubt that the crippling of Cambodia had hurt him, but he kept that pain to himself, as my father would have done.

May later told me, "That trip really was a powerful healing for us. When we got back home, we were so in sync that my mother noticed." Four years later, when I learned that Bob had died at the age of eighty-nine, I fervently hoped that he had been able to release regret and understand his important life of service.

This journey of reconciliation provided personal healing for me also. I realized that I could honor my own father by remembering precious moments when we had been in sync and thereby achieve personal healing from growing up with a father affected by war. My brother Jack, who was drafted to Vietnam right out of college, was fortunately not one of the fifty-eight thousand American casualties. But war scarred the lives of both my father and brother.

Perhaps World War II and the coincidence of my birth nine months after Pearl Harbor gave direction and purpose to my life, inspiring me to visit so many war zones over the years. None had felt so personal as Vietnam, the war that tore apart my generation of Americans. I met no enemies in Vietnam, only friendly and forgiving people. Their humanity informed my certainty that the real enemy is war itself.

OPPOSITE: I will always think of Vietnam as green, the verdant green of rice paddies, where workers stood in water, bent at the waist, and of jungles, where the young men of my generation fought and died; ABOVE: It was hard to think of this kind and gentle man as once wearing fatigues, which U.S. soldiers called "pajamas," and crawling through underground tunnels to defend his country, but he had been a Viet Cong leader.

OPPOSITE: A "tree house" on water provided shelter from the sun for a fisherman and his family; TOP: A classic street scene in Hanoi, North Vietnam; BOTTOM: When Secretary Seamans and his daughter May boarded the train from Hanoi to central Vietnam, the DMZ, it seemed clear they had experienced healing and a deeper understanding of the calamitous effect the Vietnam War had on families in both countries.

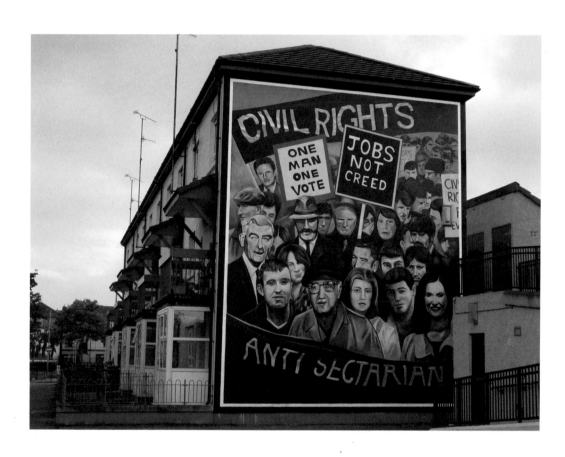

Murals painted by the Bogside Artists enlivened buildings in "Free Derry" and provided a perfect backdrop for a conference focused on protecting children in conflict.

CHAPTER TWENTY-NINE

HEALING THE TROUBLES IN DERRY

*Four days in Derry with His Holiness the Dalai Lama
to celebrate the power of forgiveness*

NORTHERN IRELAND, JULY 2007

In the early spring of 2007, I received a surprise phone call from Northern Ireland. A man in a deeply accented Irish voice said, "This is Richard Moore in Derry. Do you remember me, Jane?"

Indeed, I did remember meeting this remarkable Northern Irish peace activist from four years earlier when he had visited Pasadena and my friend Maureen Grady, an Irish American activist, had introduced Richard to our community. I could never forget hearing his tale of having been shot by a rubber bullet and blinded as a Catholic schoolboy during "the Troubles" in Northern Ireland, which lasted for thirty years, following centuries of human rights struggle for the Catholic population.

Richard continued, "We are planning a conference in July for the tenth anniversary of my organization, Children in Crossfire. I would love to have you, as the chair of Human Rights Watch, come to Derry and give a talk about children's rights." I quickly checked my calendar and assured him that I would be there. "That's good news," he said, "because I only have one other confirmed speaker so far, the Dalai Lama."

I nearly dropped the phone. I was glad that Richard had not told me about the Dalai Lama before inviting me, because now he knew that I had accepted the invitation in order to support Richard himself, not only because I wanted to meet his distinguished headline speaker—but I couldn't wait to fulfill my bucket list dream of meeting the Dalai Lama.

I greatly admired Richard Moore and loved his story. As a ten-year-old Catholic boy, in the spring of 1972, he was walking home from school through a crowd of angry protestors. A British soldier, trying to contain the chaos, shot a rubber bullet into the air. Tragically, the bullet landed on the bridge of Richard's nose, leaving him blinded for life.

When I met Richard in California, he referred to his blindness as a gift. "I live with blindness, but not in darkness," he said. "I do not feel any hatred for the man who shot me. I would like to meet him and tell him that." His words really moved me, because I had witnessed the positive effects of forgiveness in many parts of the world. Among others, I remembered Comandante Tomás Borge in Nicaragua, who forgave the men who tortured him and killed his wife, and a Bosnian Muslim mother who'd lost all her sons to the Serb militia but later embraced the choice of her daughter to marry a Serbian man she truly loved. All these stories reveal the healing power of radical forgiveness.

I learned that Richard had accomplished his goal of meeting the British soldier who shot him. He wrote a letter of compassion and forgiveness to the anonymous soldier, whose identity had always been protected by the British Army. Through circuitous means, the letter found its way to the soldier, Charles, who was then living in Scotland. In 2006, Richard and Charles met privately at a hotel in Edinburgh, Scotland, and Richard offered his forgiveness and friendship.

The story of that meeting made international headlines, quoting Richard as saying, "The soldier said he never meant to cause damage to me. I can either accept that or not." He chose to take the higher road. The Irish Film Board, together with BBC Northern Ireland, heard the story and made the documentary film, *Blind Vision*, which won acclaim and attracted international support for his organization, Children in Crossfire.

During our phone call that day in 2007, when I asked Richard how he had gotten the Dalai Lama to accept his invitation, he explained that the Dalai Lama had read an article about the incident and wrote a letter to Richard, in which he praised Richard as a "true practitioner of compassion." Richard shared his dream of creating a conference in Derry to illuminate the plight of children in war-torn countries. His Holiness immediately agreed to come.

As mythical as Derry seemed to me, maybe because of my Scots-Irish maternal great-grandmother, it had a long history of conflict and division. The Irish and British, Catholics and Protestants, Nationalists and Unionists, existed, polarized against each other. Derry is also divided geographically; the River Foyle runs from northeast to southwest and makes an "S" curve in the city center, separating Derry into the eastern "Waterside" area and the western "Bogside." Families began to separate by religious affiliations to different parts of Derry as soon as the first bridge was built in 1790, which allowed people to move across the river without resorting to boats. From that time onward, Protestant families moved across the river to the Waterside area, and most Catholics remained in the Bogside, a process that accelerated in the 20th Century when tensions grew even more heated.

A brutal bloody period called the Troubles broke out in Northern Ireland in 1968, starting with a civil rights housing protest in Derry. The unrest continued for thirty years, as people split apart over seemingly irreconcilable differences in religion and politics. Children attended separate schools, missing the opportunity to know "the other." The Troubles ended officially with the Good Friday Accord of 1998, but psychological wounds remained.

In that phone call, Richard told me that tension and stress recently had manifested more intensely for children; several teenagers had committed suicide in both Belfast and Derry. In one incident, he said, several teenagers held hands and jumped off a bridge together. I closed my eyes and shuddered, not wanting to imagine such a tragedy. Richard explained that the Troubles had ended abruptly with a political agreement, and people were supposed to carry on with their personal lives. Since families did not receive any counseling or therapy after experiencing decades of strife, Richard told me, violent and self-destructive actions of children and youth reflected generations of familial trauma.

By creating the organization Children in Crossfire, Richard sought to heal children by teaching them to focus outward and develop compassion for others who had suffered destructive violence, including members of different faiths in their own communities, and people in other war-torn countries, in order to learn they are more alike than different.

"I want kids to feel, first of all, that they are human beings who share the planet with others, many of whom have even greater problems and needs," he said. I smiled at that and told Richard he was singing my song.

I could not wait to attend the conference. The responsibility of giving a speech to an audience of traumatized teenagers from around the world excited and challenged me, as a human rights advocate, as a peacemaker, and most of all as a mother; I wanted to bring all parts of myself fully to Derry.

Maureen Grady and I flew on Aer Lingus, my first trip to Ireland. When we arrived in Derry, we took an elevator to our rooms on the fourth floor of the City Hotel. When the elevator doors opened, we nearly bumped into His Holiness, the Dalai Lama. The shock of encountering the great man and a dozen of his monks in the hallway, combined with jetlag, took my breath away. He raised his eyebrows expectantly, but we both were speechless. When we managed to utter our names, they all bowed, bending low in their scarlet and saffron robes, and we bowed in return, a ritual we repeated at least twice a day.

On the fourth day, when we met in the hallway for one last time, His Holiness put his hands on my shoulders and looked deeply into my eyes; time truly stood still. I lost all sense of time and place and may have lost my balance if he had not been holding on. Then he threw back his head and laughed, breaking the spell and filling me with "a peace that passeth all understanding." I did not need an interpreter to understand his message of love and support.

But I'm getting ahead of the story. After arriving and unpacking, I read the conference schedule and walked with Maureen to a municipal government building, where the Dalai Lama and Richard were meeting with local families in a conference room. The two men sat side by side and held hands in front of a large Children in Crossfire poster. They invited families to come forward, one group at a time, sit in the front row, and share their personal experiences, while both men, still holding hands, bent forward and listened attentively. I leaned forward also, straining to hear. I noticed that Richard tilted his head at an angle, as if trying to both hear and see with his ears.

The Dalai Lama fixed his attention on each family, with boundless patience and empathy in his eyes. I could hear only snippets of words, such as "peace," "love," and "time," but I could see the effects on these hurting families. Group after group of parents and children walked away, their arms around each other.

Needing to integrate this powerfully emotional experience, I later walked the streets of Derry, not fully present in my body and hoping not to get lost. Absentmindedly, I wandered into a neighborhood that assaulted my senses; graphic clues identified it as the "Bogside." Political urban art covered many of the buildings, enormous paintings, some in monochromatic shades of black and white and others with vivid color, which depicted grisly and heroic scenes: men with guns, gas masks, and bottle bombs; men carrying dead or wounded companions; and the heroic hunger strikers. The image that captured my attention was the haunting face of a woman wearing a headscarf and holding a cape together at her throat. A symbol of Ireland, she represented female mourners everywhere. Words were few on those walls, but they carried strong messages: *Civil Rights, Jobs Not Creed,* and *One Man One Vote.*

A sign identified the murals as having been created by the Bogside Artists in 1997 to commemorate Bloody Sunday, January 30, 1972. The over-sized art gallery seemed to represent every man and every woman who had been caught up in the insanity of war over all time. I felt both my heart and mind opening to the pain of history.

At the conference the next morning, I gave my talk on international children's rights. I had prepared my remarks carefully and included important research about the effects of war on children, planning to quote several articles of the Universal Declaration of Human Rights and give examples of how violations of those laws had impacted families in different war zones. But while Richard Moore was introducing me, I looked around at the audience of children, youth, and human rights workers who represented some of the world's most devastating conflicts. I could identify some nationalities by their attire, such as the black African teenager, who was wearing a tunic and pants in a colorful print that I recognized as West African. Others had come from Central America, the Balkans, and South Asia.

As I walked to the lectern, I felt overcome by the silent and expectant attention focused on me. I had spoken to high school, college, and law school students many times, but before me were some young children; I realized that I had to communicate with them, not lecture them. So I set down my notes, took a deep breath, and began to tell stories, as I would have done with my own children—stories that required no notes, because I had lived them—and because incidents involving vulnerable children always lived in my heart.

The final story I shared that day had been inspired by my tour of Derry, when I walked along the River Foyle and saw a large bronze statue of two men, arms reaching out to touch one another. The profound statue, called *Hands Across the Divide*, on the western side of a bridge, symbolizes reconciliation between both sides of the political divide.

I began my story with that bridge in mind. "During a recent war in a country once called Yugoslavia, I met two little girls at a hospital in Zagreb, Croatia. Both girls had been injured during a war in a city called Mostar, and they were flown to that hospital in a United Nations helicopter." I then described Mostar as a city that looked a lot like Derry, because a river divides it, just like the River Foyle divides Derry.

"When the war began," I explained, "Christian families got to stay on one side of the river, the more modern side, but Muslim families had to move to the old city across the river. One of the girls I met in the hospital was a Muslim girl named Sabina, who was seven years old. Sabina had been shot, and pieces of bullets remained in her spine. She was suffering from paralysis and a disease called 'meningitis.'"

I continued, "The other girl, named Asida, was nine years old, and she came from a Catholic family on the opposite side of the river. Asida also had been shot, and the bullets had caused extensive nerve and tissue damage in both of her legs." I stopped for a minute to measure the reaction and felt glad to see the audience leaning forward, waiting to hear the rest of my story.

"Neither of the girls could walk, and both were very ill when they arrived at this hospital," I said. "The doctors put them next to each other in a room where a nurse stayed with them all the time." The nurse told me that for a long time, both girls had been sad and afraid, lonely for their families; slowly they began talking to each other. During the five months they stayed in the hospital, she added, they gave each other support and became friends.

"By the time I met them, Asida smiled and laughed, and Sabina could walk. The girls performed a little dance for me with their arms around each other. After the girls left the hospital, they flew together home to Mostar, but they ended up again on different sides of the river, opposite sides of the bridge."

I stopped again for a few seconds. I had made my point, that tragedy had brought these two girls together from disparate sides of the conflict, and that during their recovery, they had become good friends. But now they were going back to their homes, where they would again be separated by a conflict that had gone on for generations. I waited, letting those words sink in before ending on a note of hope—telling the audience that I strongly believed those two Bosnian girls would maintain their friendship, and that they would be able to bring their families together. Then I ended with a favorite quote: *Hope is the ability to listen to the music of the future, and faith is the courage to dance to that music in the present.*

While telling the story, I had mostly kept my gaze above the heads of the audience, hoping to get through it without crying. But when I ended and looked down and saw the eyes of children fixed on me, I felt like encircling them all in my arms.

Suddenly, the teenager wearing a West African costume approached me and held out his hand. He grinned widely. "You look just like my mother," he said. I asked his name, "Michael Femi-Sodipo," and his country, "northern Nigeria." I asked Michael to tell me about his mother. "She died when I was only five years old," he responded, "and you look just like her." From his warm smile, I knew this was a very high compliment indeed.

For the rest of that week, Michael called me "Mother," and he barely left my side. Michael and I have maintained our relationship ever since. Inspired by Richard's conference, Michael, a Christian, initiated a program in his home city of Kano, northern Nigeria, a region dominated by Muslims with a conservative government and culture based on strict Islamic Sharia law. Michael's program, called the Peace Initiative Network, brings together teenagers from different tribes and different religions to work together on mutually beneficial projects, such as picking up trash and planting trees along streets, both to beautify Kano and to bring peace to their neighborhoods.

(When the International Board of Human Rights Watch held a board meeting in Nigeria a few years later, I took members of the board and staff to meet Michael and visit his impressive program. Michael has become a key spokesperson on humanitarian and human rights issues at the United Nations and other important venues, sometimes representing all of Africa on peace initiatives, and I see him in New York, California, and Washington, D.C.)

To conclude the Derry conference, the Dalai Lama gave a keynote speech in a large municipal auditorium, and people came from all around Northern Ireland. Every seat was filled. The audience buzzed with anticipation until the curtains opened, then hushed to silence while His Holiness walked to center stage and stood beside bouquets of golden sunflowers and crimson gladioli that matched his robes. After bowing, the Dalai Lama recognized the tension in the room and brought in some levity, as was his nature, by opening with these words:

"Seven hundred years of violence here. Catholics and Protestants. Same God. Same Jesus." He paused and gave a quizzical look, raising both his eyebrows and his shoulders. Then he threw back his head and laughed from deep within his being at the absurdity of the human condition. Many people in the audience squirmed. A few giggled nervously. His seemingly simple statement had offered a profound reality, and people clearly needed time to digest his meaning.

At first, I didn't know what to think, even though I agreed with the complexity he had reduced to those few words. I remembered having had similar feelings in many of the war zones I visited, especially in the former Yugoslavia, where I could not tell the difference between the Serbs, Croatians, and Bosnians. They were all Southern Slavs. Small differences, which seemed insignificant to an outsider, had divided people in so many countries and led to violent conflicts with devastating outcomes of destruction and death. Still, I didn't know whether to laugh or cry, and everyone around me seemed suspended by that question.

Then Richard came onto the stage. The Dalai Lama took his right hand, guided him to a chair, and sat down beside him. Richard turned his head to face the Dalai Lama, feeling rather than seeing the sparkle of kindness in his eyes that radiated throughout the auditorium. With the help of an interpreter, a young monk seated on his other side, His Holiness talked about the importance of religious harmony, warm-heartedness, and tolerance. He quoted a teaching from 13th Century Buddhist sages: *If one lights a fire for others, it will also brighten one's own way.*

"Inner peace is good for health and mental function," he said. "The most important thing is to forgive, whether or not the other person accepts his fault or your forgiveness."

He added that the 20th Century brought one hundred years of violence, but the 21st Century must be about dialogue and peace. "Children will lead the way," he said, his voice strong with assurance. After my previous afternoon with all those teenagers, I shared his hope and his belief that children will indeed demonstrate the way forward to peace and justice.

The Dalai Lama had spoken only a few words, but he needed few words. His power came through his very being. His loving energy and his light-filled eyes communicated for him. When he raised Richard's hand at the end of his speech, a hand he had been holding the entire time, I felt a calm come over the audience.

Then, during the question period, a woman stood up and introduced herself as the single mother of a troubled teenaged boy. She listed several of her son's failings and asked what should she, as a mother, do to help him. The Dalai Lama leaned forward, placing an elbow on his knee and stroking his chin as if considering his response very carefully. Then he raised both arms in the air and answered, "I don't know. I am a monk!"

This time everyone joined his joyful laughter. At that moment, I understood the foundation of the Dalai Lama's magical impact. While he took the human condition very seriously, he took himself lightly. How else could he bear the burdens that he carried for all of Tibet and the whole world?

When there were no more questions, the Dalai Lama took Richard's hand and they both stood up. His Holiness proclaimed that Richard was his hero because of the radical forgiveness he had extended to the man who blinded him. Then Richard turned to the curtain behind them and surprised the Dalai Lama with a special gift. He had invited the British soldier who had shot him, Charles, to come to Derry so he could stand beside Richard and receive a blessing from His Holiness.

Charles walked forward with a military bearing and stood, as if at attention, three feet to Richard's left. The Dalai Lama, visibly moved, reached under his robe, took out a long white silk scarf, wrapped it around the shoulders of Richard and Charles, and pulled them close to each other. Then he threw back his head and laughed, his joyous laugh again, uniting every one of us as witnesses to this moment of universal love. I felt the sting of tears and closed my eyes to contain them and all the emotions rising from my heart.

If only we could wrap a white scarf around the entire world.

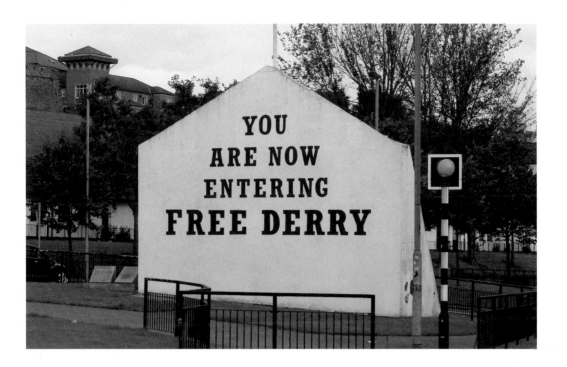

Images of Bloody Sunday, a violent and devastating event in Derry's history, evoked prayers of "Never Again." To enter Free Derry was to enter an outdoor art museum, with beautiful monuments and murals that boldly advocated for equality, peace, and justice.

OPPOSITE: Twenty years after Bloody Sunday and the worst of "The Troubles," the city of Derry
unveiled this inspirational bronze sculpture called *Hands Across the Divide*, which captured the spirit
of hope and reconciliation; ABOVE: When His Holiness the Dalai Lama came to Derry for a Children in
Crossfire global conference, he spent four days with local families. HHDL and Richard Moore, founder
of Children in Crossfire, demonstrated the healing power of love, hope, and forgiveness.

EPILOGUE

---

*The strength of community provides roots and wings
to all who wish to make a difference*

When I began to speak publicly about my experiences, I felt a need to impress people with facts and statistics, but I soon learned that such details simply overwhelmed audiences, causing eyes to glaze over. When I dropped my notes and began telling stories about inspirational people I met, survivors who exhibited courage and resilience, people leaned forward in their seats.

Stories of real-life experiences put a face on victims of war, disease, poverty, and other conditions beyond their control. Because it is important not to glamorize victims, exaggerate their situations, or generalize their individuality, I reported only what I witnessed and how I felt about what I learned.

My small-town Midwestern childhood grounded me in a culture that valued each person as being important to the community without regard to wealth or circumstances. I considered the courageous people I met on my travels to be important to the global community. They taught me the basic truth that we all are connected, more alike than different.

Most stories in this book came from my journeys with humanitarian organizations, especially the Women's Refugee Commission and Landmine Survivors Network, whose boards I chaired and whose staff members worked collegially with volunteers. I always served as a volunteer and paid my own expenses, thanks to the support of my husband, Ron. My notes and photographs found their way into many trip reports and advocacy efforts.

When I traveled with Human Rights Watch, our professional research staff wrote all the reports. My greater value came in supporting that extraordinary staff by building communities of people who care about human rights abuse and want to end its brutal impact around the world. There is no more potent agent of change than a group of influential people armed with facts and grounded in laws.

Because victims who shared intimate details about their personal suffering looked to me as a lifeline, I carry a responsibility to share their stories—and to secure help through my connections with extraordinary humanitarian and human rights organizations. Making connections became easier after one extraordinary man created an electronic service to link the world, the World Wide Web (WWW). Sir Tim Berners-Lee, a British scientist, invented the WWW in 1989—and he gave it freely to the world. He could not have given the service a better name!

"World Wide Web" accurately describes what I believe to be the true nature of humanity. Imagine that, like a bamboo grove or a forest of aspen trees, we are bound together as a single organism, knitted together energetically through a shared root system. What harms one, hurts all. What helps one, benefits all. And that is how lives are changed.

A LETTER TO MY CHILDREN

Kristin Olson McKissick, Steven James Olson,
and Amy Olson Duerk

While writing this memoir, I realized how different my life has been from that of my parents, who were part of the Greatest Generation. Because of the Great Depression, they were poor and could not dream of going to college, but they were lifelong learners, and they introduced their children to a world beyond rural Iowa.

When World War II hit, my father went to the South Pacific with the U.S. Navy, and Mother raised three young daughters alone in a small house in Iowa. She had to deal with food rationing, a wringer washing machine, a coal-burning furnace, and long, cold, and dark Iowa winters. I think of her whenever I am tempted to feel sorry that "women's liberation" came too late to support my ambitions for graduate school and a profession. I got to go to college, and I am grateful for my parents' sacrifice to educate all five of their children.

It is said that "life is what happens when you're busy making other plans." I'd put a period after "happens." I really don't remember making any plans. Every important relationship and event in my life, it seems, just came to me, including you three children. I must have said "no thanks" a few times when asked to take on a responsibility, but I found that the invitations I accepted led to extraordinary experiences I could not have imagined.

My roles as mother and grandmother have always been the most gratifying. I have loved every minute spent with you and with your children, our eight fabulous grandsons. As you know, I have informally adopted children all over the world. Most of them called me "Mother Goose," and many still reach out for comfort and advice, which the internet facilitates.

Volunteer work has provided more enriching opportunities and relationships than any paid job I could have imagined. The ladder of volunteerism served as my graduate school, and I became a "professional volunteer." Most women must work outside the home to support their families, but your father, with his eight years of higher education, all of it paid by athletic and academic scholarships, built a successful career that gave us a privileged life and supported my work and travel. I hope he knows how much I appreciate the love and support he gave to me over our marriage of fifty-eight years, and counting.

A friend once called me a "privileged do-gooder." I knew he was teasing, but I admit that it hurt my feelings. Over time, however, I decided to accept that judgment as a compliment, and to realize that it's true. Anyone born white in America began life with privilege, especially those who grew up in the heartland. And "do-gooder"? Indeed! I have tried to do good all my life, and am glad that he noticed, because the alternative must be to do nothing or do bad.

Above my desk is a framed poster of Eleanor Roosevelt that says: "No one can make you feel inferior without your consent." Never allow another person's judgment to stop you from doing what you know is right.

I am gratified that all of you have excellent educations and have established your own satisfying careers. But I am most proud that you volunteer your time, expertise, and leadership to many important causes. As my mentor, George Regas, once said, "People often complain to me that they are burned out, when I know for certain they have never once been on fire."

My beloved children, your efforts to make a positive difference in the world will set your hearts on fire! Always shine your light, understanding that LOVE is the operating energy of the Universe.

ACKNOWLEDGMENTS

With great respect and gratitude, I want to thank the incredible staff members of the esteemed humanitarian and human rights organizations that invited me to journey with them into some very dark places around the world, regions suffering from catastrophic wars, devastating poverty, and diseases unknown in more developed countries. I would drop in for few weeks, but they stayed for the long haul and hard work of meeting the basic needs of desperate people. They are my heroes and heroines, the champions who risk their own lives to save those of strangers.

I served as an informed and compassionate witness, recording and sharing stories of the victims I met in order to influence people with resources to care and to help improve conditions. Through hearing personal stories, we can recognize humanity, celebrate resilience, and realize our own vulnerability.

This book would never have been written had my busy life not come to a halt as the result of a terrible fall several years ago that caused the triple fracture of an ankle. The recovery lasted many months and provided time for me to write, with the help of pain pills. Luckily, I could reach file drawers and photo albums from the wheelchair that kept me mobile.

Although I had told many of these stories during public speaking opportunities, I soon learned that writing a book was much more difficult. I would have given up if not for help I received from the Lunch Bunch, a group of successful local women writers who had been meeting weekly for decades. At the invitation of my "other mother," Martha Tolles, the Lunch Bunch came to my house every Tuesday morning. We read aloud and critiqued each other's work, up to ten pages every week, a deadline that kept me motivated. Their invaluable feedback could be tough, but it inspired me to keep working and improving. I am forever indebted to Martha Tolles, Tony Johnston, Jenny Johnston Taylor, Lael Littke, and Susan Rubin. During the coronavirus pandemic, we continued to meet virtually.

I received early encouragement from my husband, Ron, and our children, from my sisters, Judy Holm and Cynthia Dusenbury, and from friends who generously suffered through reading early chapters. They include Karen Averitt, Joel Berke, Gaye Browne, Bettina Chandler, Dr. Mary Lee and Shelby Coffey, Mary Daly, Laurie McKinley, Colleen Nunn, Heather Sturgess, Vicki Riskin, and Diane Wittenberg.

Helpful suggestions also came from Ken Brecher, Jonathan Fanton, Jerrold Green, Carol Loomis, Becky Quick, and Davan Maharaj, who liked the story "Knitting Lives Together" and suggested it should be chapter one. Jerry White, my travel companion who always made me laugh until I cried, gave me important advice and corrections.

I am grateful to Dave Dierks at the University of Iowa, who shared an early manuscript with James McCoy at the University of Iowa Press and then passed on McCoy's helpful advice that the book should be a memoir, not a journalism exercise, and that I needed to go deeper into my personal feelings and reactions. That challenged me, because I had wanted to focus on inspirational survivors, but soon after receiving that suggestion, I began working with the talented Annie Gilbar. I sent her a "completed" manuscript of more than one hundred thousand words, and she magically put me into my own story.

I am indebted to Aviva Layton, who edited my early chapters with scissors and Scotch tape, helping me to contain and organize thematic chapters. My friend Maureen Grady, a published poet, creative writing teacher, and college counselor, helped to smooth out clumsy phrases and correct punctuation, style, and so much more. She and I also found time to watch our favorite World War II movies about the Holocaust, a passion we share.

I have been gifted by association with organizations that hold the love and welfare of humanity as core values of their missions, among them All Saints Church, Human Rights Watch, the International Rescue Committee, the Women's Refugee Commission, Direct Relief, Landmine Survivors Network, Promoting Enduring Peace, World Vision, the Global AIDS Interfaith Alliance, and Children in Crossfire. All are devoted to creating a more equitable world of justice and peace.

I would have continued to fuss over this book for much longer if a tragic world event had not jolted me into action. In February 2022, Russia committed a brutal, unprovoked invasion of Ukraine, killing thousands of innocent civilians and demolishing cities. The immediate outflow of desperate refugees, mostly women and children, brought back memories of war zones and refugees I had visited.

When courageous journalists broadcast scenes of the wanton shelling of Ukrainian cities, I recognized landmarks I had visited in 1989 and 1990. Blue and yellow being waved in defiance reminded me of having been there at the very moment the citizens of Kyiv (then spelled "Kiev") tore down the Soviet flag and raised up that blue and yellow flag. I have continued to communicate with people I met in Ukraine thirty years ago, and they have sent emails describing the terror and turmoil, messages that begin, "Dear Mother Goose" and end with "love from your Gosling, _____." Those poignant messages motivated me to publish this book for them.

A dream team came together for World Citizen in support of that urgent goal. Brilliant book designer Yolanda Cuomo and her assistant Bobbie Richardson made the photo selection and design process so much fun that our virtual sessions all ended with laughter. We shared our computer screens, a commitment to excellence, and our hearts. I would write another book just for the joy of working with them.

Daniel Frank at Meridian Printing in Rhode Island agreed to a tight printing schedule despite the global shortage of paper and other supply chain issues. He has been a delight to work with in an industry that is stressful in normal times. Tony Manzella and his crew at Echelon Color, Los Angeles, worked overtime for several days to improve the quality of my photographs, negatives, and slides, many of which are several decades old, by digitizing them at a higher resolution.

Most of all, my dear friend Tippy Bushkin served as an extraordinary producer, using skills she honed at Lucasfilm to keep everything moving perfectly and on time. I am forever indebted to Tippy for resolving every issue by turning problems into opportunities.

And finally, my thanks and love to my husband, Ron. Without his love and support, I would not have been able to live these chapters or all those I left on the cutting room floor, just in case there is a sequel.

UNIVERSAL DECLARATION OF HUMAN RIGHTS (1948)

PREAMBLE

Whereas recognition of the inherent dignity and of the equal and inalienable rights of all members of the human family is the foundation of freedom, justice and peace in the world,

Whereas disregard and contempt for human rights have resulted in barbarous acts which have outraged the conscience of mankind, and the advent of a world in which human beings shall enjoy freedom of speech and belief and freedom from fear and want has been proclaimed as the highest aspiration of the common people,

Whereas it is essential, if man is not to be compelled to have recourse, as a last resort, to rebellion against tyranny and oppression, that human rights should be protected by the rule of law,

Whereas it is essential to promote the development of friendly relations between nations,

Whereas the peoples of the United Nations have in the Charter reaffirmed their faith in fundamental human rights, in the dignity and worth of the human person and in the equal rights of men and women and have determined to promote social progress and better standards of life in larger freedom,

Whereas Member States have pledged themselves to achieve, in cooperation with the United Nations, the promotion of universal respect for and observance of human rights and fundamental freedoms,

Whereas a common understanding of these rights and freedoms is of the greatest importance for the full realization of this pledge,

Now, therefore,

The General Assembly,

Proclaims this Universal Declaration of Human Rights as a common standard of achievement for all peoples and all nations, to the end that every individual and every organ of society, keeping this Declaration constantly in mind, shall strive by teaching and education to promote respect for these rights and freedoms and by progressive measures, national and international, to secure their universal and effective recognition and observance, both among the peoples of Member States themselves and among the peoples of territories under their jurisdiction.

ARTICLE 1

All human beings are born free and equal in dignity and rights. They are endowed with reason and conscience and should act towards one another in a spirit of brotherhood.

ARTICLE 2

Everyone is entitled to all the rights and freedoms set forth in this Declaration, without distinction of any kind, such as race, colour, sex, language, religion, political or other opinion, national or social origin, property, birth or other status.

Furthermore, no distinction shall be made on the basis of the political, jurisdictional or international status of the country or territory to which a person belongs, whether it be independent, trust, non-self-governing or under any other limitation of sovereignty.

ARTICLE 3

Everyone has the right to life, liberty and the security of person.

ARTICLE 4

No one shall be held in slavery or servitude; slavery and the slave trade shall be prohibited in all their forms.

ARTICLE 5

No one shall be subjected to torture or to cruel, inhuman or degrading treatment or punishment.

ARTICLE 6

Everyone has the right to recognition everywhere as a person before the law.

ARTICLE 7

All are equal before the law and are entitled without any discrimination to equal protection of the law. All are entitled to equal protection against any discrimination in violation of this Declaration and against any incitement to such discrimination.

ARTICLE 8

Everyone has the right to an effective remedy by the competent national tribunals for acts violating the fundamental rights granted him by the constitution or by law.

ARTICLE 9

No one shall be subjected to arbitrary arrest, detention or exile.

ARTICLE 10

Everyone is entitled in full equality to a fair and public hearing by an independent and impartial tribunal, in the determination of his rights and obligations and of any criminal charge against him.

ARTICLE 11

1. Everyone charged with a penal offence has the right to be presumed innocent until proved guilty according to law in a public trial at which he has had all the guarantees necessary for his defence.

2. No one shall be held guilty of any penal offence on account of any act or omission which did not constitute a penal offence, under national or international law, at the time when it was committed. Nor shall a heavier penalty be imposed than the one that was applicable at the time the penal offence was committed.

ARTICLE 12

No one shall be subjected to arbitrary interference with his privacy, family, home or correspondence, nor to attacks upon his honour and reputation. Everyone has the right to the protection of the law against such interference or attacks.

ARTICLE 13

1. Everyone has the right to freedom of movement and residence within the borders of each State.

2. Everyone has the right to leave any country, including his own, and to return to his country.

ARTICLE 14

1. Everyone has the right to seek and to enjoy in other countries asylum from persecution.

2. This right may not be invoked in the case of prosecutions genuinely arising from non-political crimes or from acts contrary to the purposes and principles of the United Nations.

ARTICLE 15

1. Everyone has the right to a nationality.

2. No one shall be arbitrarily deprived of his nationality nor denied the right to change his nationality.

ARTICLE 16

1. Men and women of full age, without any limitation due to race, nationality or religion, have the right to marry and to found a family. They are entitled to equal rights as to marriage, during marriage and at its dissolution.

2. Marriage shall be entered into only with the free and full consent of the intending spouses.

3. The family is the natural and fundamental group unit of society and is entitled to protection by society and the State.

ARTICLE 17

1. Everyone has the right to own property alone as well as in association with others.

2. No one shall be arbitrarily deprived of his property.

ARTICLE 18

Everyone has the right to freedom of thought, conscience and religion; this right includes freedom to change his religion or belief, and freedom, either alone or in community with others and in public or private, to manifest his religion or belief in teaching, practice, worship and observance.

ARTICLE 19

Everyone has the right to freedom of opinion and expression; this right includes freedom to hold opinions without interference and to seek, receive and impart information and ideas through any media and regardless of frontiers.

ARTICLE 20

1. Everyone has the right to freedom of peaceful assembly and association.

2. No one may be compelled to belong to an association.

ARTICLE 21

1. Everyone has the right to take part in the government of his country, directly or through freely chosen representatives.

2. Everyone has the right to equal access to public service in his country.

3. The will of the people shall be the basis of the authority of government; this will shall be expressed in periodic and genuine elections which shall be by universal and equal suffrage and shall be held by secret vote or by equivalent free voting procedures.

ARTICLE 22

Everyone, as a member of society, has the right to social security and is entitled to realization, through national effort and international co-operation and in accordance with the organization and resources of each State, of the economic, social and cultural rights indispensable for his dignity and the free development of his personality.

ARTICLE 23

1. Everyone has the right to work, to free choice of employment, to just and favourable conditions of work and to protection against unemployment.

2. Everyone, without any discrimination, has the right to equal pay for equal work.

3. Everyone who works has the right to just and favourable remuneration ensuring for himself and his family an existence worthy of human dignity, and supplemented, if necessary, by other means of social protection.

4. Everyone has the right to form and to join trade unions for the protection of his interests.

ARTICLE 24

Everyone has the right to rest and leisure, including reasonable limitation of working hours and periodic holidays with pay.

ARTICLE 25

1. Everyone has the right to a standard of living adequate for the health and well-being of himself and of his family, including food, clothing, housing and medical care and necessary social services, and the right to security in the event of unemployment, sickness, disability, widowhood, old age or other lack of livelihood in circumstances beyond his control.

2. Motherhood and childhood are entitled to special care and assistance. All children, whether born in or out of wedlock, shall enjoy the same social protection.

ARTICLE 26

1. Everyone has the right to education. Education shall be free, at least in the elementary and fundamental stages. Elementary education shall be compulsory. Technical and professional education shall be made generally available and higher education shall be equally accessible to all on the basis of merit.

2. Education shall be directed to the full development of the human personality and to the strengthening of respect for human rights and fundamental freedoms. It shall promote understanding, tolerance and friendship among all nations, racial or religious groups, and shall further the activities of the United Nations for the maintenance of peace.

3. Parents have a prior right to choose the kind of education that shall be given to their children.

ARTICLE 27

1. Everyone has the right freely to participate in the cultural life of the community, to enjoy the arts and to share in scientific advancement and its benefits.

2. Everyone has the right to the protection of the moral and material interests resulting from any scientific, literary or artistic production of which he is the author.

ARTICLE 28

Everyone is entitled to a social and international order in which the rights and freedoms set forth in this Declaration can be fully realized.

ARTICLE 29

1. Everyone has duties to the community in which alone the free and full development of his personality is possible.

2. In the exercise of his rights and freedoms, everyone shall be subject only to such limitations as are determined by law solely for the purpose of securing due recognition and respect for the rights and freedoms of others and of meeting the just requirements of morality, public order and the general welfare in a democratic society.

3. These rights and freedoms may in no case be exercised contrary to the purposes and principles of the United Nations.

ARTICLE 30

Nothing in this Declaration may be interpreted as implying for any State, group or person any right to engage in any activity or to perform any act aimed at the destruction of any of the rights and freedoms set forth herein.

INDEX

WORLD CITIZEN: JOURNEYS OF A HUMANITARIAN
JANE OLSON

Net proceeds from the sale of this book will go to author designated humanitarian
and human rights organizations.

Cover: Jane with Duru, a refugee woman in Azerbaijan, who with her daughter and three
grandchildren lived in a reed house with a cardboard ceiling.
Page 2: Ukrainian Motherland Monument in Kyiv.
Page 5: Knitting projects helped refugee women to focus on the future.
Page 6: This woman sifting grain in a field in northern Ghana made eye contact,
communicating her strength and dignity.

Page 46: La Patria La Revolucion—poster. F.S.L.N. Secretaria Nacional De Propaganda
Y Educación Política
Page 142: © Getty Images, *Ex-Yugoslavia* by Dario Mitidieri
Page 147: © Getty Images, *Bosnia and Herzegovina—Mostar: Stone bridge "Stari Most"*
over the river Neretva by Ullstein Bild
Page 420: © diego_cue, *"Hands Across the Divide" sculpture, Derry*

Producer: Tippy Bushkin
Reproduction and Print Preparation: Echelon, Los Angeles
Color Separations: Meridian

BOOK DESIGN BY YOLANDA CUOMO DESIGN
Associate Designer: Bobbie Richardson
Proofreading: Sally Knapp
Maps: Rachel Botbyl

PRINTED BY MERIDIAN PRINTING IN 2022, RHODE ISLAND.
The printing and paper for this book were produced with 100% wind-powered electricity.
The paper by Monadnock Paper is made with 100% post-consumer fiber sourced from responsibly
managed forests.

ISBN 978-1-5136-9569-3